IMAGES
of America

BOSTON
NEW YORK

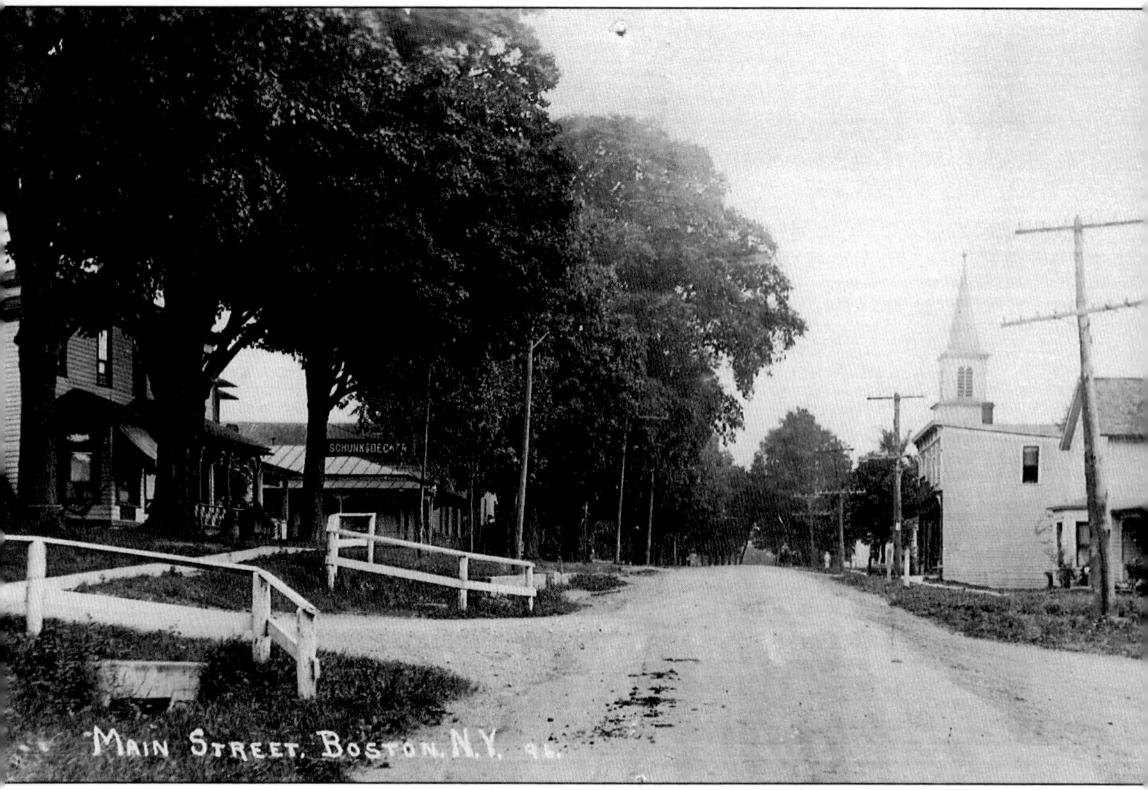

Looking south, one can see part of downtown Boston in 1896. On the left is the establishment of Shunk and Decker and the giant elm tree that withstood two centuries of history. On the right is the flat-topped roof of the building that would become first the Wurtz Furniture Store and then the Wurtz Funeral Home. Behind it is the spire of St. Paul's Church.

On the cover: Please see page 19. (Courtesy of Boston Historical Museum.)

IMAGES
of America

BOSTON
NEW YORK

Sherrie L. Pluta

ARCADIA
PUBLISHING

ISBN 978-0-7385-6288-9

Published by Arcadia Publishing
Charleston SC, Chicago IL, Portsmouth NH, San Francisco CA

Printed in the United States of America

Library of Congress Catalog Card Number: 2008930178

For all general information contact Arcadia Publishing at:
Telephone 843-853-2070
Fax 843-853-0044
E-mail sales@arcadiapublishing.com
For customer service and orders:
Toll-Free 1-888-313-2665

Visit us on the Internet at www.arcadiapublishing.com

To my father, who taught us to revere the past
as we planted flowers in the cemetery every Memorial Day.

Contents

Acknowledgments

I wish to thank those who helped me research the history of our town for this treatise: Charles B. Bradley, our first town historian, who tirelessly documented interviews and collected newspaper clippings from the people who lived our history; James J. Jehle and Mary Ann Jehle, who took the reins from Charles Bradley and continued the honored traditions of research and documentation of each event in town that needed to be remembered; David J. Shenk, our town clerk, who gave me unfettered access to the town's historic archives of town meetings, births, and deaths; Norman Gern, who shared his collection of school district photographs and showed me his uncanny ability to remember historic events that was miraculous at times; Jane Ellen Dalziel Clarke, a Dye family descendant, for sharing with me her mother's and grandmother's photographs and her knowledge of the Dye family genealogy; Bessie Enser, for sharing her mother's (Florence Winkelman Theil) memories of her childhood and many wonderful photographs; Dorothy Berger, for sharing her memories of Boston and of her husband, Warren Berger; Clive "Tom" and Marilyn Rucker, for their photographs and memories of the Rucker family; and the Boston Historical Society for allowing me to share its collection of historic photographs with all of you and the next generation of the Boston community. Finally, I would like to thank Jim Pluta for his undying support.

INTRODUCTION

Western New York was an unexplored wilderness in the late 18th century. Inhabited by Iroquois Indians, deer, wolves, bear, and raccoons, summers were warm and winters were harsh.

In 1803, brothers Charles and Oliver Johnson came from Cayuga County to put down a homestead and start a new life. They arrived in November of that year, unprepared for the winter, so they stayed with the Didemus Kinney family of East Hamburg, now called Orchard Park, until travel was easier in the spring.

Most of the valley and the east and west hill were heavily wooded, except for a remarkably clear 50-acre section of the valley. This expanse of meadow was the perfect place to put down roots next to the meandering 18 Mile Creek. Charles erected a small wooden cabin along an American Indian path at the bottom of the east hill, where Liebler Road is now. He traded with the American Indians for food and supplies until he could get settled enough to travel to Buffalo.

The Johnson brothers, who were the first to buy land from the Holland Land Company at $2.25 per acre, were followed by Samuel Eaton, Samuel Beebe, Deacon Richard Cary, Jonathon Bump, Benjamin Whaley, Job Palmer, Calvin Doolittle, Eliab Streeter, Joseph Yaw, and Kester and Serrill Alger. Richard Cary, a hero of the Revolutionary War, had just 3¢ in his pocket and was $2 in debt when he arrived with his sick wife and eight children.

Even though it was a hard life, each man settled the land, grew wheat and corn, and tamed the land in order to form a new town. On April 5, 1817, the town of Boston was formed from a portion of the town of Eden. Samuel Abbott became the first town supervisor, and Truman Cary, Richard Cary's nephew, became a member of the board of assessors.

Gristmills, sawmills, churches, and cheese factories were established along 18 Mile Creek, the greatest natural resource that the pioneers could have had.

At the first town meeting, the people held elections for many positions—town clerk, poor masters, commissioners of highways, constable, collector, and commissioners of common schools. They were a growing community of people from many different parts of the country, but they all had a common goal. They would build relationships and roads. Their children would have organized schools, and the farmers would have organized procedures. The first town meeting in 1818 documented each goal they all agreed upon. The most unusual goal they had was the rule that "any person who shall suffer a stalk of Canada thistle to bloom on his or her lot or farm, shall pay a fine of fifty cents for each and every blossom to any person suing for the same." The farmers had experience with this hardy weed. They knew that the thistle would crowd out the wheat and corn they wanted to raise and that their cattle would find it unpalatable.

A great many of the settlers in Boston were Quakers, good men and women, religious and peace loving. Quakers refused to serve in a government army, so in lieu of military service or jail, the men were taxed $4 each. Early Bostonians who paid this tax were Matthew Middleditch, John Kester, Stephen Kester, William Pound, David Laing, Thomas Twining Jr., Aaron Hampton, and James Miller. In 1818, there were 153 settlers in Boston.

As the work continued to build this small town, harness shops, hardware stores, wagon shops, dress shops, and post offices were built. Many of the business owners also performed civic duties and held office of some type in addition to their business duties.

Talcutt Patchin, an officer during the War of 1812, built a tannery near Boston Center around 1820. He also ran a general store. In his daily ledger, he documented each customer, each item they purchased, and its cost. This journal is part of the collection of the Boston Historical Museum. One entry shows that Rheuben Ensign purchased one wood saw and a file on October 14, 1831, at a cost of $1.22. On October 17, Roswell Rice bought a quarter of a pound of tea and a quarter of a pound of snuff for 31¢. Joseph Carey made a large purchase on October 21 of 16 yards of flannel, 30 yards of sheeting (spelled "sheating"), 10 skeins of yarn, pins, 10 buttons, two bowls (spelled "bols"), a basin, one chamber mug, two tumblers, 42 eggs, and tea for a total of $24.35.

Talcutt Patchin's legacy would prove to be more than just as another businessman in town. He was wounded in the Battle of Chippewa during the War of 1812 and became friends with another officer, Richard Cary of Boston. He eventually married Richard's daughter Clarissa and made his home in Boston after his discharge from the army. Not only did he build and run many businesses, he also became a religious teacher at the Free Will Baptist Church at the bottom of Liebler Road. He also preached to the Society of Friends (Quakers).

His business dealings began to suffer hardships, and in 1833, he moved his wife, two sons, and one daughter to Texas, which was then a province of Mexico, in an effort to forget his financial embarrassments.

His friends back in Boston missed his larger-than-life presence and honored his contributions in 1850 when a new post office in Boston Center was opened. The petition for a Boston Center Post Office was rejected, as there already existed a North Boston Post Office and a Boston Post office. They were told to name it something else. So in homage to their absent friend and mentor, they decided to call their new post office Patchin. So not only did the post office take on the name of Patchin, the whole area known as Boston Center became forever known as Patchin, even after the post office was closed in 1909.

In another example of renaming, the southernmost portion of Boston was first known as Torrey's Corners. Immediately after the War of 1812, Captain Torrey and his family, including sons Erastus and Uriah settled in the area. In 1820, when a new mail route was established, Erastus Torrey became the first postmaster. The intersection of Boston State Road and Boston Cross Road, as they are known today, was the main hub of all business activity for the town. The post office was named the Boston Post Office, and the nickname "Torrey's Corners" faded to become Boston Corners, and eventually, just Boston.

One

The Early Years

From 1818 to the mid-1820s, the focus for the new settlers was survival. The woods were full of bear and wolves, competition for the occasional rabbit dinner. They built log homes, shacks really, with a blanket covering the doorway and maybe one window. They had to build a fireplace that would be able to keep the family warm in the winter months when the snow and the cold threatened their very lives. The lake effect snow that came off Lake Erie for five months of the year was heavy and unforgiving. When spring came, one could finally venture out and begin farming the land to grow enough food to stock up for the next brutal winter. Businesses most important to survival—sawmills and grain mills—started to appear. Money was practically nonexistent, so the barter system was used. One could trade wheat for lumber, or a chicken for a supply of flour and sugar. Many men could not pay in full for the land they bought from the Holland Land Company, so they worked out a deal where they would pay in five or six yearly installments, after which they received a deed. Some families could not afford even portions of the annual payments and ended up losing their land as it was taken back by the seller. Hardship was a daily companion, but settlers with spirit, a strong work ethic, and a sense of duty to their families built barns, churches, and the first semblances of commerce. They enjoyed the summer and fall with corn-husking parties, dances, and cider sipping. In time, rough-hewn log homes were replaced with frame houses, dirt floors were covered with wood planks, and primitive glass for windows could be made from the black salts derived from wood ash they produced from hundreds of acres of trees that were cut down to make way for corn fields.

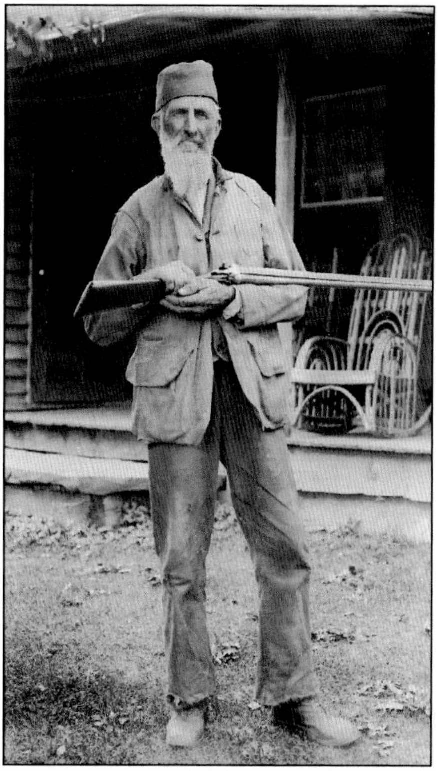

Rollin Alger was a descendant of Kester and Serrill Alger, who came to Boston sometime between 1803 and 1807. Rollin, obviously a very rugged man, was appointed overseer of highways for Road District No. 32 in 1862 and for District No. 31 in 1865. The overseer of highways was responsible for gathering teams of residents together to repair roads and bridges, which in the 1860s were always in need of such repair.

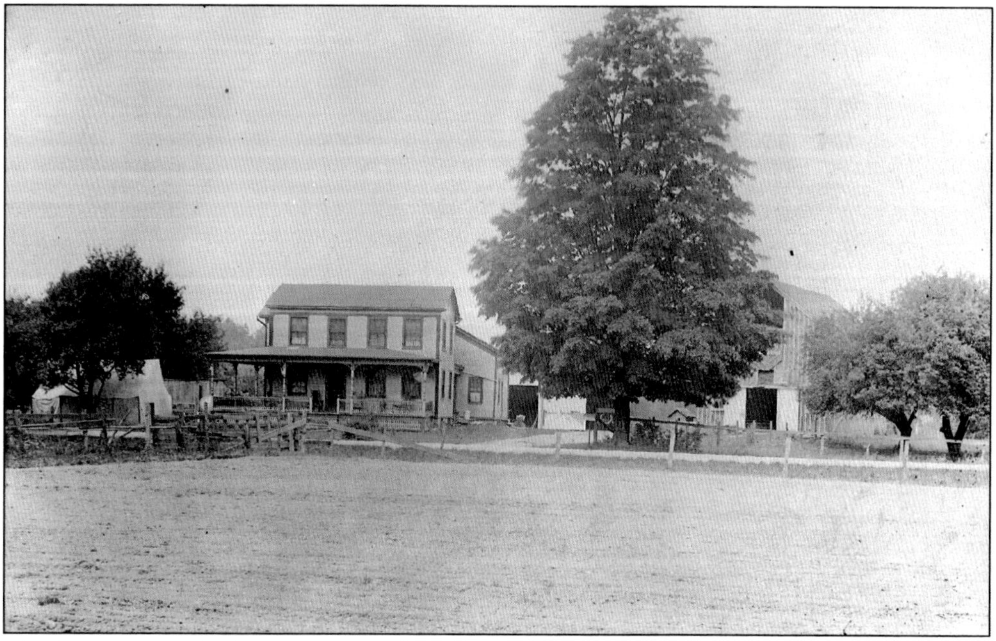

This home in North Boston is one of the oldest in town, and this photograph was taken in the early 1900s. It was built in the mid-1850s by Jonathon Hoag and was eventually handed down to his grandson Perry Kester. The large tree on the right still stands, and the house is a private residence and an antique shop. (Courtesy of Vincent and Arlene Weiss.)

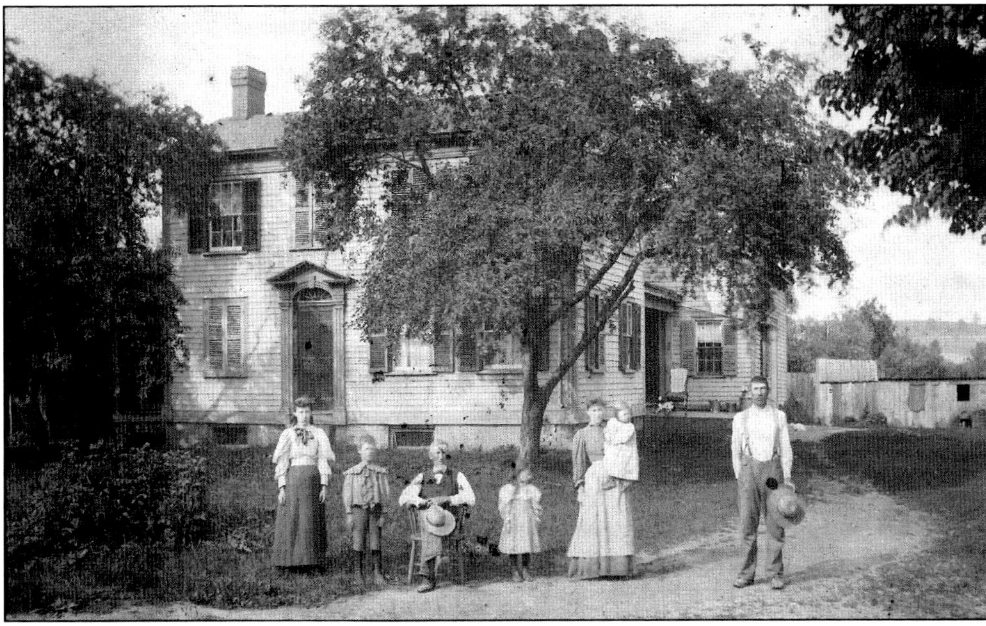

Here is an earlier photograph of the Hoag house around 1896. One can see one of the two chimneys from the fireplaces used to heat the home, which were removed in later years. The family, from left to right, includes Charlotte Dunkin, Leon Kester, Benjamin Kester (seated), Genevieve Kester, Jennie Kester, Stuart Kester (the baby), and Perry Kester. (Courtesy of Jack Kester, descendant of Perry Kester.)

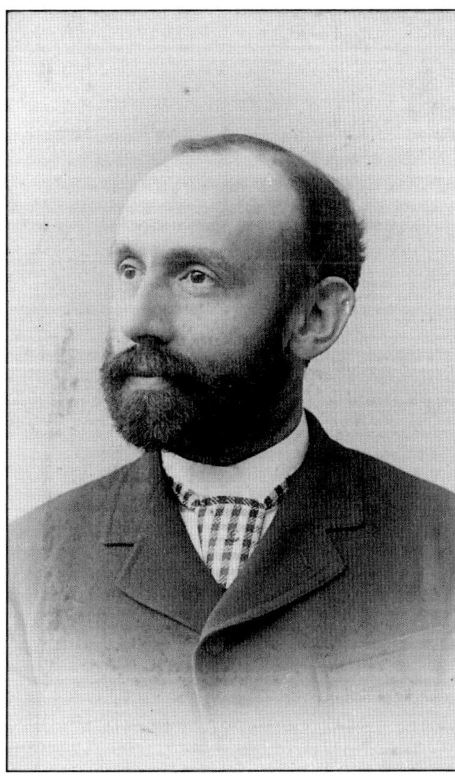

Pictured is Frank Sheldon Fosdick around 1889. Frank was the son of John Spencer Fosdick, who built the Free Will Baptist Church in 1832. Frank was the first college graduate in his family and began a teaching career as an instructor of Latin and Greek at the Buffalo Classical School. After a year's time, he moved to the public school system because he believed that a good public school education was the "foundation of democracy."

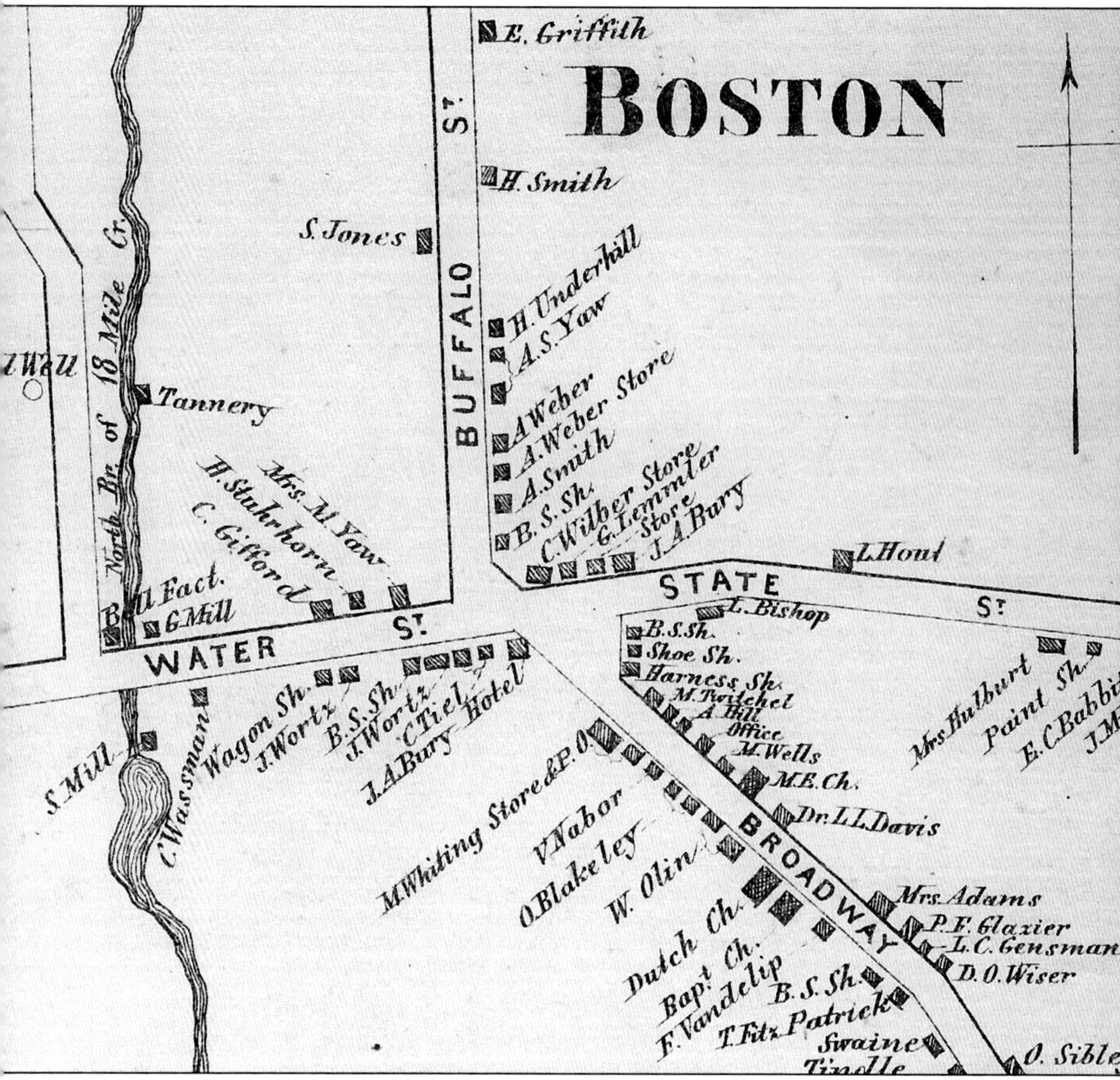

This map of Boston, from the F. W. Beers atlas of Erie County, was published in 1866. All the street names are different from the names now known. State Street is now Boston Cross Road. Water Street is now Mill Street. Buffalo Street and Broadway are now State Route 391. One can see 18 Mile Creek traveling north and south, with the Yaw Bell Factory located where the creek goes under Water Street. Along Broadway on the south side one can see Capt. Mark Whiting's store, which also was the location for the Boston Post Office; the Dutch church, which now holds the Boston Historical Museum; and the Baptist church, which was later torn down. On the other side of the road can be seen Dr. L. L. Davis's medical office and S. N. Blakeley's Harness Shop. At the intersection of all the streets is J. A. Bury's Hotel, which is now where the Boston Hotel stands. Along Buffalo Street are G. Lemmler's store and Anthony Weber's store, among others.

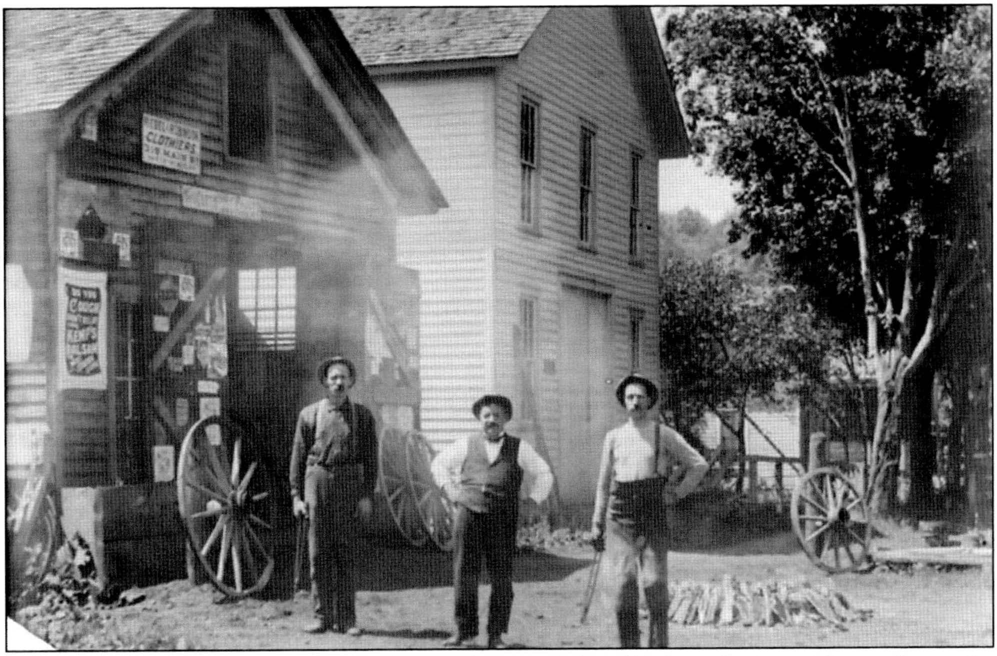

These fellows are standing in front of one of the town's four blacksmith shops. Notice the smoke from the fire they used to heat the horseshoes in order to bend them. The large sign on the very left of the picture advertises Kemp's Balsam. The *New York Times* advertised this miracle cure for coughs, colds, and sore throats as early as 1891.

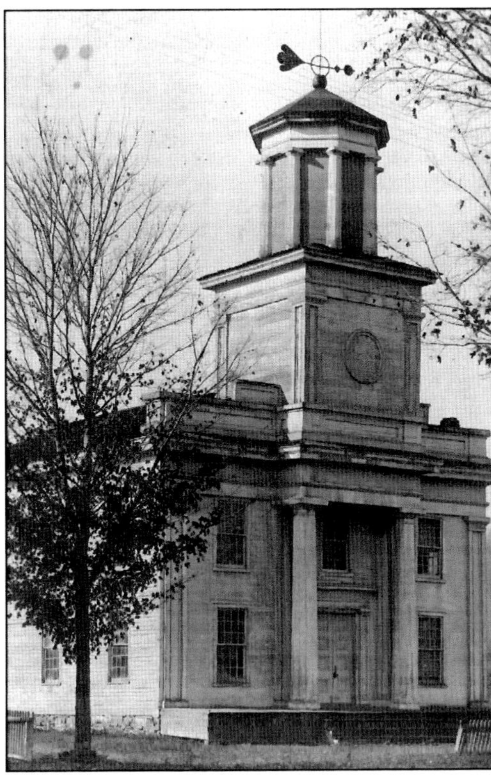

This photograph shows the Baptist church that was built in Boston in 1834. The congregation was first organized in 1811 with only 11 members. This church stood right next to the Dutch church, which was erected several years earlier. After building this structure, membership never increased and eventually decreased to the point where the building fell into disrepair and was eventually torn down.

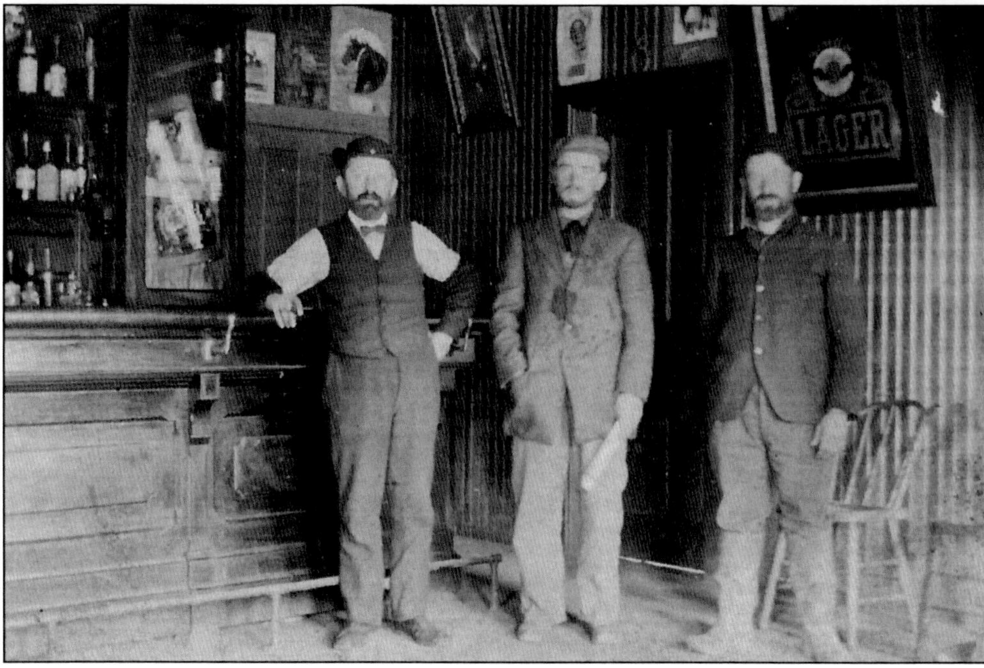

There has always been a hotel in Patchin, and this photograph show the inside of the bar around 1908. In addition to beer on tap, including William Simon lager as seen on the sign on the wall, patrons could wet their whistles with the scotch, bourbon, or gin that was kept along the back wall. Standing with the owner Edward Kaufman (left) are Al Gisman (center) and Cleveland Anthony.

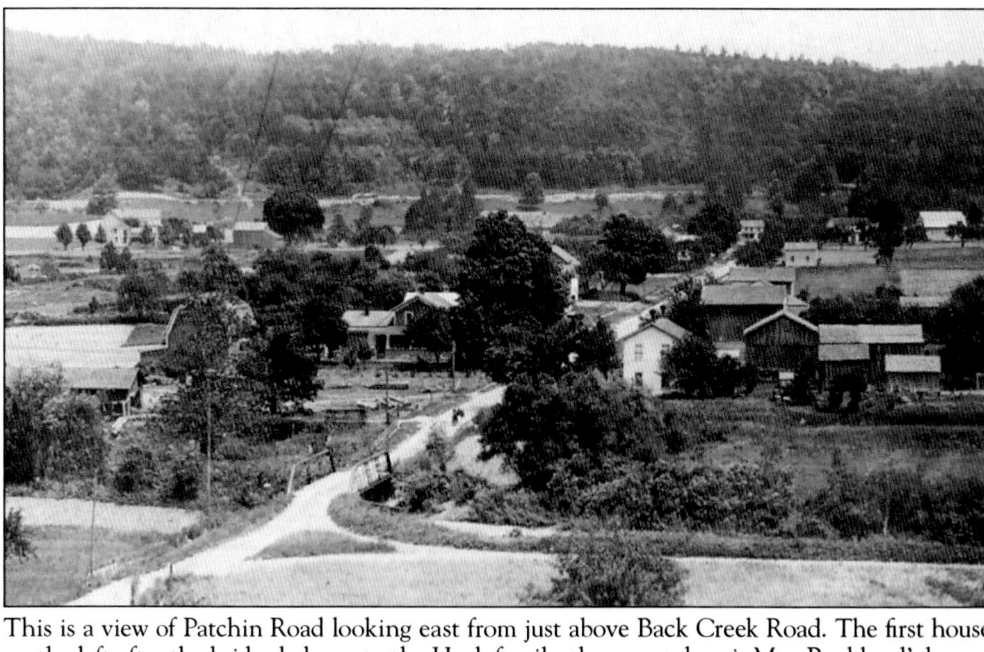

This is a view of Patchin Road looking east from just above Back Creek Road. The first house on the left after the bridge belongs to the Haab family, then next door is Mrs. Buckland's house. Right across the street is Michael Steffan's tannery. At the far end of the street, where Patchin Road meets the state road, is Flickinger's store and the Patchin Post Office.

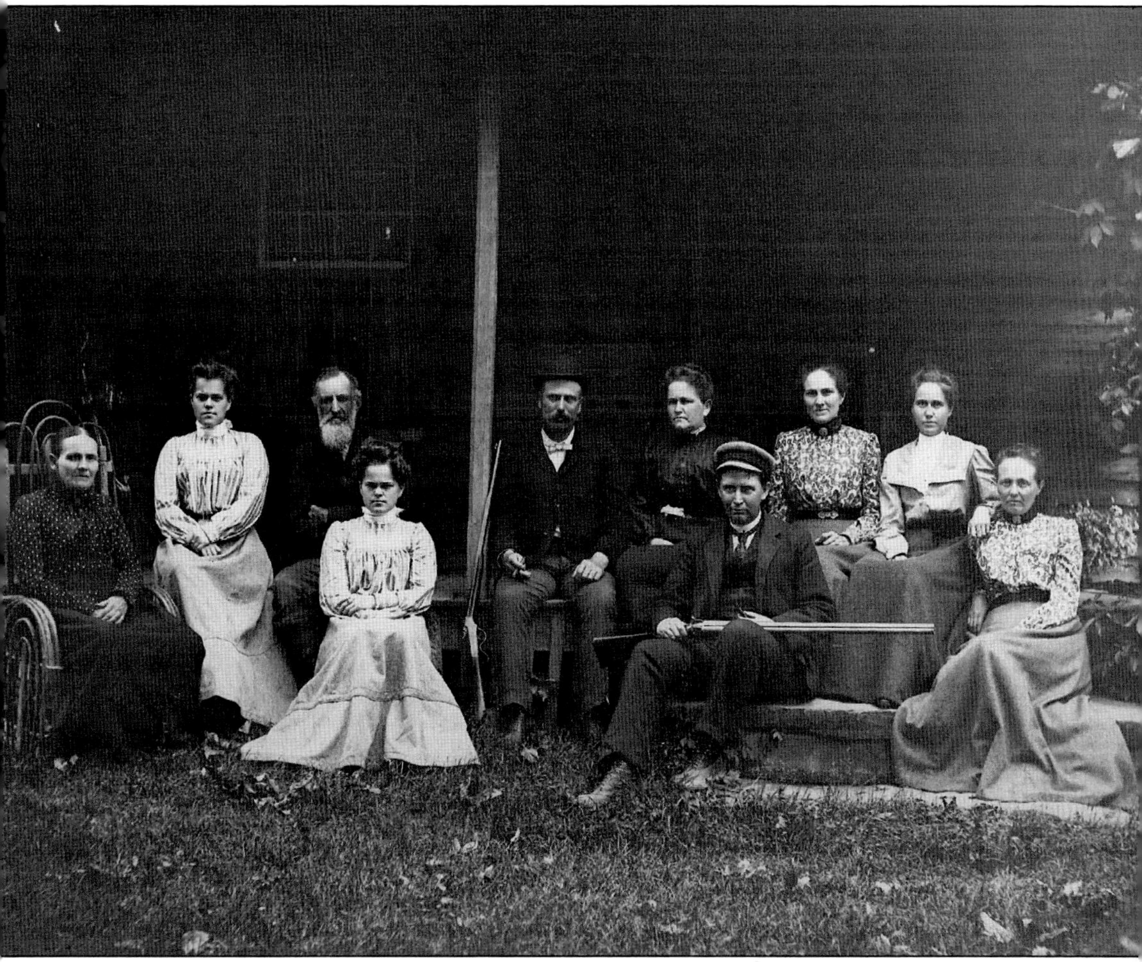

One of the founding families of Boston was the Algers. Kester and Serrill Alger came to Boston and helped build the community with their hard work and courage. Not only did the family have to fight off wild animals and the weather, but when the War of 1812 came along, the men and their sons had to leave the women to fend for themselves while they went off to fight the British and retain control of Lake Erie. Joseph Alger, Charles Johnson, Tallcut Patchin, and Richard Cary were among the Boston men who went to war. The Alger family members seen here are, from left to right, (first row) Fannie Alger, Dr. William Jennings, and his wife, Fannie Alger Jennings; (second row) Mrs. Rollin Alger, Carrie Alger (Fannie's sister), Rollin Alger, Frank Alger, Mrs. Frank Alger, Carrie Alger (Rollin and Frank's sister), and Edith Alger Dye.

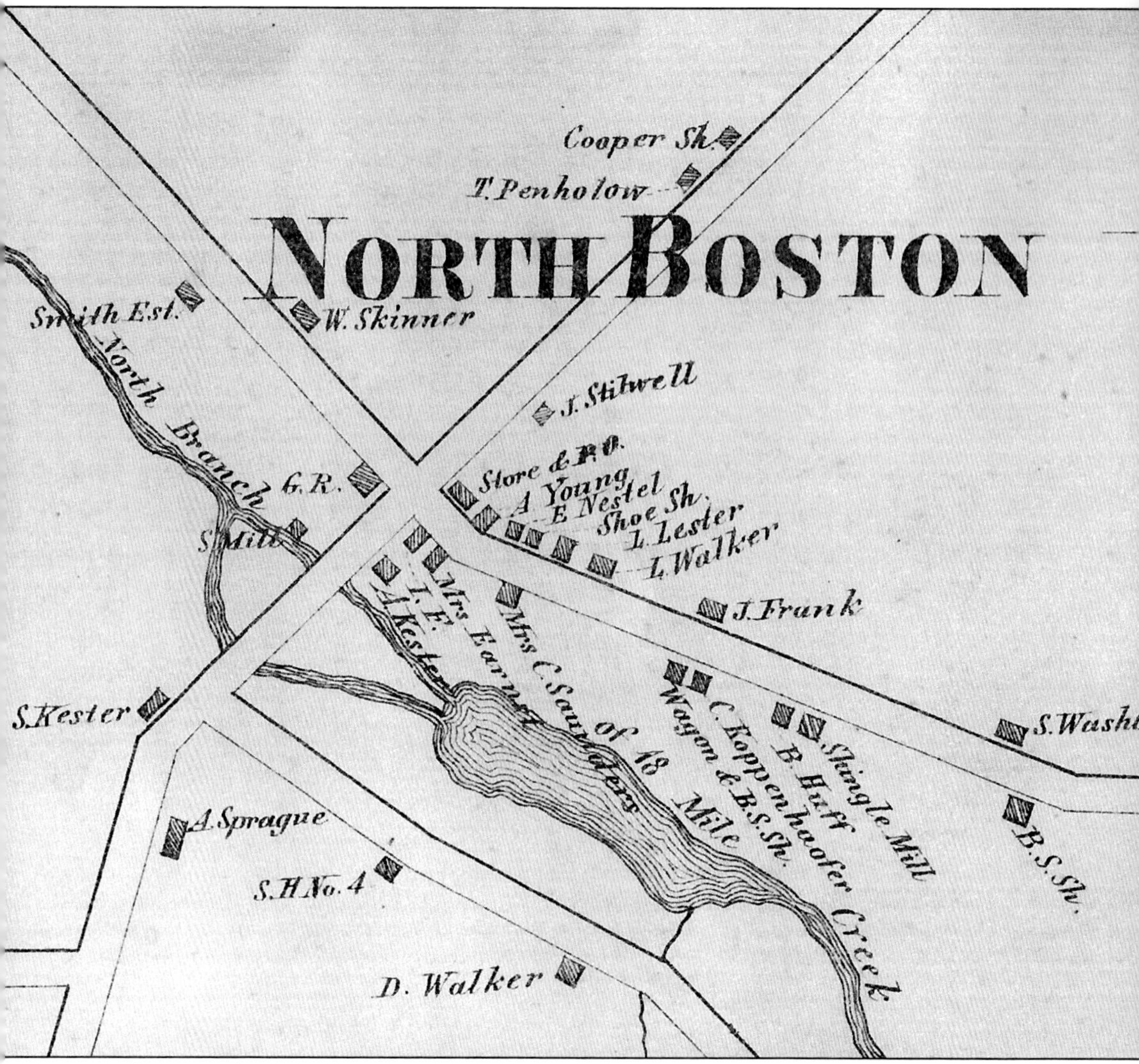

This map, also from the F. W. Beers atlas of Erie County, shows something that not many people know. Back then, 18 Mile Creek was diverted from its normal course and split into two runs, one of which would be for the exclusive use of the sawmill. The sawmill is seen on the map as a small block marked "S. Mill." The rest of the map shows the current State Route 391 intersecting with Zimmerman Road, with 18 Mile Creek shown parallel and in between Route 391 and Back Creek Road. "S.H. No. 4" is schoolhouse No. 4, which used to stand next to Boston Valley School but was torn down several years ago because the foundation was crumbling. Maps of later years show the creek running in a single path, evidently because the sawmill was no longer in use and the diversion of the water was no longer necessary. Now there is no visible evidence that the path of the water was anything other than the way it travels now.

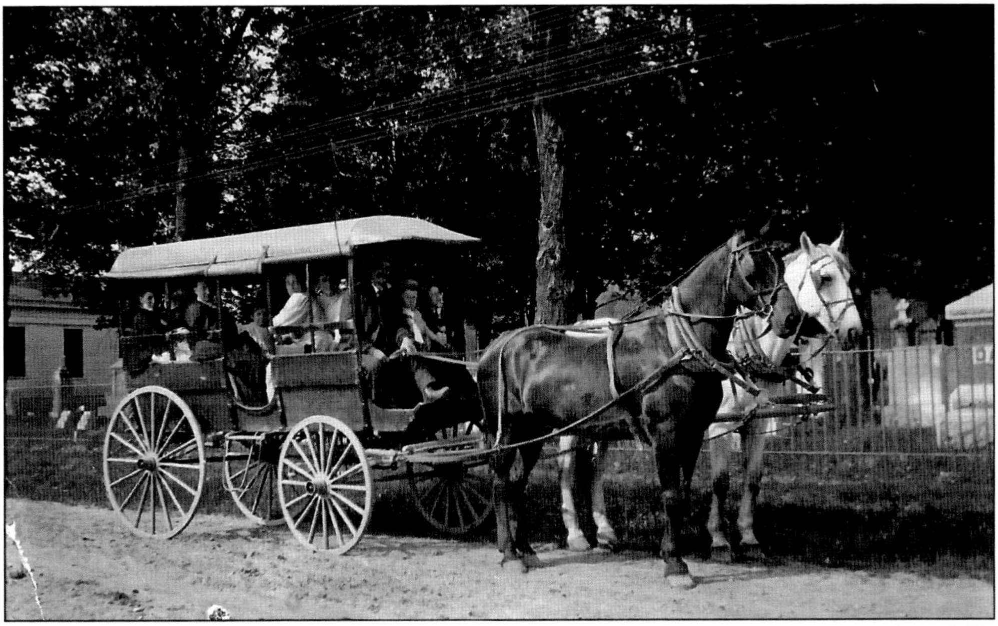

The stagecoach was the only form of public transportation in the late 19th century. These folks are headed south toward Springville on the state road. They probably got on the stage in front of the Patchin Hotel. They are sitting in front of Maplewood Cemetery, which is a stone's throw from the hotel. The lines that look like scratches at the top of the picture are actually telegraph and telephone lines.

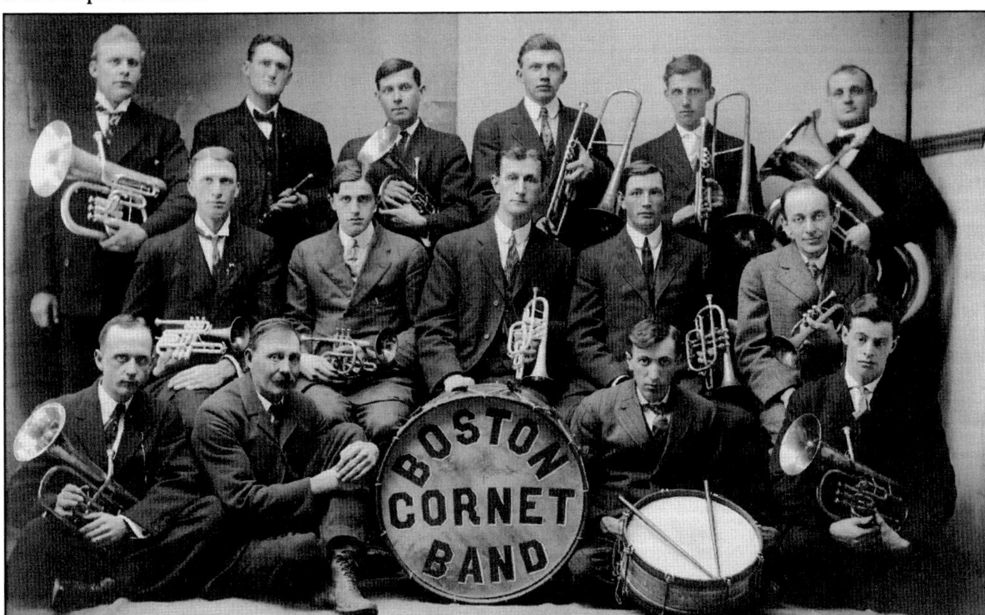

This c. 1910 photograph shows one of two cornet bands that existed in Boston at the beginning of the 20th century. From left to right are (first row) George Weber, Frank Fiveshilling, John Nabor, and Albert Rucker; (second row) Henry Trevett, Clifford Drake, Jacob Busch (leader), Carl Emerling, and Lee Blackley; (third row) C. J. Thurber, John Parkinson, H. S. Owen, Harry Trevett, Herbert Wurtz, and Frank Brunner.

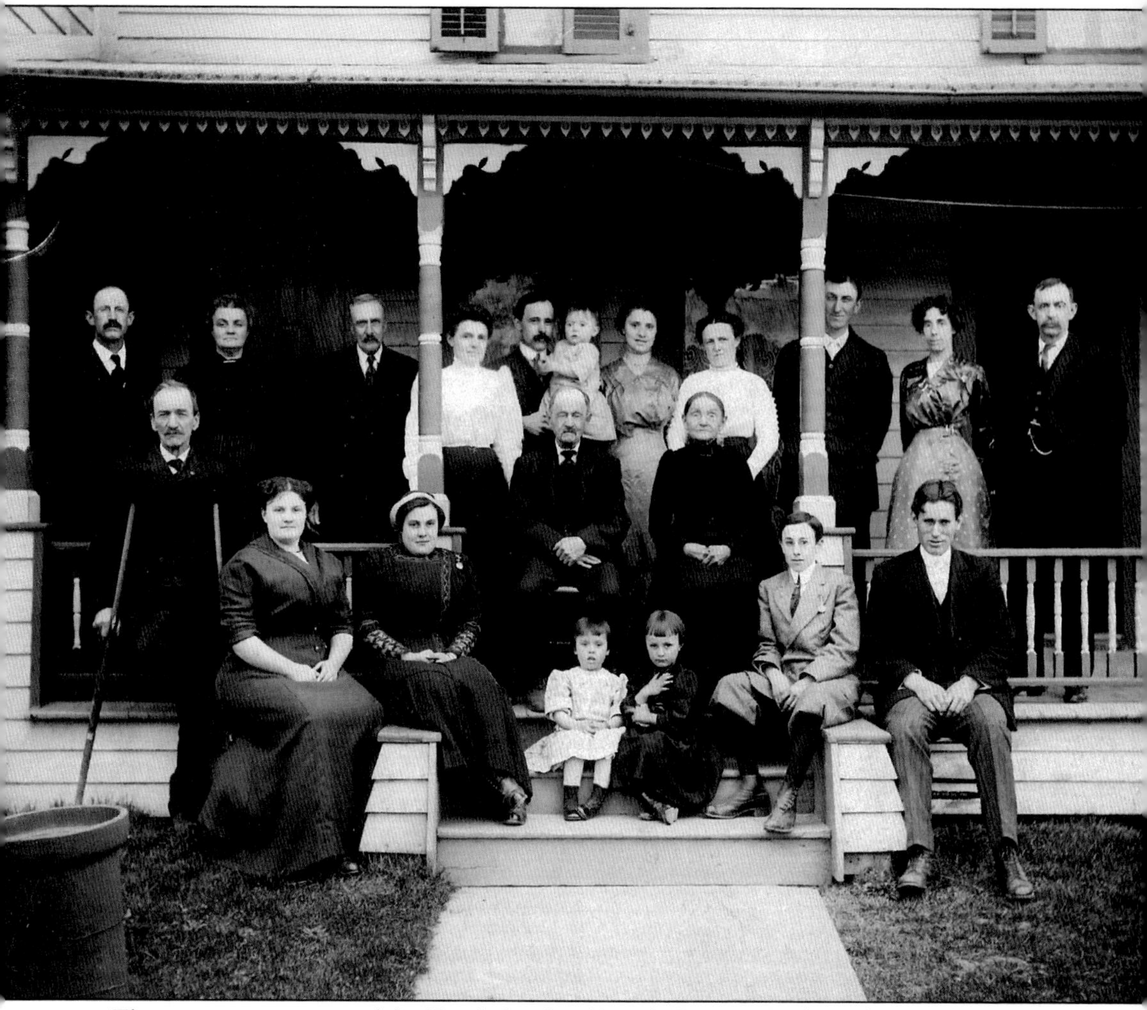

This is a great portrait of the Frank family of North Boston. Fred Frank owned and operated several businesses in town: a grocery and hardware store on the corner of Zimmerman Road and Boston State Road and a harness shop a little way down the street from his store. He donated some of the land he owned to the newly formed North Boston Fire Company in 1904. He was also involved in the North Boston Cornet Band as a leader and a player. From left to right are (first row) Leonora Monckton, Georgia Massing, Violet Frank, Bernice Monckton, Lyle Frank, and Leonard Monckton; (second row) Mr. Brodbeck (who lost his leg fighting during the Civil War), Fred's father Jacob Frank, and his mother Emma Haab Frank; (third row) Fred Frank, Amelia Frank (his wife), James and Lena Titus, Henry Frank holding his son Horris, Adeline Frank, Rose and Jake Brodbeck, and Rose and Jake Frank. (Courtesy of Norman Gern.)

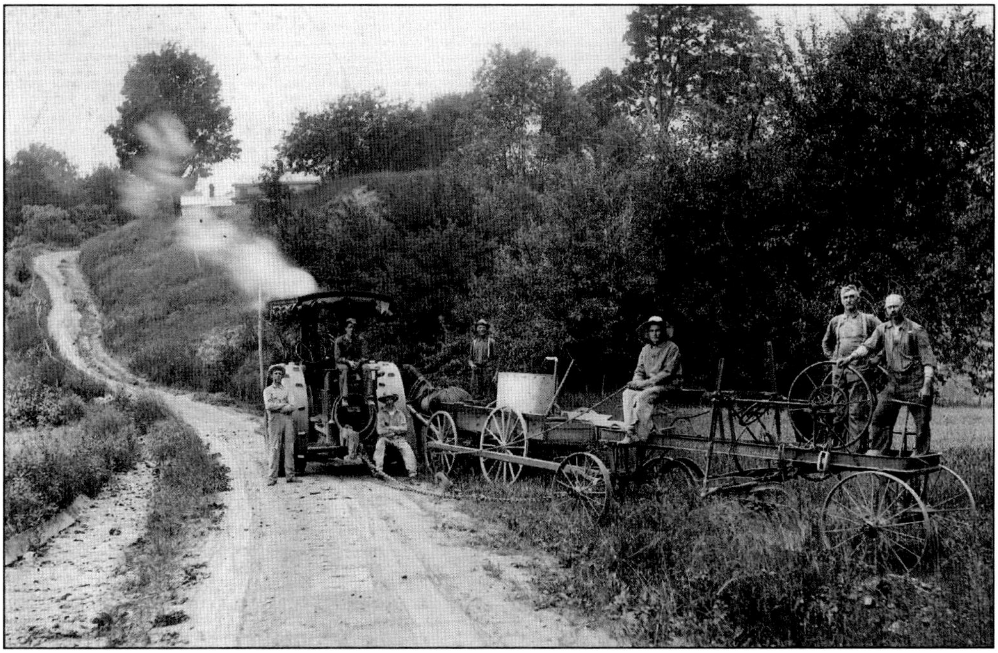

The Boston Highway Department has a long history of working hard to keep the town roads in good shape. Beginning with the overseers of highways in 1818, the job has always been necessary and sometimes troublesome. Of course, every job is easier as long as one has the right tools. Pictured from left to right are Guy Thurber, Charles Klein, Clarence Klein, Dick Walker, Fred Blanchard, Frank Bond, and Jake Hauck.

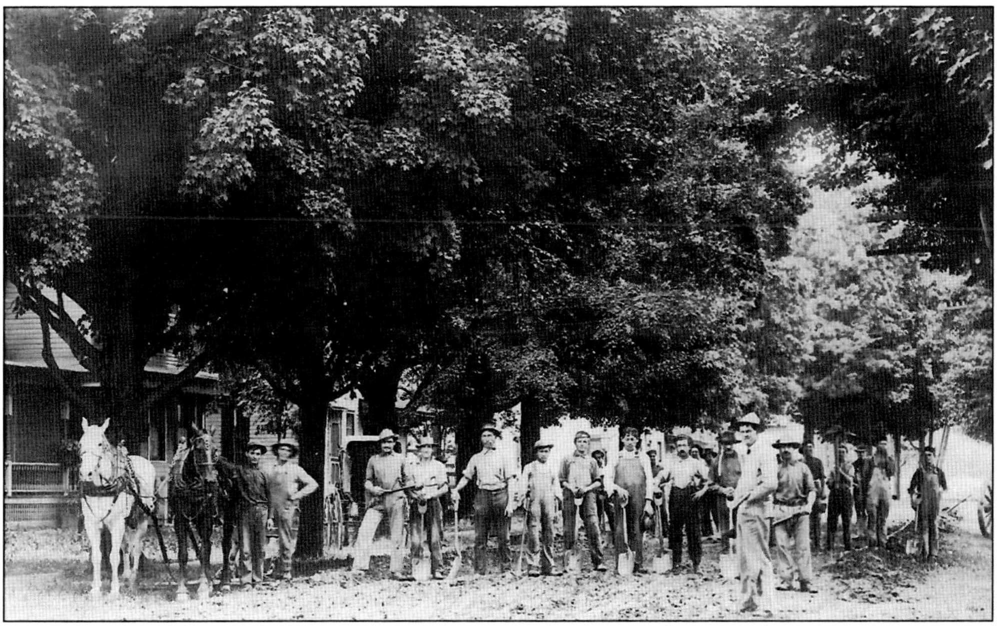

This is an earlier photograph showing the job of keeping up the roads. At the beginning of the 20th century, men could work off their taxes rather than come up with the money to pay them. Here a group is getting ready to take care of the state road, not far from where Emerling Chevrolet now stands.

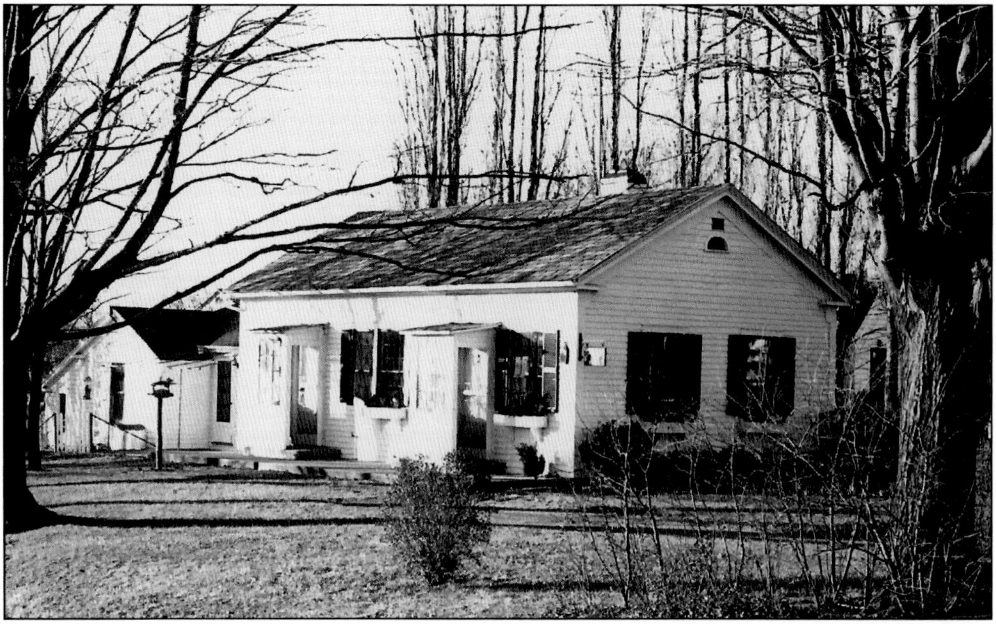

The Quakers who came to this area at the beginning of the 19th century began holding their meetings in East Hamburg (now Orchard Park). In 1828, the group had differences that caused a split; the two factions became known as the Hicksites and the Orthodox Quakers. The orthodox group built a log meetinghouse in North Boston and replaced it in 1840 with this frame building that still stands today as a private residence.

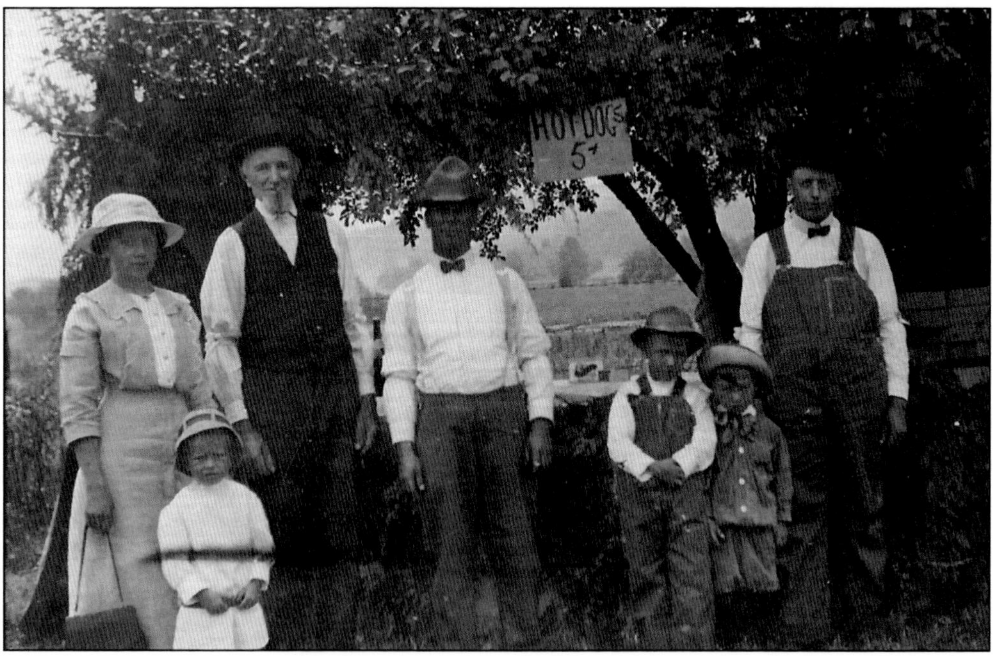

Seen here with her family, Mrs. Burr decided, well before her time, that the men were not the only ones who could earn money. Selling hot dogs for 5¢ apiece probably would not make her rich overnight, but it was a good way to teach the children a lesson in entrepreneurial spirit and how to count money.

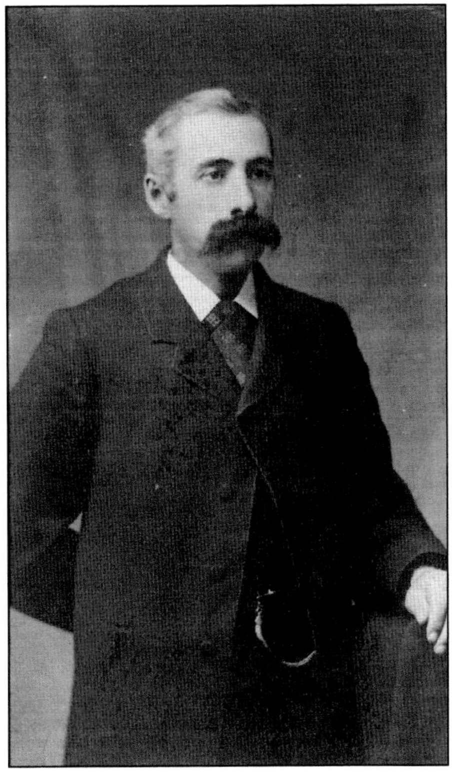

A. A. Underhill was born in 1850 and first lived on his grandfather's farm on Horton Hill, two miles from the Boston village. After a few years, his family moved to a dairy farm in the valley. He wrote a diary of his life experiences, showing rare insight into what motivated and affected people who lived during the days of horse and buggies and no electricity. As a child, he wrote of walking to school everyday, leaving at lunchtime to move the family cow herd to another pasture a mile away, eating his small lunch on the way, walking back to school, and walking back home to start his chores. At age 12, a year after the photograph below was taken, he started working for neighboring farms for his room and board. By the age of 19, he was running a cheese factory, teaching school, and working in a tannery.

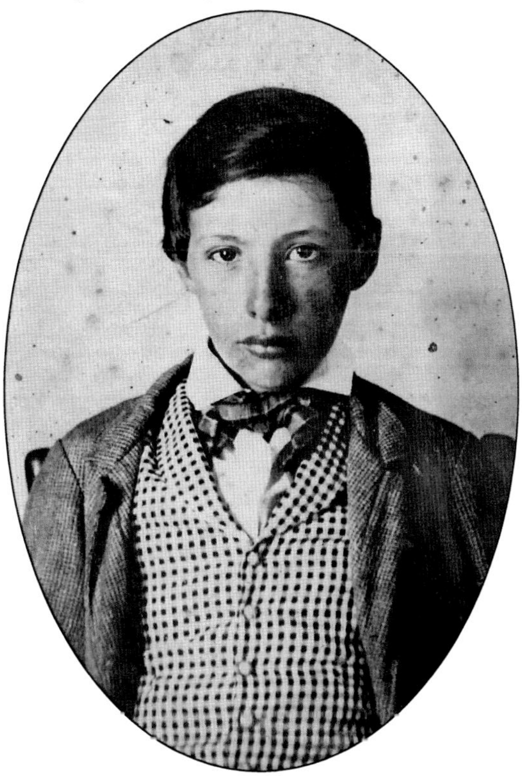

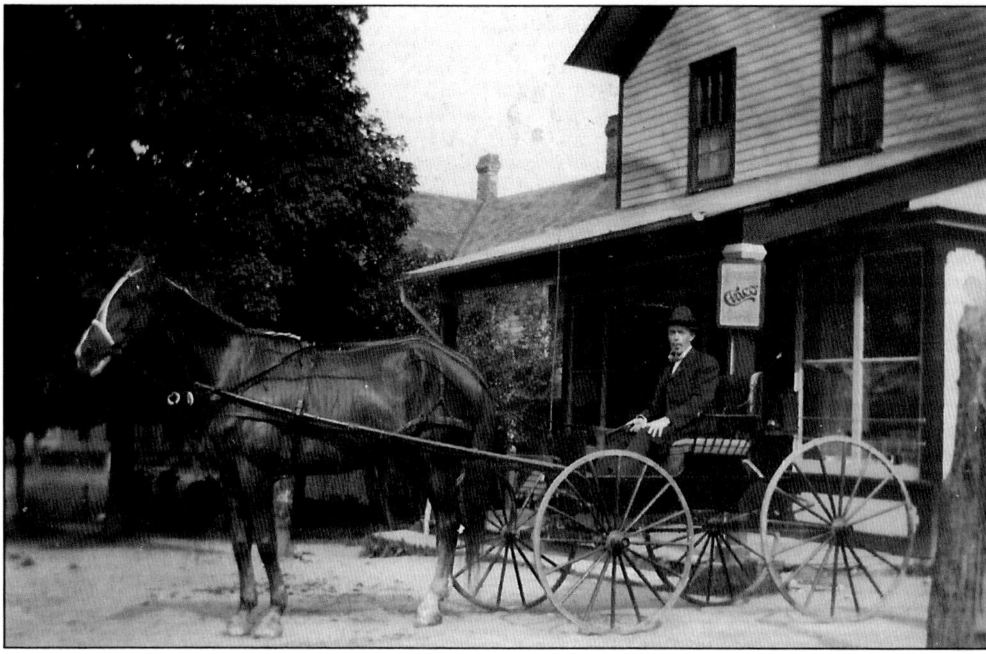

Riding in an excellent example of a 19th-century buggy, this Dye family ancestor poses in what was called a "cut under" buggy. It might even have been a Concord buggy, invented in Concord, New Hampshire, in 1813, that had special springs built into it for a smoother ride. The horse is wearing a loosely woven black shawl. (Courtesy of Jane Clarke.)

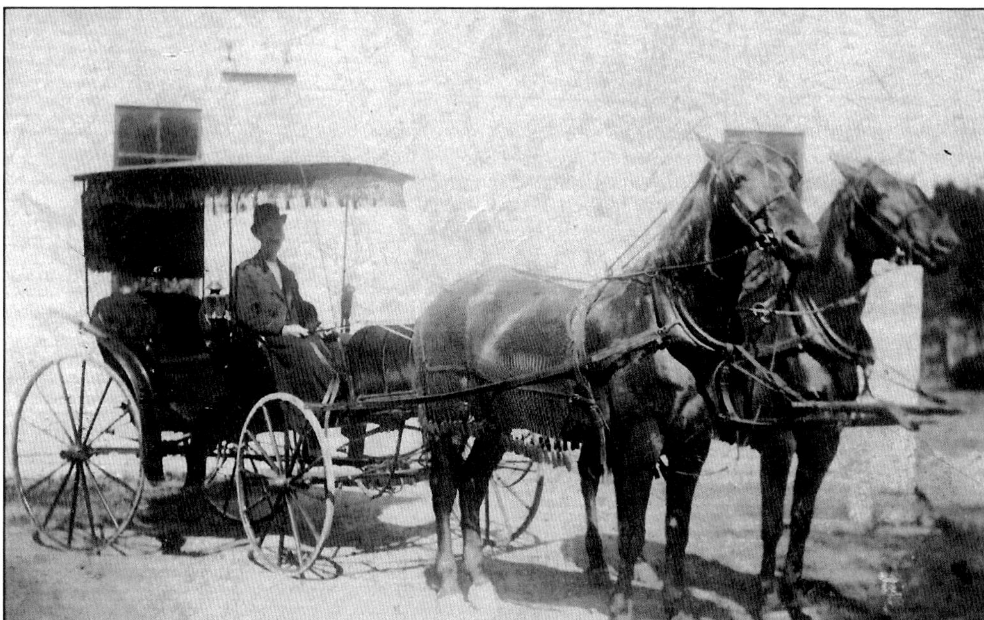

Here another Dye family ancestor travels in a popular mode of transportation in the late 19th century. This was one of the "surries with the fringe on top" popularized by the song of the same name. Here again, the horses are fitted with shawls customized with matching fringe to the buggy. (Courtesy of Jane Clarke.)

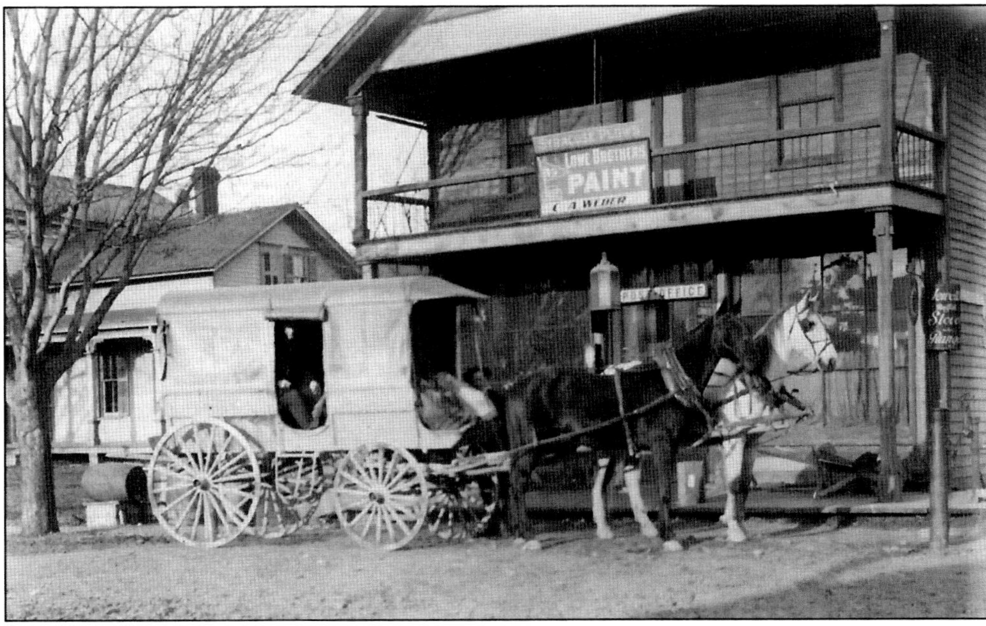

Post offices started out being located within a store, since there really were not that many people who received mail. This was the location of the Patchin Post Office in the 1900s inside C. A. Weber's store, which was in the building that now stands next to Goehler's Produce Market. The signs show that one could buy plows, paint, stoves, and ranges in the store. The mail stage shown here carried mail and occasionally passengers.

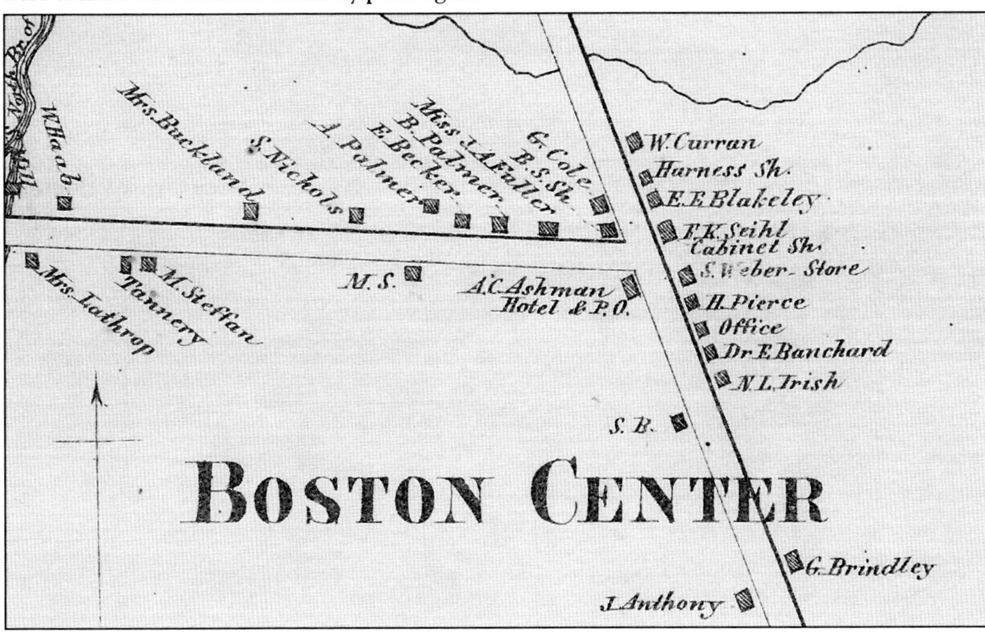

Finally, the F. W. Beers atlas of Erie County shows a map of Boston Center, now called Patchin. One can see Michael Steffan's tannery on what is now Patchin Road, a harness shop, a cabinet shop, Weber's store, and Dr. Blanchard's office on the main road and evidence that the post office in 1866 was then located within Ashman's Hotel, which became the Valley View Inn 100 years later.

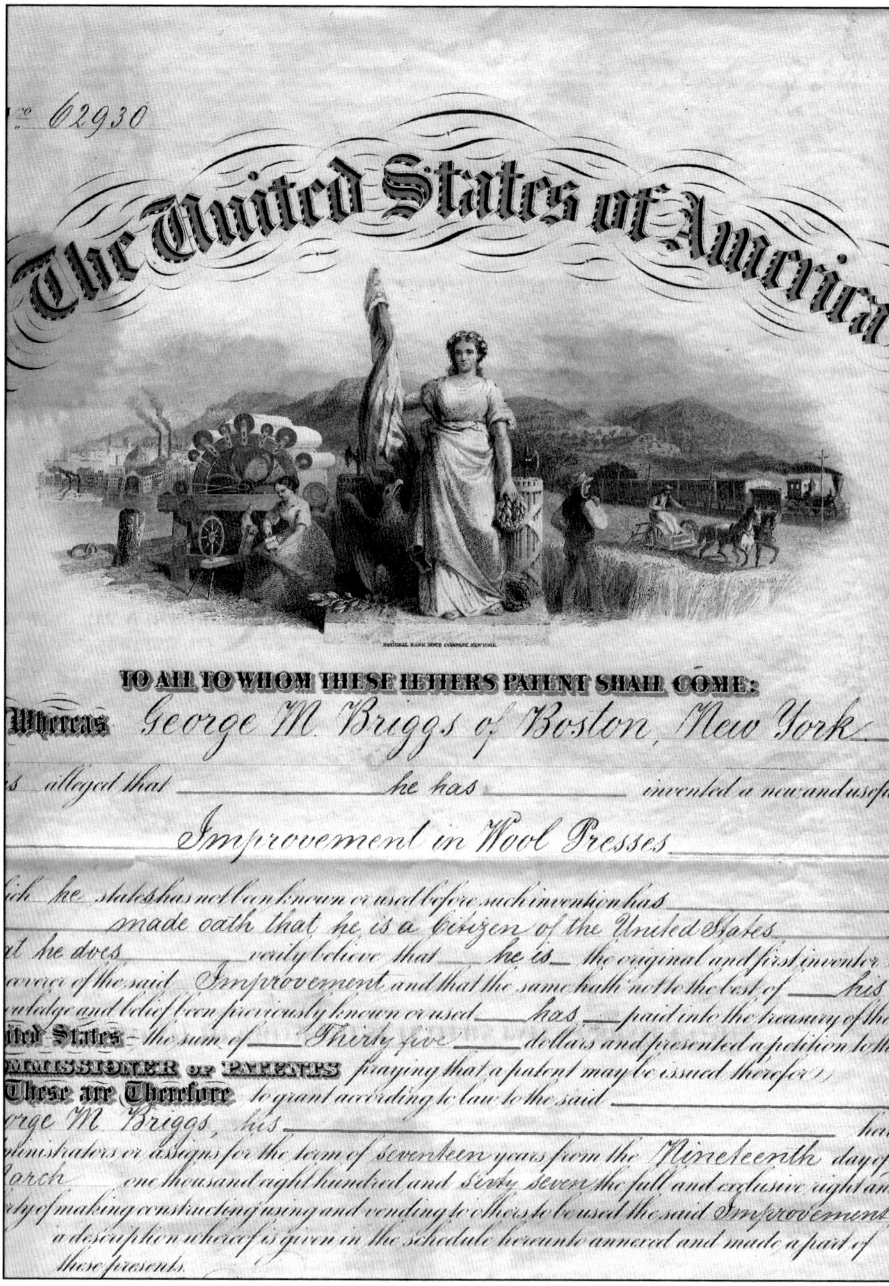
Nº 62930

The United States of America

TO ALL TO WHOM THESE LETTERS PATENT SHALL COME:

Whereas George M. Briggs of Boston, New York

s alleged that he has invented a new and usef

Improvement in Wool Presses

ich he states has not been known or used before such invention has made oath that he is a Citizen of the United States t he does verily believe that he is the original and first inventor overer of the said Improvement and that the same hath not to the best of his owledge and belief been previously known or used has paid into the treasury of the ited States the sum of Thirty five dollars and presented a petition to the MMISSIONER OF PATENTS praying that a patent may be issued therefor.

These are Therefore to grant according to law to the said rge M Briggs, his hei ministrators or assigns for the term of seventeen years from the Nineteenth day of arch one thousand eight hundred and sixty seven the full and exclusive right an ty of making constructing using and vending to others to be used the said Improvement a description whereof is given in the schedule hereunto annexed and made a part of these presents.

The resourcefulness and ingenuity of the townspeople in the 19th century did not go unrecognized. In 1867, George Briggs was awarded patent No. 62,930 from the U.S. Patent Office for his invention of improved wool presses used in baling fleeces together for transport. Further pages of the patent showed very detailed drawings of his invention. The patent was awarded to him after he paid a huge sum of $35 and the patent was personally signed by W. T. Otto, acting secretary of the interior, and Gen. A. M. Stout, acting commissioner of patents. It was good for 17 years from March 19, 1867. This patent was awarded at the beginning of this country's industrial revolution, moving the agricultural community from using simple tools to do their job to using complex machinery to get the job done faster and with less work.

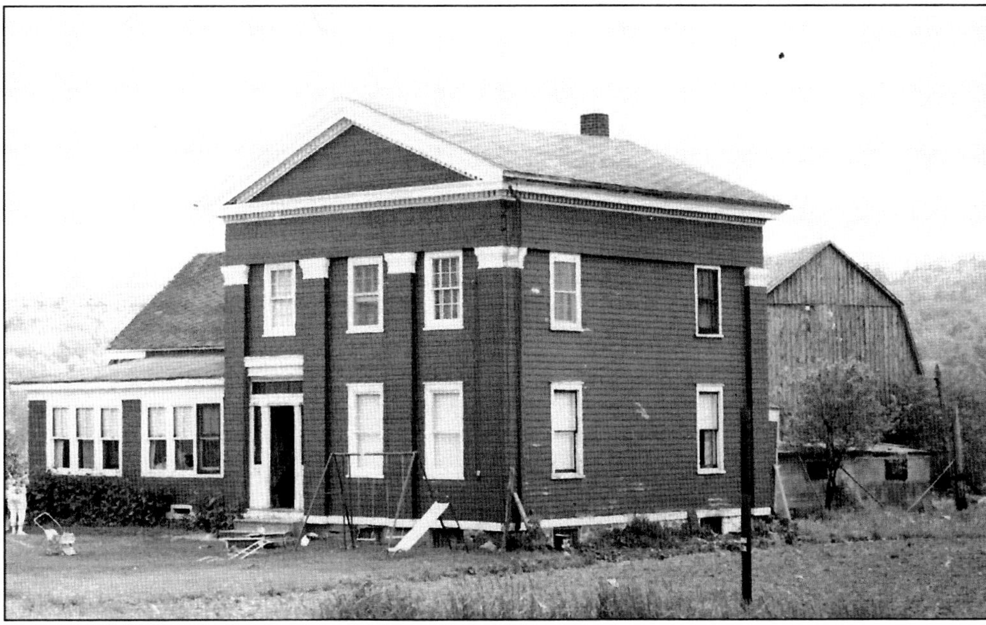

This photograph shows the original home of Talcutt Patchin. He built the house just after he moved into town around 1820. The house was also used at one time as a tollhouse where travelers were stopped to pay a toll for the privilege of using the road, then built with hewn wooden planks that replaced the dirt and mud. A toll had to be taken to make enough money for the upkeep of the planks.

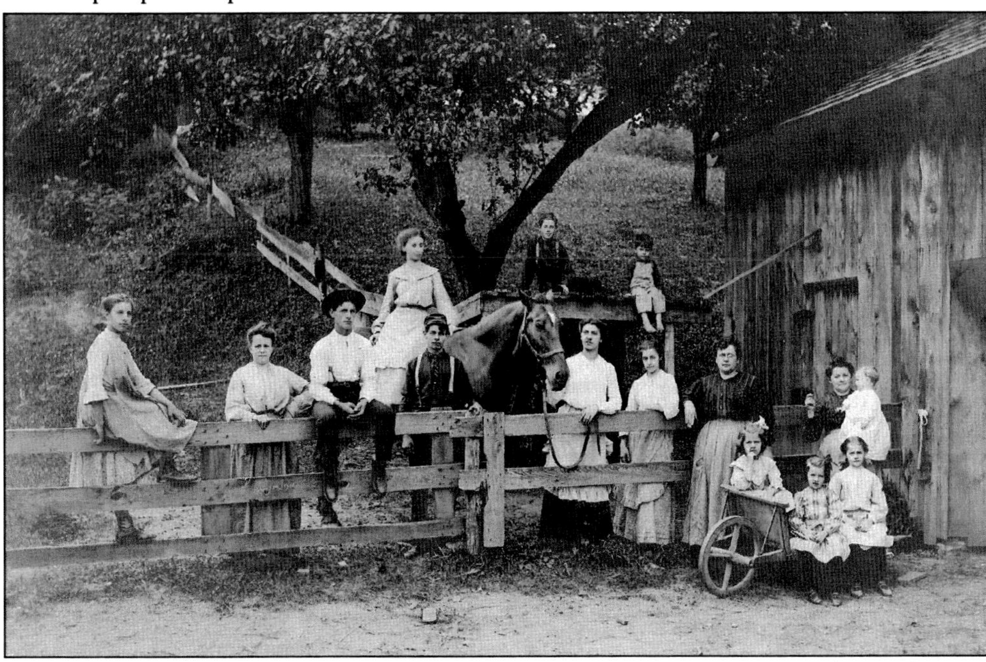

The farm was the base camp of the pioneer family. By the time the boys were in their early teens, they were working for neighboring farmers as well as their family's farm, and the women and girls had to take care of the animals and spend many hours every day canning, salting and smoking meat, and baking. Here they are taking a short break to pose for a family portrait.

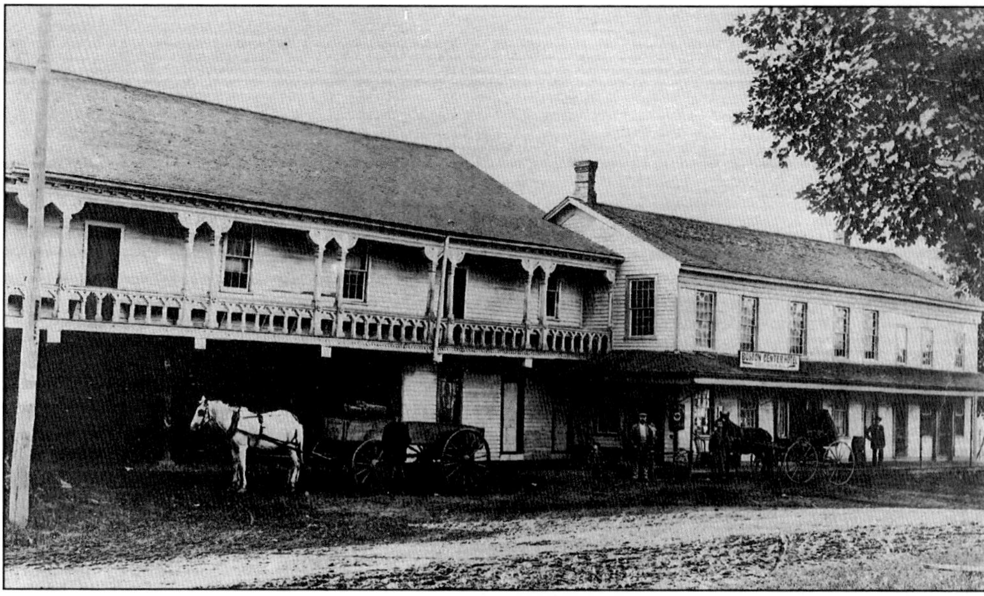

In this pre-1904 photograph, the Boston Center Hotel in Patchin is seen. The building on the left was used for the storage of wagons and a stable for the horses for tenants of the hotel. The hotel and stable stood on the corner of the state road and Patchin Road where the Valley View now stands. The original buildings burned down on Valentine's Day 1904.

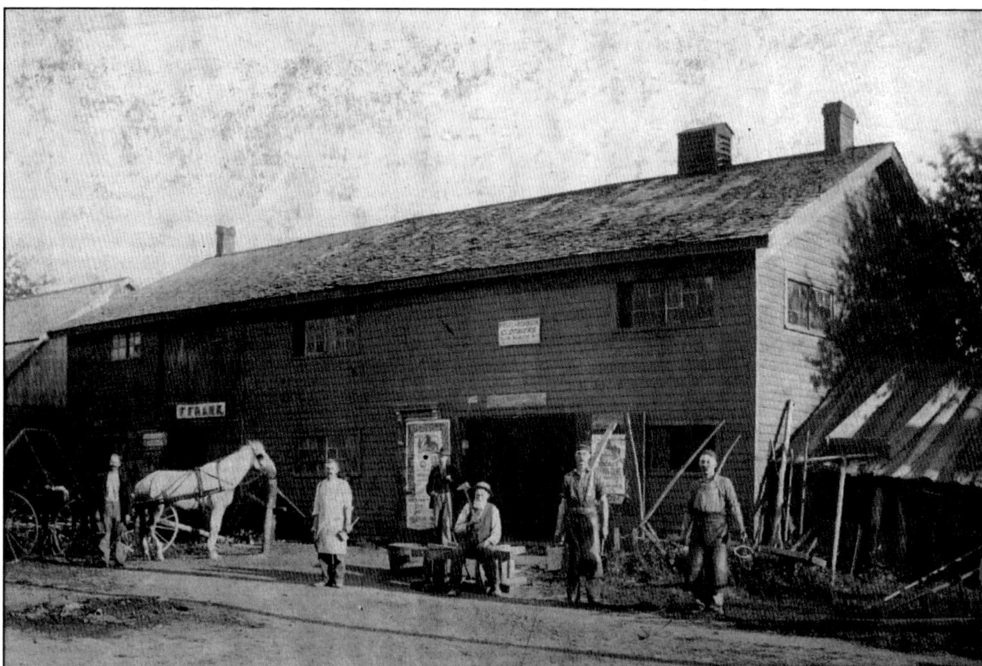

This is Fred Frank's harness shop in North Boston. The posters on either side of the main door advertise Kendall's Spavin Cure. Spavin was a joint inflammation suffered by horses that caused lameness. It is now known that it is caused by osteoarthritis. So not only did Fred Frank produce custom-made harnesses, he also provided medicinal cures for the treatment of horse diseases. The building still stands and has been remodeled into an apartment building.

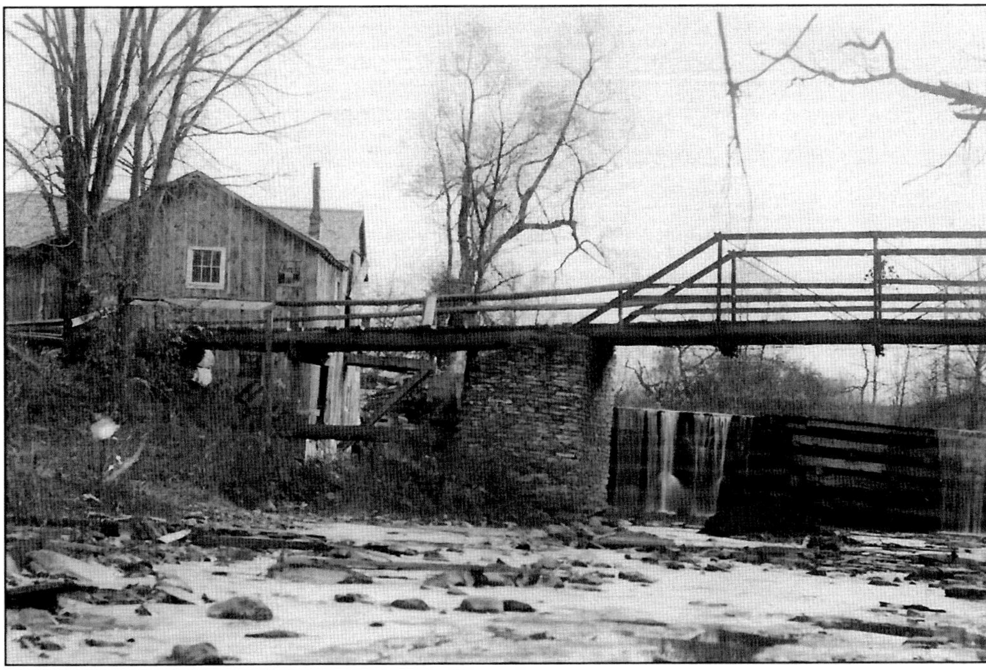

Sawmills were built all along 18 Mile Creek, like this one at Mill Street and Back Creek Road. The creek was dammed up to control the flow of the water that was used to power the mill. This bridge does not look very sturdy, but after replacing it a few times over the years, it is quite sturdy now.

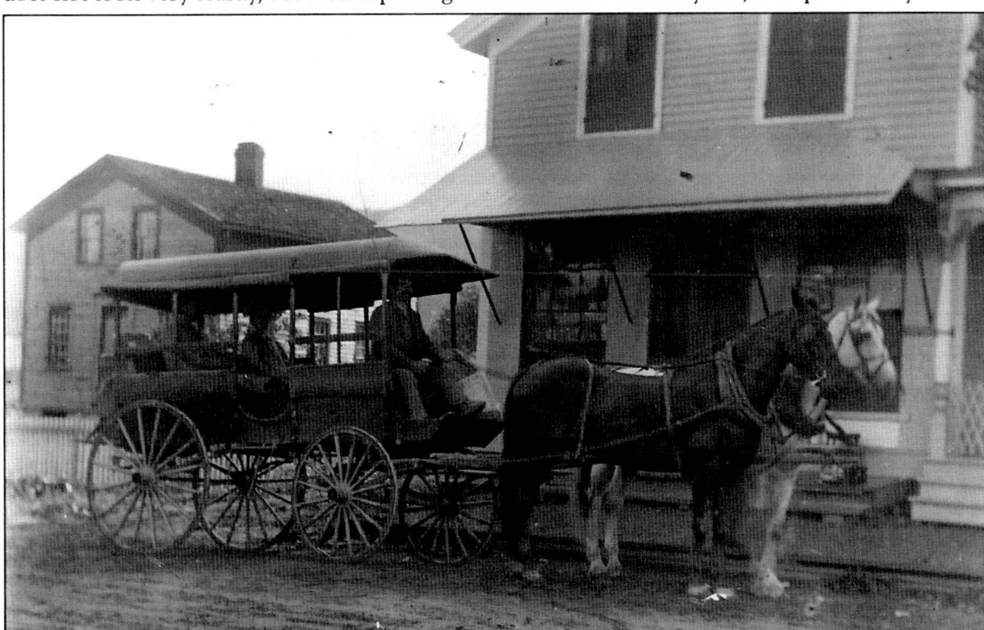

Just like people now usually know their mailman, everyone used to know the stagecoach driver. Boston's driver was John Gasper. He knew everyone in town and would tip his hat and call people by name when he passed them by. Not only did John Gasper carry the mail, he carried travelers and sometimes, when it was especially cold outside, he would pick up the children who were walking home from school and give them a ride home.

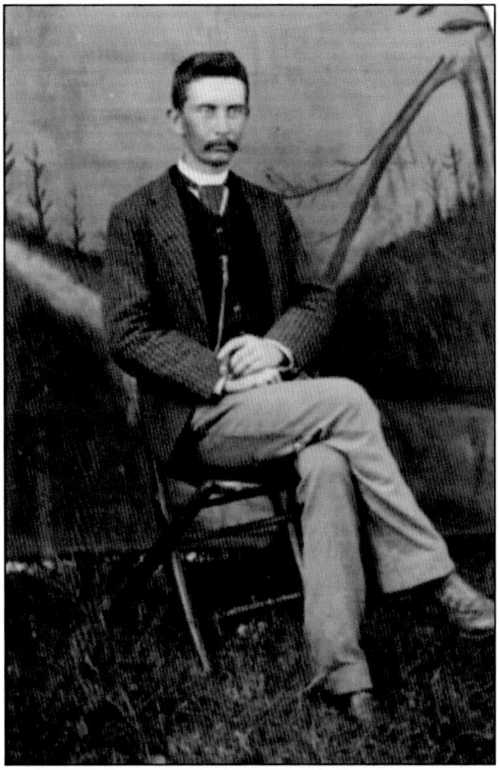

This photograph is a tintype of Dr. William Jennings, one of the first doctors to take up residence in Boston. He looks handsome in his button-top shoes and golden watch chain. Dr. Jennings married into the Alger family and owned a home in Boston across the street from St. Paul's Church.

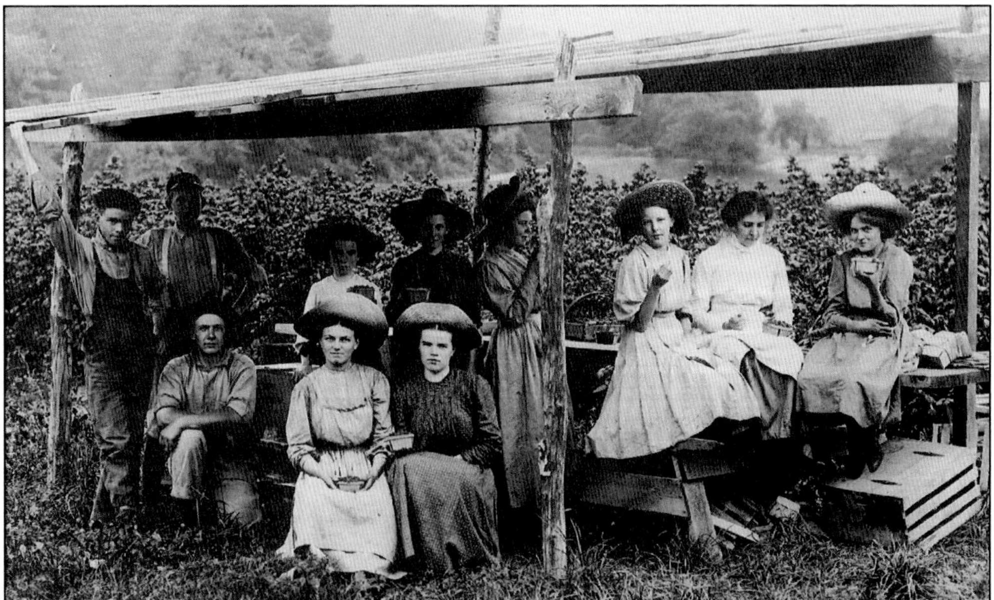

Not everything about farming was hard work. Many times, when a crop was ready to be picked, it was turned into a social occasion. Neighbors would come over, bring picnic lunches, and enjoy one another's company while they all helped to get the ripe fruit or the tender beans and peas off the vines before the insects and the birds got them.

Two

Important People and Events

In 1824, John Love came to western New York looking for work. He took a job on a ship that traveled the Great Lakes, and during the winter of 1824–1825, he boarded with a family in North Boston. His landlords, three brothers by the name of Isaac, Israel Jr., and Nelson Thayer, were not prosperous men. Their families were starving, so Love lent them money and the thanks they gave him involved a shotgun blast to the head. The brothers had planned his murder so they could claim all his money. They buried his body in a ravine in back of the house. The townspeople found his dead body, and the brothers were arrested and taken to jail in Buffalo. There they were tried for their crime, and all three were hanged in Niagara Square in front of thousands of spectators.

In 1843, a sick traveler came through town and stopped at Fuller's Tavern in North Boston. He took to a bed in one of the rooms to rent, and within a few days he died. No sooner had the authorities been notified when several townspeople started getting sick, and almost a quarter of the town's population died. A medical expert from Buffalo, Dr. Austin Flint, was summoned. His conclusion was that the traveler had been suffering from typhoid fever, and the spread of the disease was caused by the pestilence finding its way into the well, which supplied the townspeople with their water supply. This revelation was the first discovery in this country that disease could be spread by tainted water.

Ellen Beach Yaw was born on September 14, 1868. As Ellen grew up, her family discovered that she had a remarkable singing voice and was often heard outside mimicking the birds as she picked raspberries. When she was 17 years old, several women from Hamburg sent her to take singing lessons in New York City, and her great talent took her all the way to Paris and London, where she starred in many great opera companies. She became a world-famous coloratura soprano and performed all over the world, including Carnegie Hall in 1896. She lived out her last 30 years in California where her great charity work became as legendary as her singing.

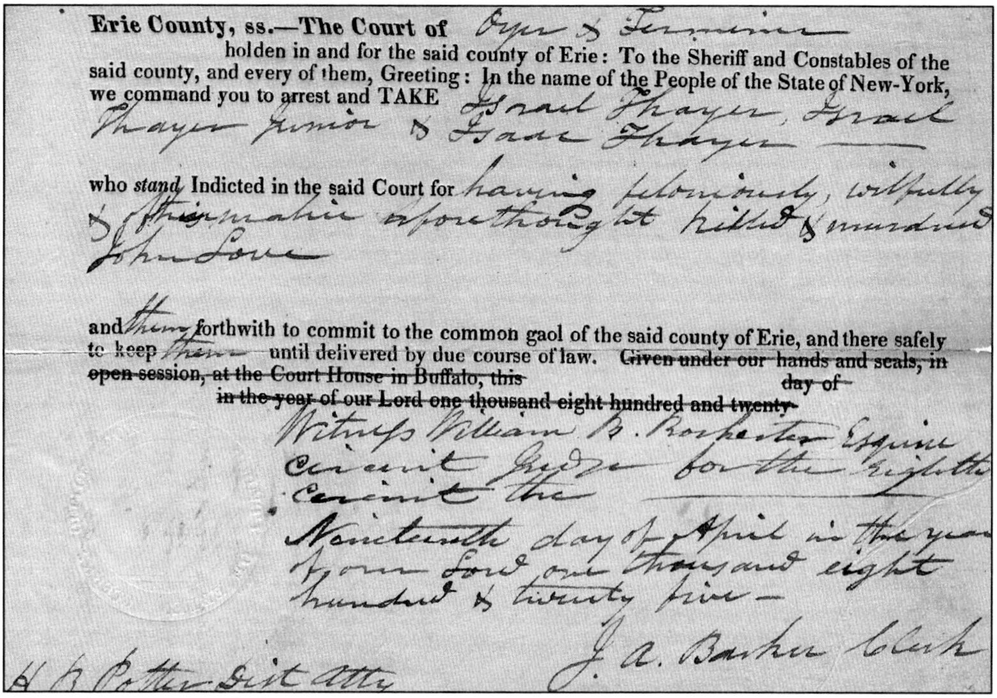

Erie County, ss.—The Court of Oyer & Terminer
holden in and for the said county of Erie: To the Sheriff and Constables of the said county, and every of them, Greeting: In the name of the People of the State of New-York, we command you to arrest and TAKE Israel Thayer, Israel Thayer Junior & Isaac Thayer —

who *stand* Indicted in the said Court for having feloniously, willfully & with malice aforethought killed & murdered John Love

and them forthwith to commit to the common gaol of the said county of Erie, and there safely to keep them until delivered by due course of law. ~~Given under our hands and seals, in open session, at the Court House in Buffalo, this day of in the year of our Lord one thousand eight hundred and twenty~~

Witness William B. Rochester Esquire Circuit Judge for the Eighth Circuit the Nineteenth day of April in the year of our Lord one thousand eight hundred & twenty five —

J. A. Barker Clerk

H B Potter Dist Atty

When the townspeople became suspicious of John Love's absence, they also noticed that the Thayers seemed to be flush with extra money. They put together a search party, suspecting foul play. After several days of searching, they found Love's frozen body in the ravine with his toes sticking out of the snow. This is the original warrant that was made out for the Thayer brothers' arrest, along with their father, whom everyone suspected might also be involved. The warrant names Israel Thayer, Israel Thayer Jr., and Isaac Thayer and indicts them for "having feloniously, willfully and with malice aforethought, killed and murdered John Love." The warrant is signed by H. B. Potter, district attorney for the city of Buffalo. A separate warrant was made out for the third brother, Nelson.

Oyer & Terminer
The People
vs.
Israel Thayer
Israel Thayer Jun.
Isaac Thayer
Bench warr.
H. B. Potter
Dist. Atty
Filed October 31. 1825

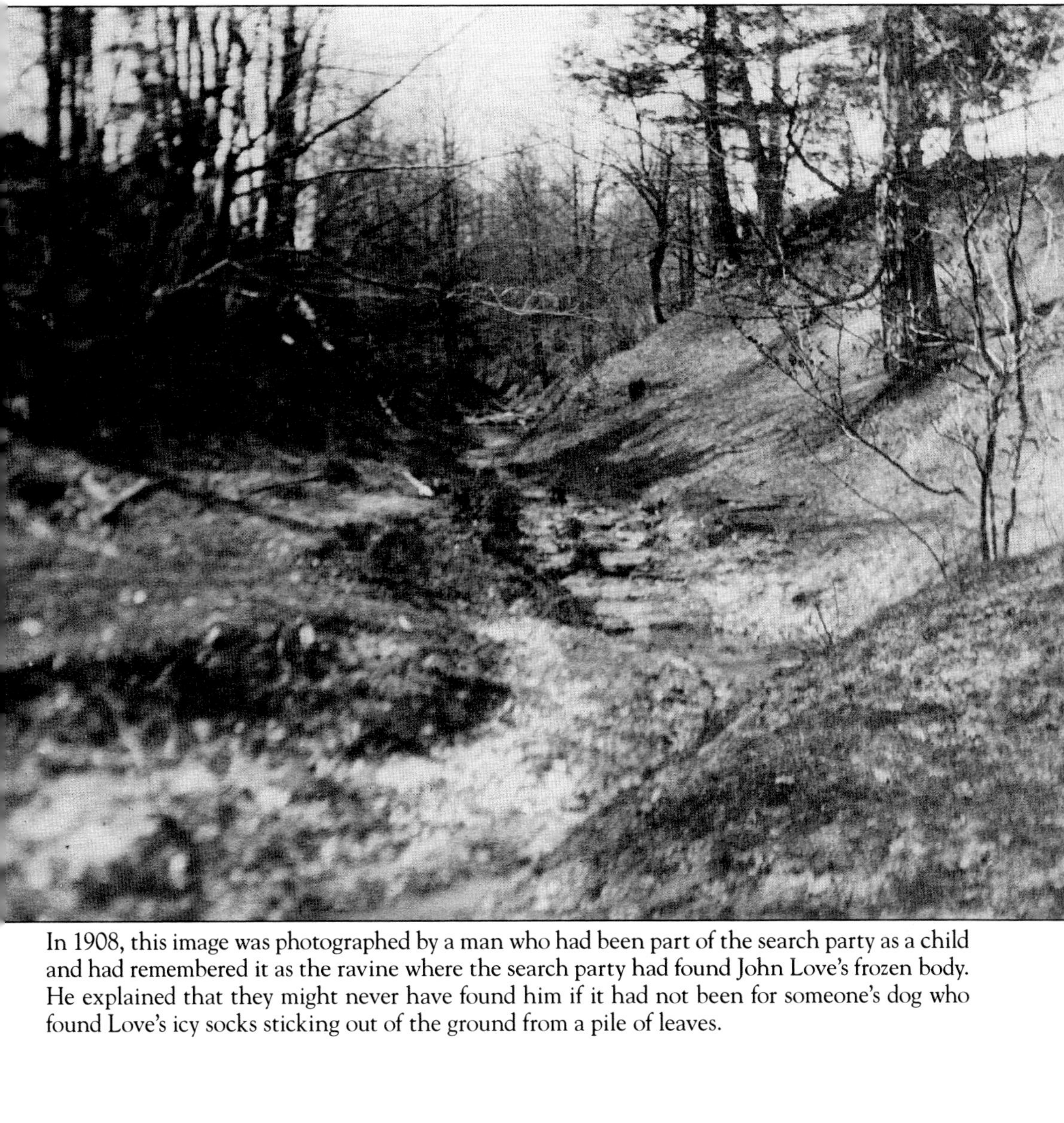

In 1908, this image was photographed by a man who had been part of the search party as a child and had remembered it as the ravine where the search party had found John Love's frozen body. He explained that they might never have found him if it had not been for someone's dog who found Love's icy socks sticking out of the ground from a pile of leaves.

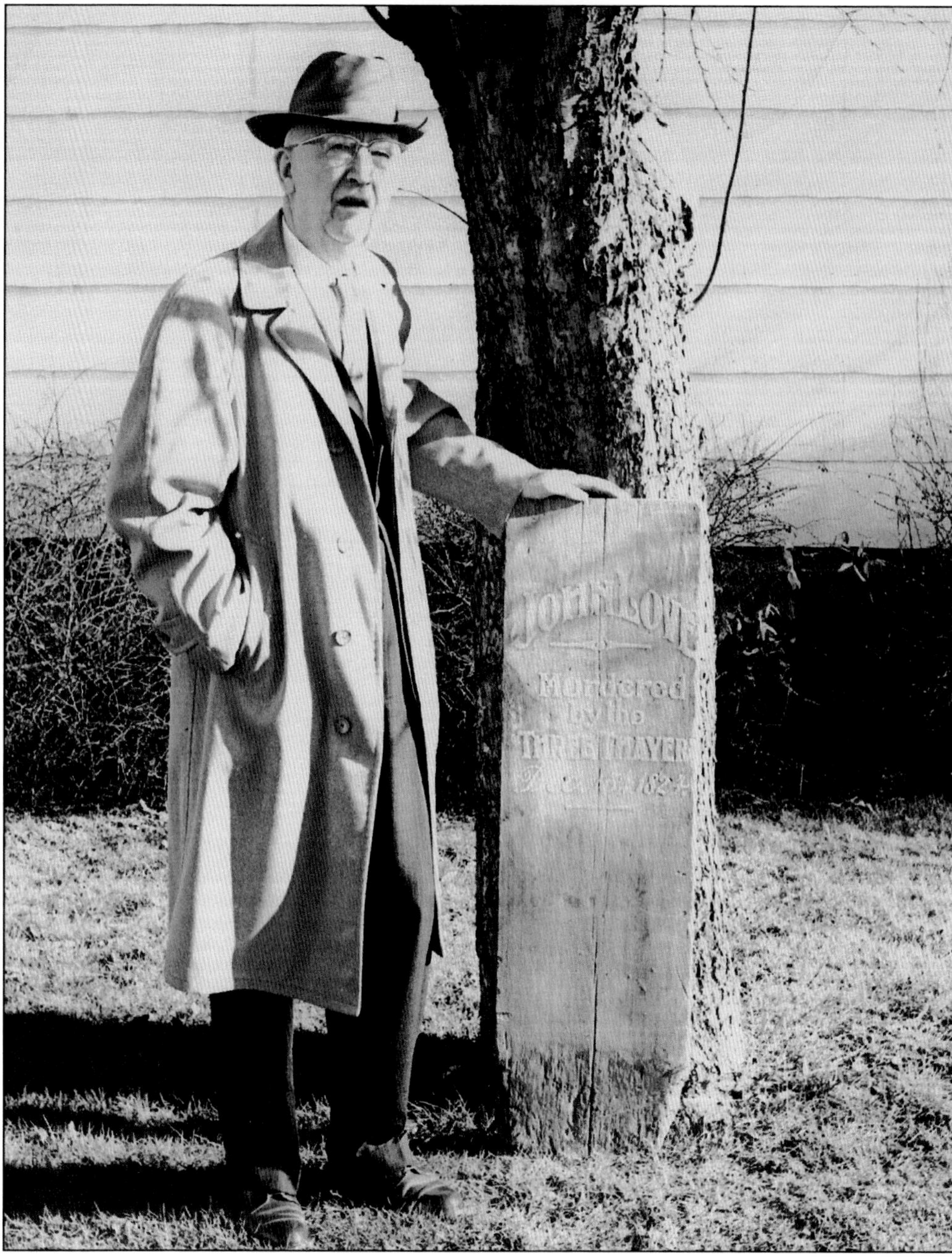

Boston town historian Charles B. Bradley is standing next to the original grave marker that was made to distinguish the final resting place of John Love's body in Maplewood Cemetery. It was carved in wood and is currently on display in the Boston Historical Museum.

The close-up of the old marker seen on the right informs readers that John Love's life was cut short by the three Thayers—Isaac, Israel Jr., and Nelson—on December 15, 1824. Love's grave was one of the first in Maplewood Cemetery, after pioneer Charles Johnson donated part of his land to be set aside for remembering those who passed before. No one knows exactly when the stone marker shown below replaced the wooden marker. Eliza Trevett, in an interview in 1953 with the town historian, said she thought that Hamilton Ward might have replaced it during the time that he was caretaker for the cemetery. One day he was inspecting the grounds and found the wooden marker missing. A few days later, it mysteriously returned. He decided that the marker was too important to go missing, so he engaged a stonecutter to make a more permanent remembrance.

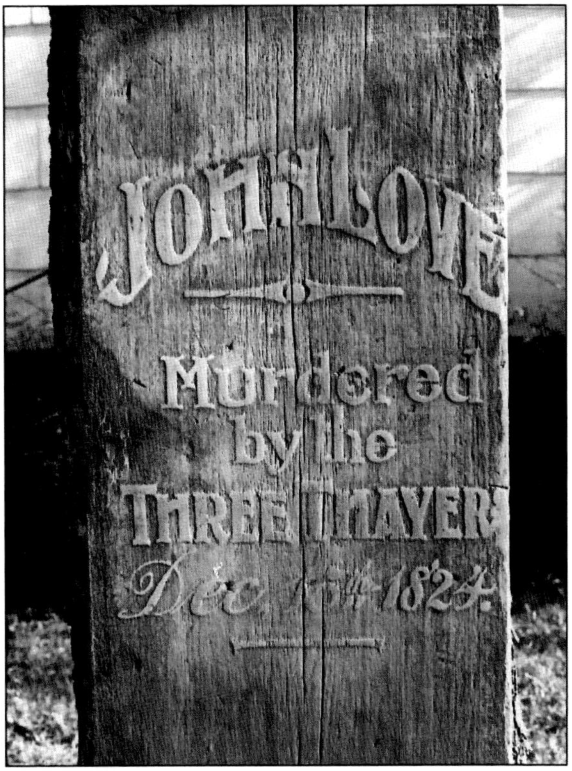

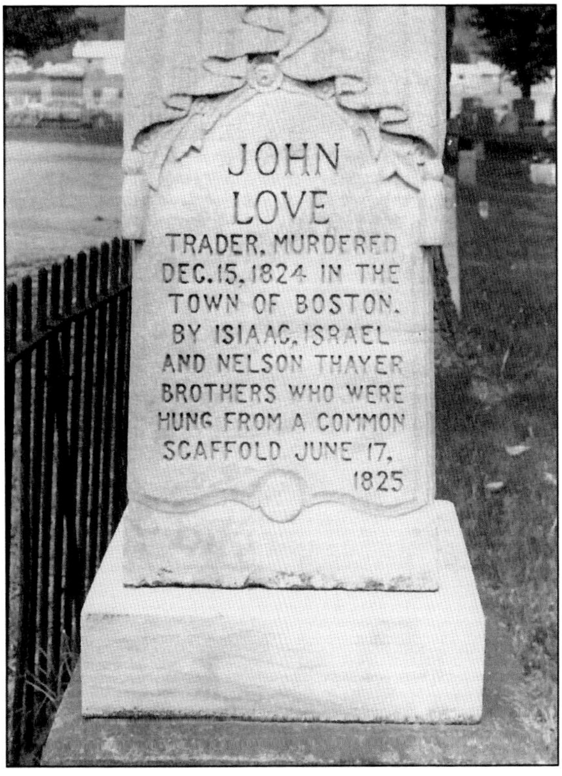

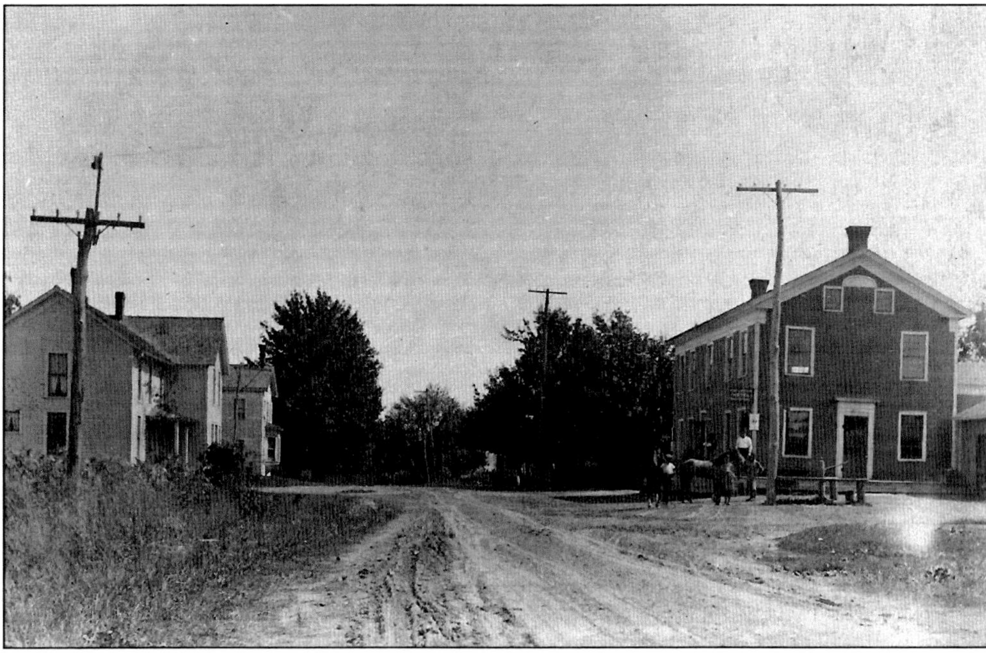

Fuller's Tavern, in this photograph probably taken between 1906 and 1910, is on the right side of the picture. The photographer is looking south at the corner of what is now Zimmerman Road and Boston State Road in North Boston. The inn had many owners over the years and was finally torn down in the 1970s in order to widen the state road.

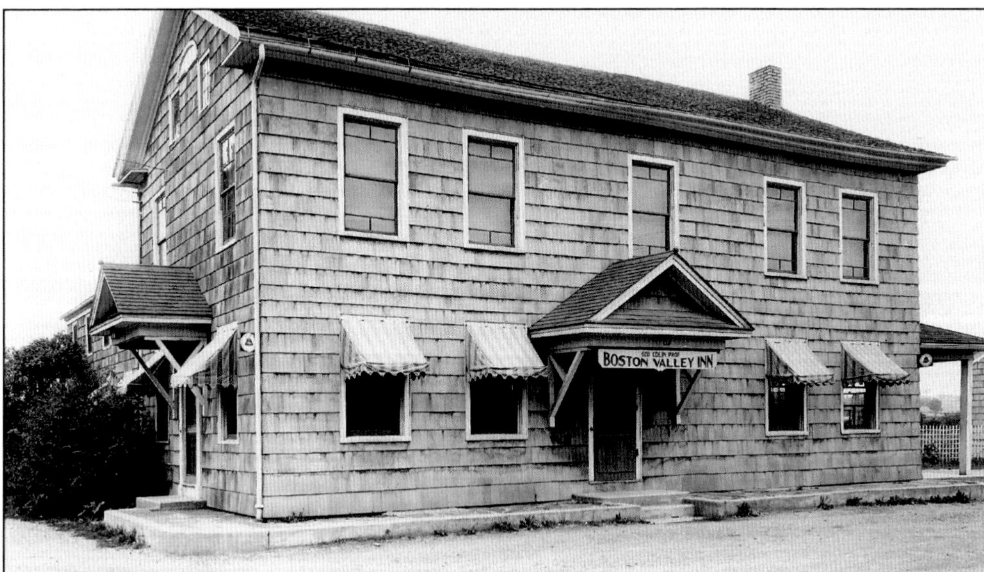

This view of the tavern was taken sometime in the 1940s, when it was called the Boston Valley Inn. The view is looking west while standing on Boston State Road. George Colin and his wife Augusta owned and operated the inn at this time. The chain of owners from the time of the typhoid fever included the Fullers, Anthony Sporney, Edward Frych, the Schunks, the Wittmeyers, the Colins, and finally the Seiders.

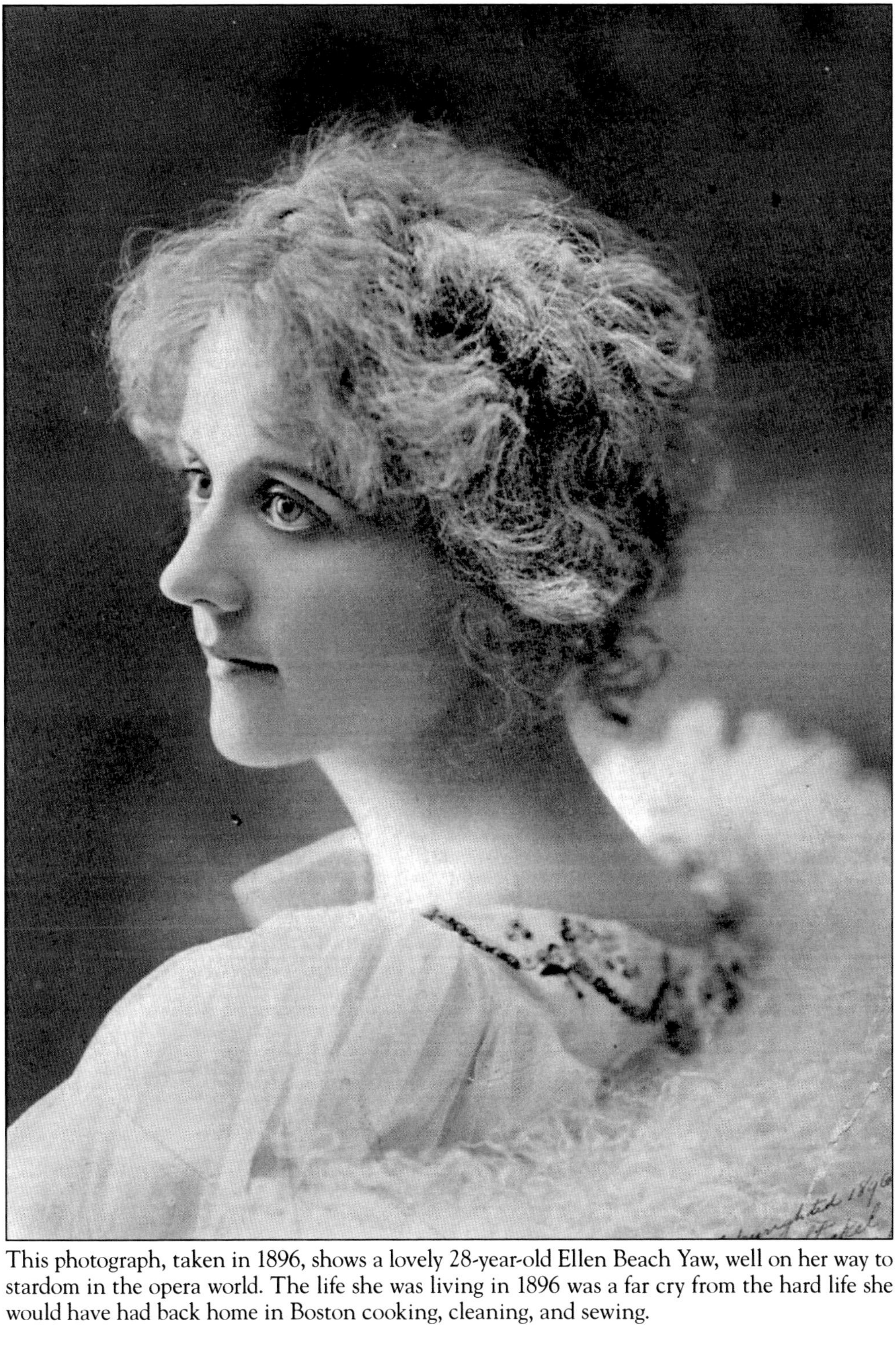

This photograph, taken in 1896, shows a lovely 28-year-old Ellen Beach Yaw, well on her way to stardom in the opera world. The life she was living in 1896 was a far cry from the hard life she would have had back home in Boston cooking, cleaning, and sewing.

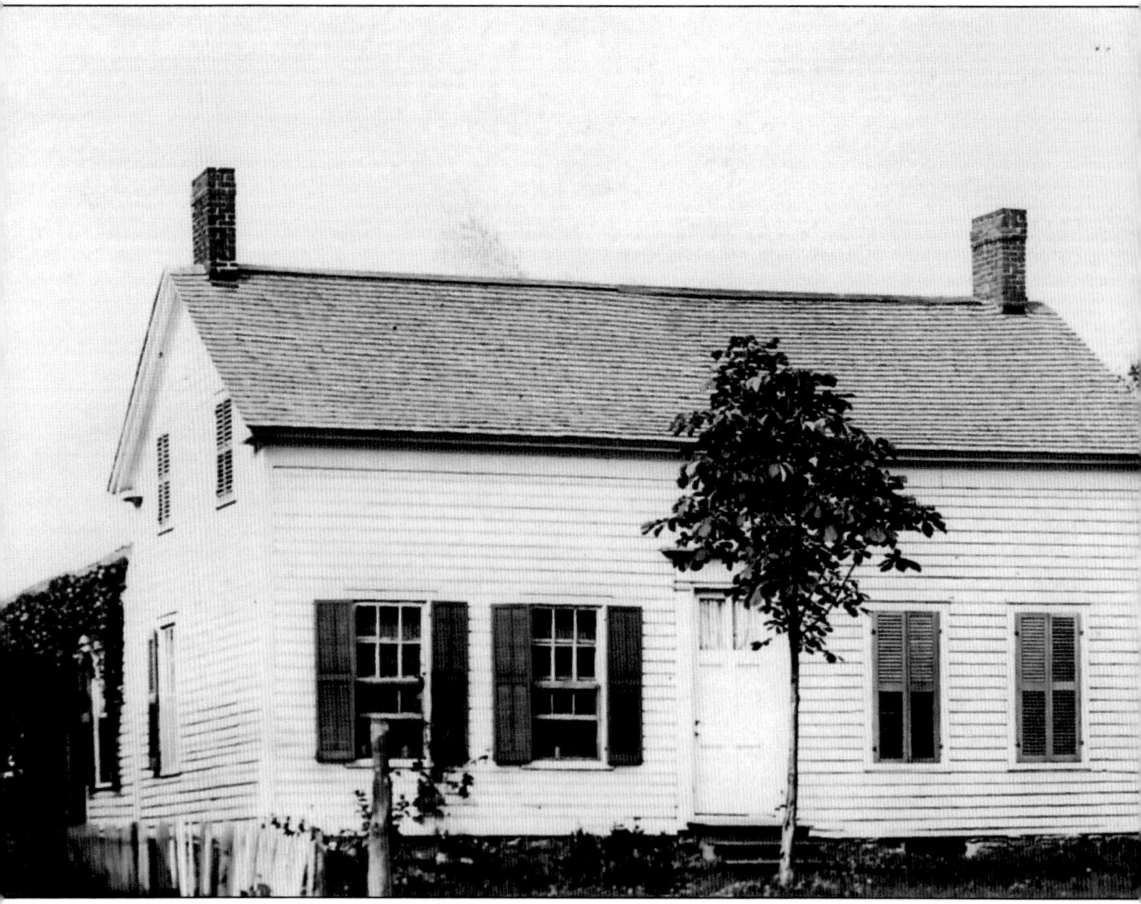

This is the home that Ellen Beach Yaw was born in. It still stands, but it has been drastically remodeled. It sits at the bottom of Boston Cross Road and has a historical marker in front of it, placed there by the Boston Historical Society. The two chimneys, funneling smoke up from the two fireplaces that were needed to keep the home warm, are no longer there.

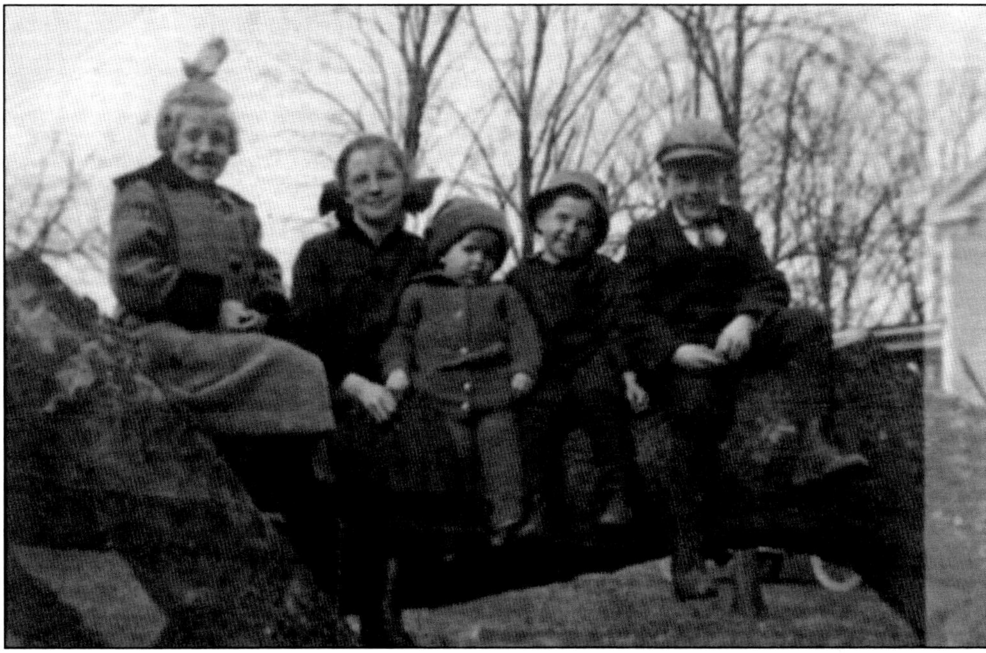

Ellen Beach Yaw is seen as a child here, sitting in the arms of a giant tree with her brothers and sister. From left to right are Ellen, Anna, Page, Charlie, and Richard. So many children in such a small house was a challenge to keep organized, but the family worked together and made the best of whatever fate gave them.

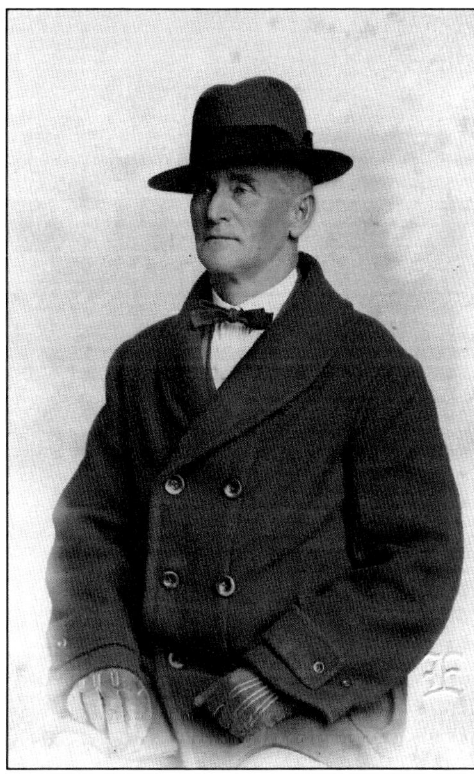

Ellen Beach Yaw's big brother Richard B. (Dick) Yaw poses here in 1919 showing off his new double-breasted coat and dapper hat. This photograph was donated to the Boston Historical Society inside a brown envelope that had a note typed inside. "To my dear friend, Mrs. William Rice. Sent to her June 27, 1919 by C.L. Drake from Pittsburgh, PA".

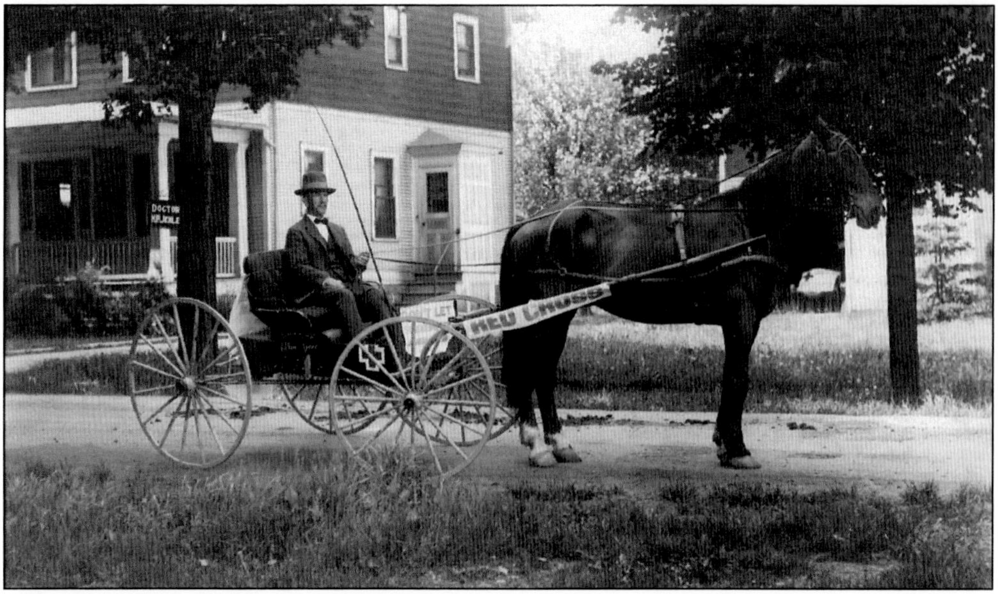

Ellen Beach Yaw would return many times to her hometown to perform free concerts for the community. This buggy, driven by family friend Clinton Leonard (C. L.) Drake, was used to transport Yaw from her concert in Boston to her next stop in Glenwood, on the other side of the east hill. It is parked in front of a well-known physician's house on the state road in Boston, Dr. H. P. Jehle.

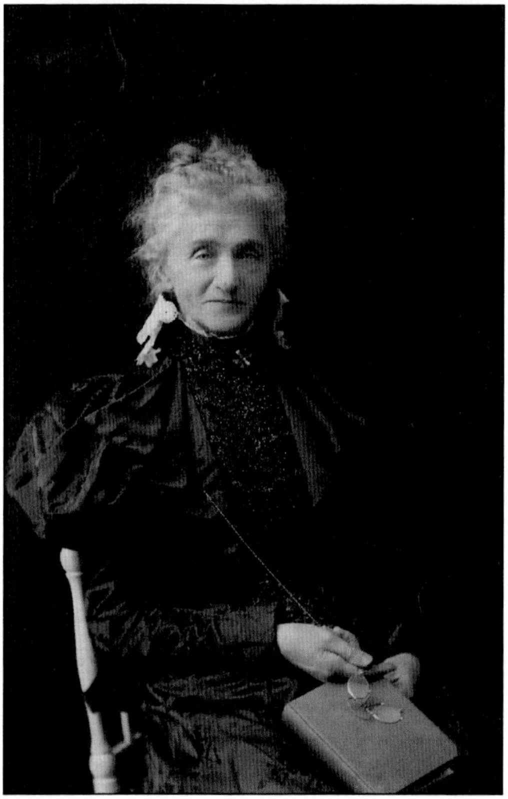

This handsome woman is Ellen Beach Yaw's mother, Mary Jane Beach Yaw, around 1916. She joined her daughter in her worldwide travels and sent home pictures taken in London and Paris to remind the family at home in Boston that she was thinking of them. She is wearing a very lovely silk dress bearing embossed oriental flowers. Her spectacles are attached to a chain clipped to her jacket.

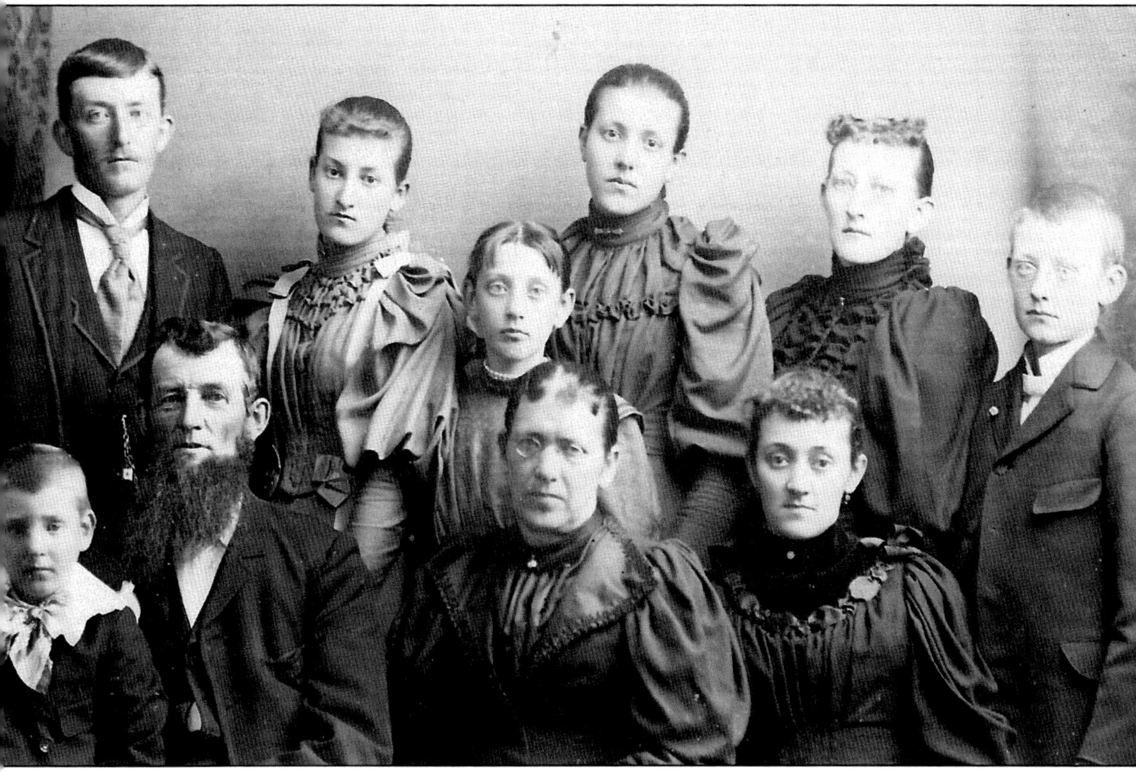

These are the Winkelmans around 1897. The father and mother are John and Elizabeth. Their large family of three boys and five girls grew up working hard on the farm on Rice Road. From left to right are (first row) William, John, Elizabeth, and Emma; (second row) John Jr., Hattie, Mary, Rose, Libby, and Joseph. (Courtesy of Bessie Enser.)

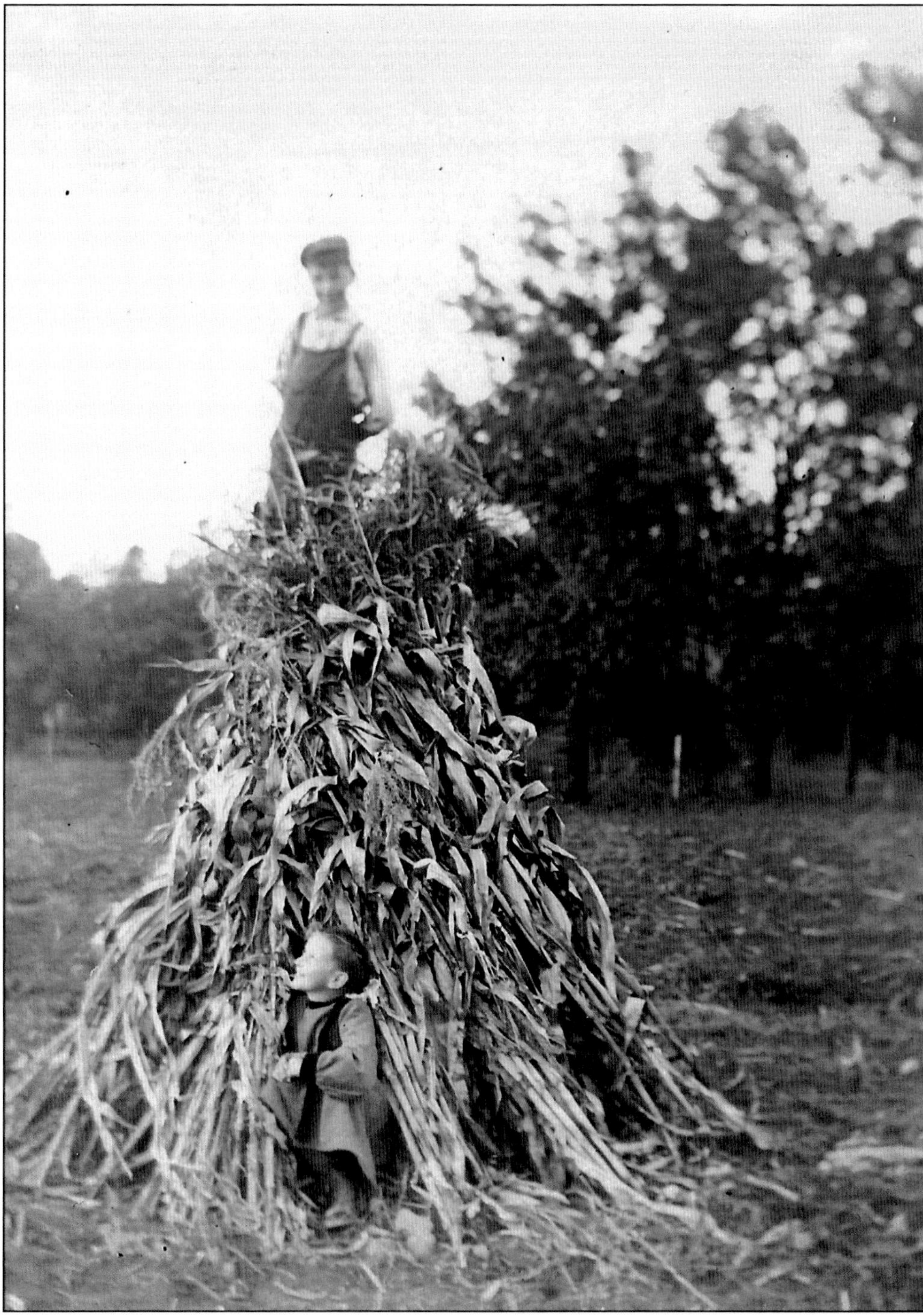

When the work was done, there was always time for play. These children spent all day gathering the cornstalks and filling the silo with corn for the cows. So when the day was done they took turns playing king of the hill.

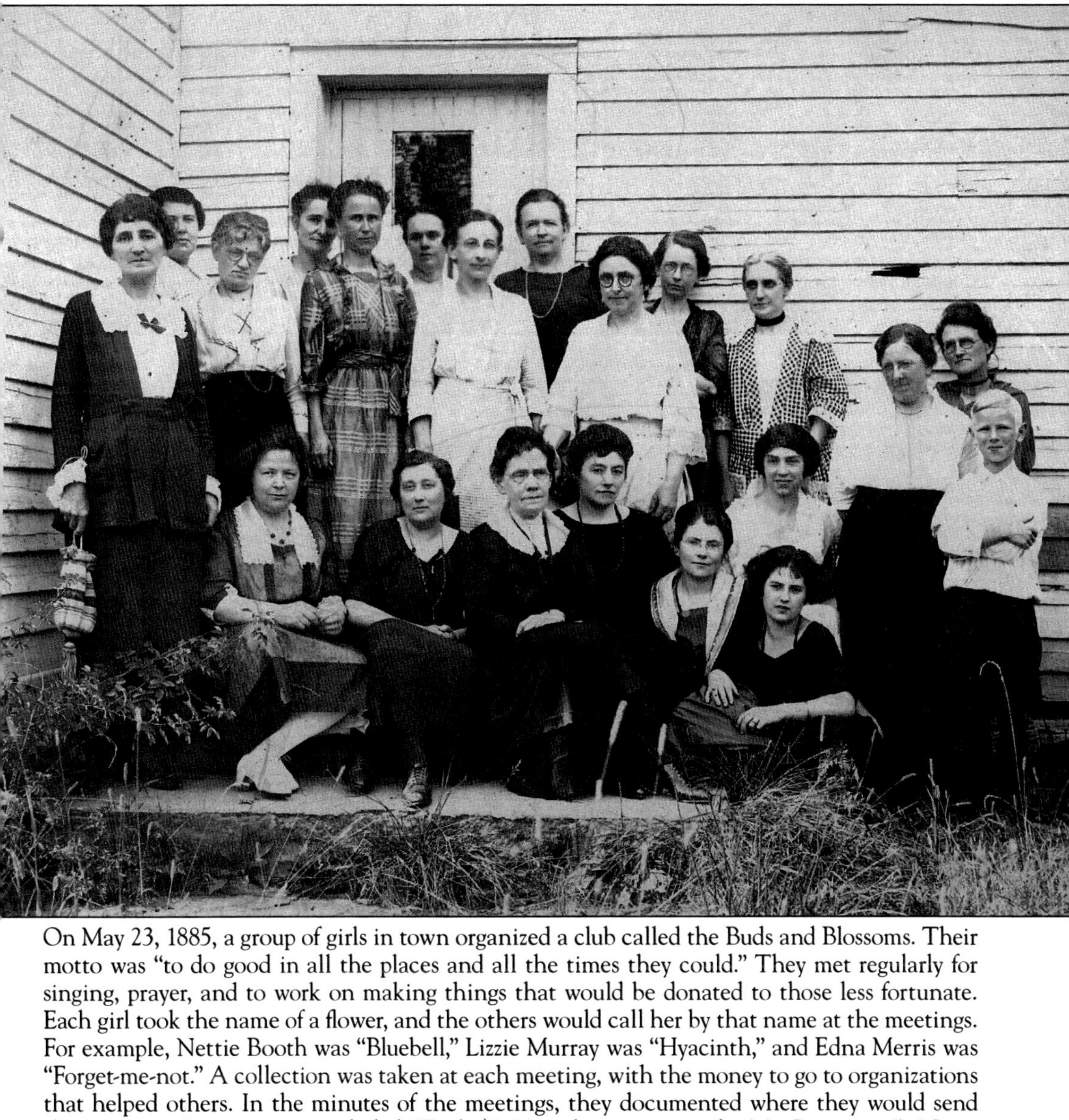

On May 23, 1885, a group of girls in town organized a club called the Buds and Blossoms. Their motto was "to do good in all the places and all the times they could." They met regularly for singing, prayer, and to work on making things that would be donated to those less fortunate. Each girl took the name of a flower, and the others would call her by that name at the meetings. For example, Nettie Booth was "Bluebell," Lizzie Murray was "Hyacinth," and Edna Merris was "Forget-me-not." A collection was taken at each meeting, with the money to go to organizations that helped others. In the minutes of the meetings, they documented where they would send their money. Some entries included "Took $2.00 to buy groceries for Mr. Parmenter"; "Gave quilt, three holders to Home for Friendless, Buffalo"; and one year on December 24, "special meeting to buy shoes and rubbers for Mrs. Green and knife for E. Palmerton, book for Myrtle Palmerton." This photograph shows the members of the group in 1920. They continued meeting and doing good until their last reunion in 1950.

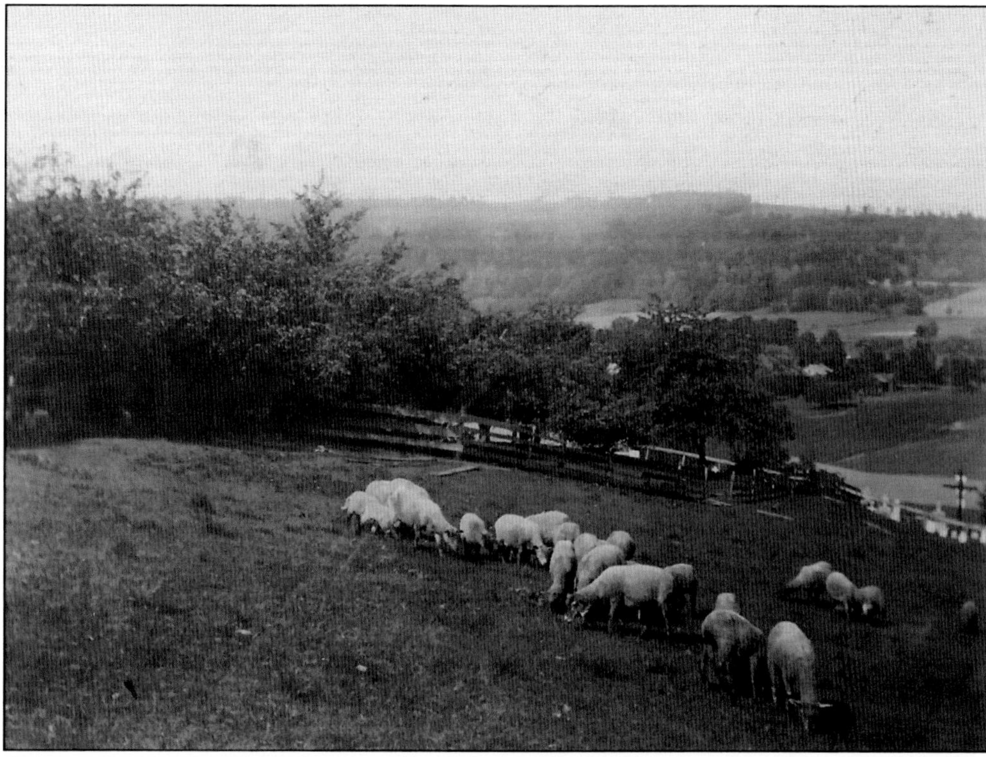

Sheep were very plentiful in Boston, since many people used the wool to make warm clothes for the winter. These sheep, grazing up the hill from St. John's Cemetery, look as if they have been shorn quite recently. In the years before fences were built, they would all have been wearing bells around their neck that were manufactured by the Yaw Bell Factory.

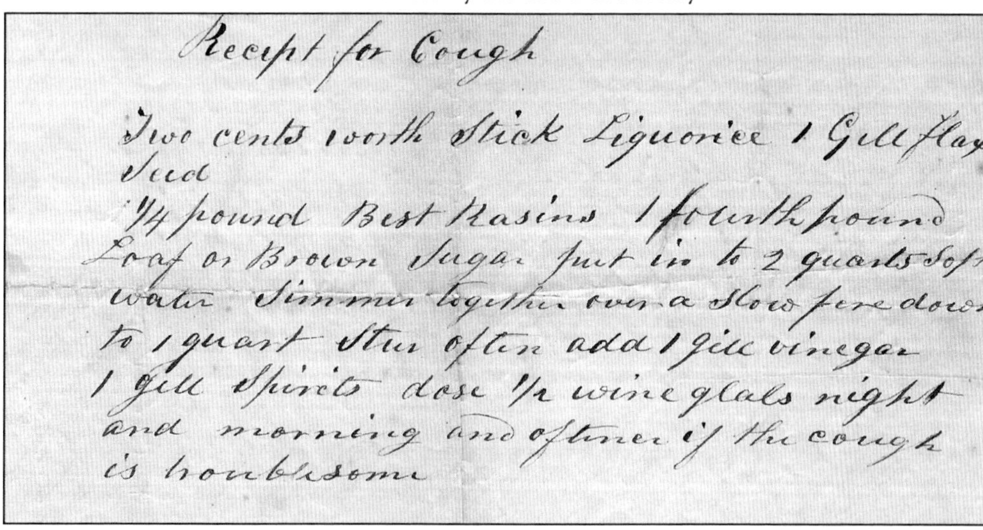

Recept for Cough

Two cents worth Stick Liquorice 1 Gill flax
Seed
1/4 pound Best Rasins 1 fourth pound
Loaf or Brown Sugar put in to 2 quarts Soft
water Simmer together over a Slow fire down
to 1 quart Stir often add 1 gill vinegar
1 gill Spirits dose 1/2 wine glass night
and morning and oftener if the cough
is troublesome

This recipe for cough syrup was in every mother's kitchen. "Two cents worth stick licorice, 1 gill flax seed [a gill was equivalent to ¼ pint or five fluid ounces], ¼ pound best raisins, 1 fourth pound loaf of brown sugar. Put in to 2 quarts soft water. Simmer together over a slow fire down to 1 quart. Stir often. Add 1 gill vinegar, 1 gill spirits. Dose ½ wine glass night and morning and oftener if the cough is troublesome."

For some, traveling in the new horseless carriage was hard to get used to. It had to be stored in the barn where the wagons and horses were kept, and the animals were not happy when this giant machine coughed and wheezed to life when the family needed to go somewhere. (Courtesy of Jane Clarke.)

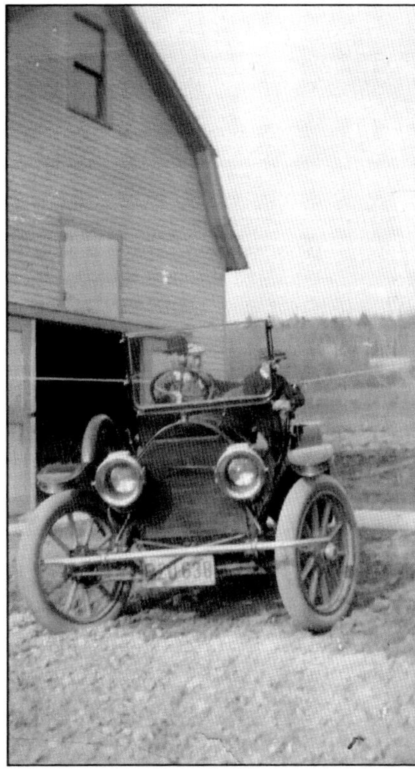

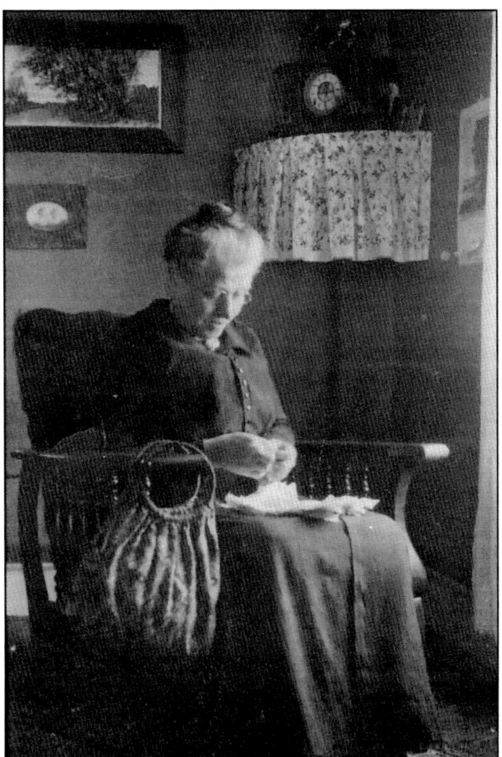

Ellen Fields was born in the town of Concord on September 16, 1851. She married Harvey Dye and raised a family, which consisted of a daughter, Jennie, and two sons, Perry and Earl. Harvey died at a young age, so Ellen had to raise their children on her own. Here grandma Ellen is working on her sewing in her favorite chair by the window, where the light was better. (Courtesy of Jane Clarke.)

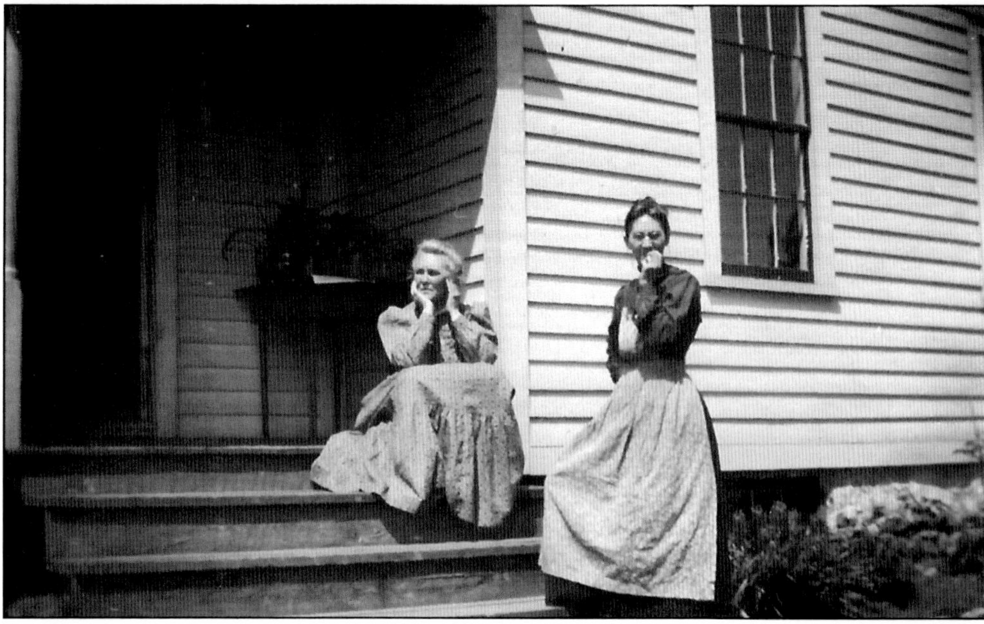

Children had a great many responsibilities in the old days, which sometimes challenged their judgment. It was natural for a mother to worry that her child had made a mistake or made a bad decision. The woman on the steps has a faraway look in her eyes with just a twinge of worry, perhaps for a child late getting back from an errand. The woman standing also looks like she fears the worst.

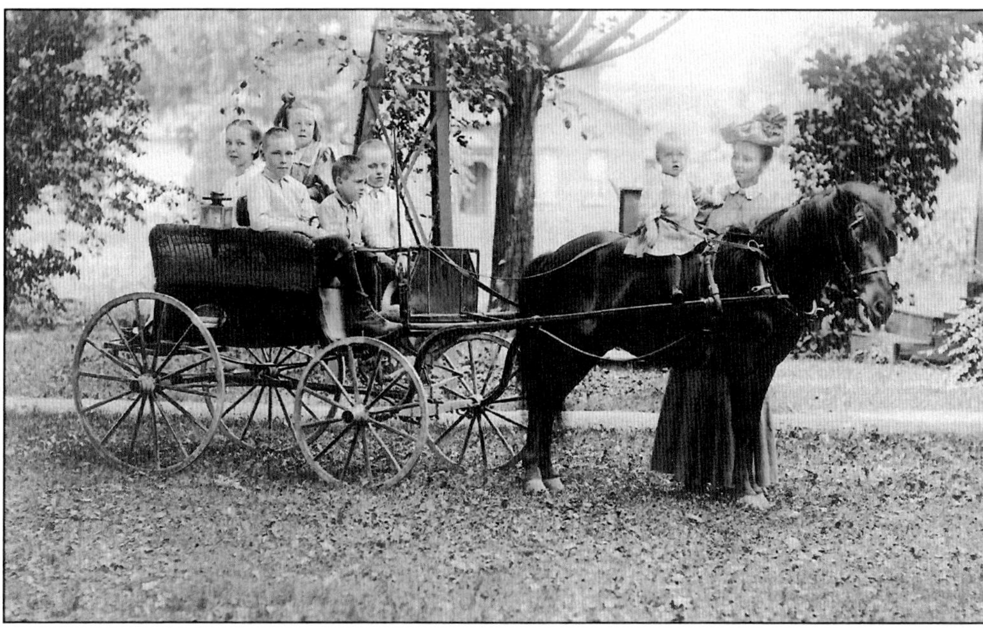

Sundays were days spent with family. Everyone would get all dressed up in their Sunday best to go to church and then have supper with grandma and grandpa. The children always enjoyed climbing into the wagon and asking their mother if they could take turns guiding the pony's reins.

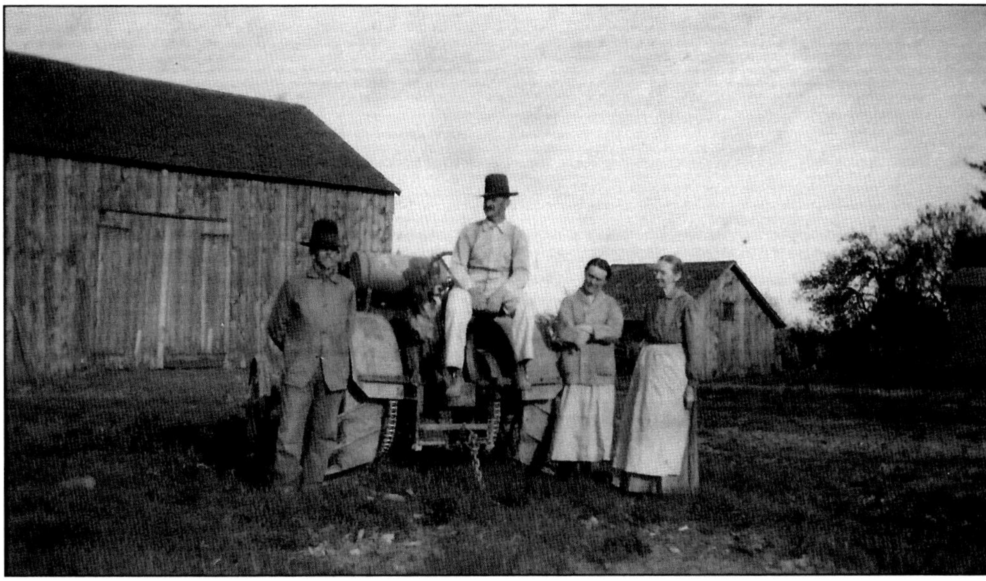

The Rice brothers and their wives are seen here resting after a long day working in the fields and doing chores. The tractor was able to do so much more work than a team of horses, but it was still tiring. Even their dog joined in the portrait, sitting up on the tractor with his master.

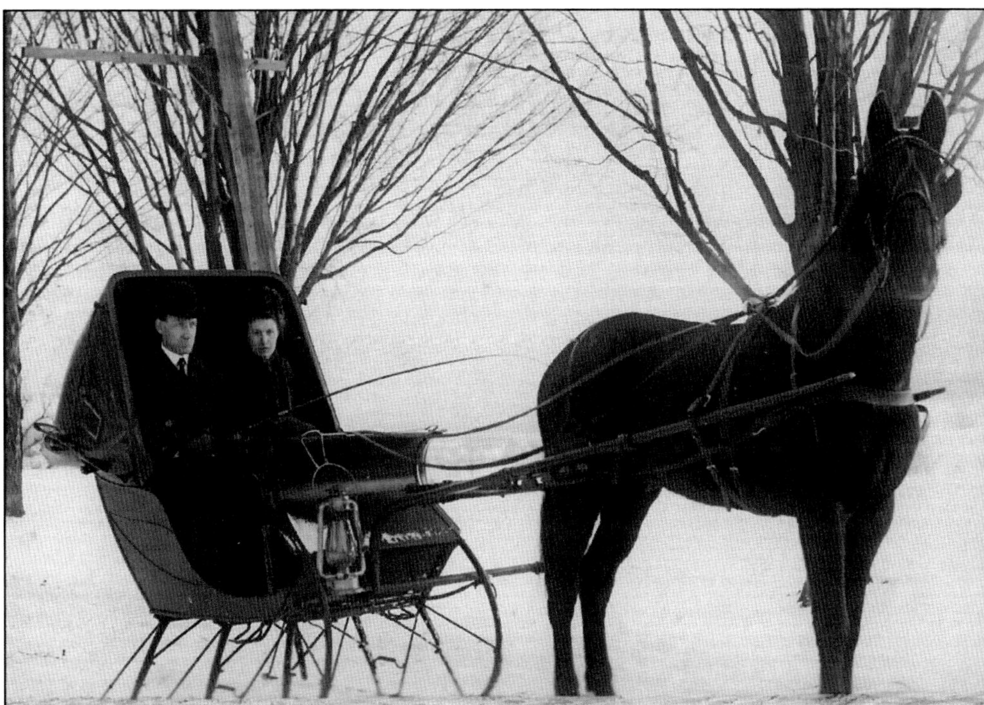

In the winter, horses were hitched up to the family's cutter. (This was the name they gave a sleigh.) This handsome animal belonged to Mr. and Mrs. R. T. Doherty, who decided to take the cutter for a ride either to Sunday church or to visit relatives, wearing their winters finest. They have brought along a lantern, in case they came home after dark.

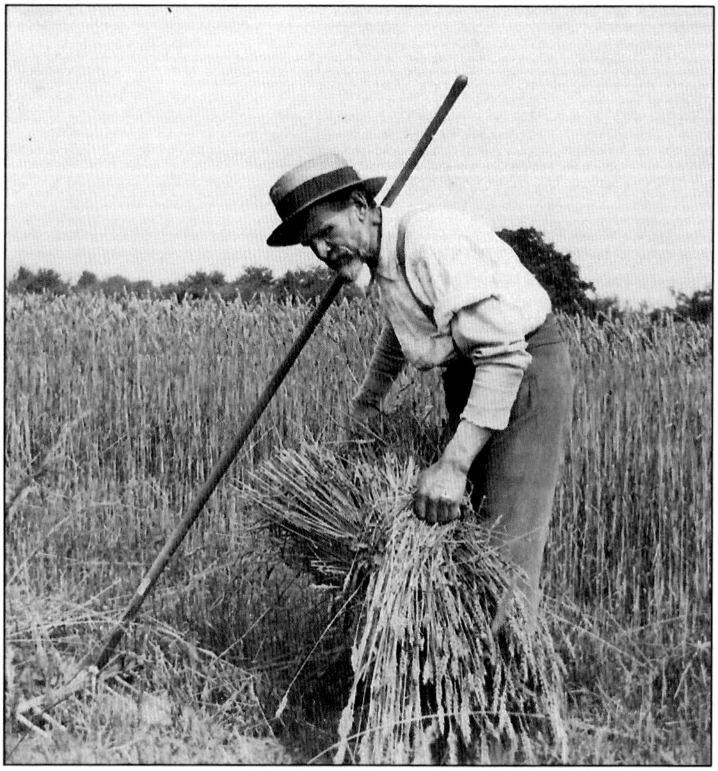

The Cary family owned a great deal of farmland in Boston, and here Elgin Cary uses a wheat rake to gather his crop. There were many gristmills in Boston, which made it convenient to have the wheat ground into flour. When Charles Johnson first came to the valley, he had to travel 40 miles to have his wheat ground into flour.

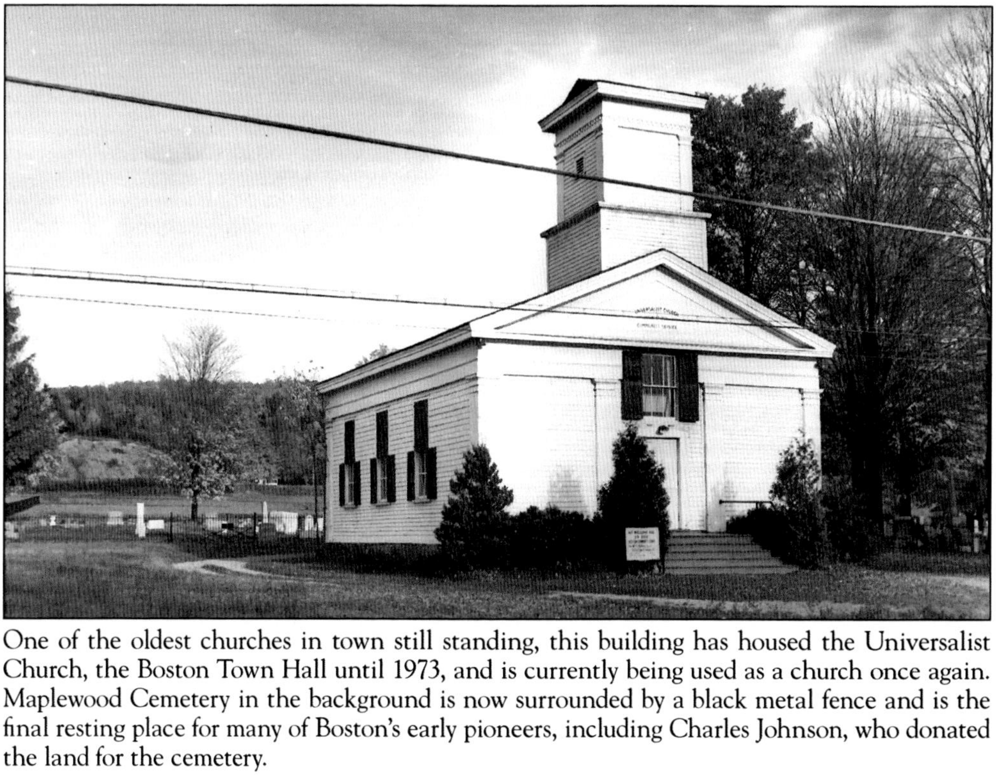

One of the oldest churches in town still standing, this building has housed the Universalist Church, the Boston Town Hall until 1973, and is currently being used as a church once again. Maplewood Cemetery in the background is now surrounded by a black metal fence and is the final resting place for many of Boston's early pioneers, including Charles Johnson, who donated the land for the cemetery.

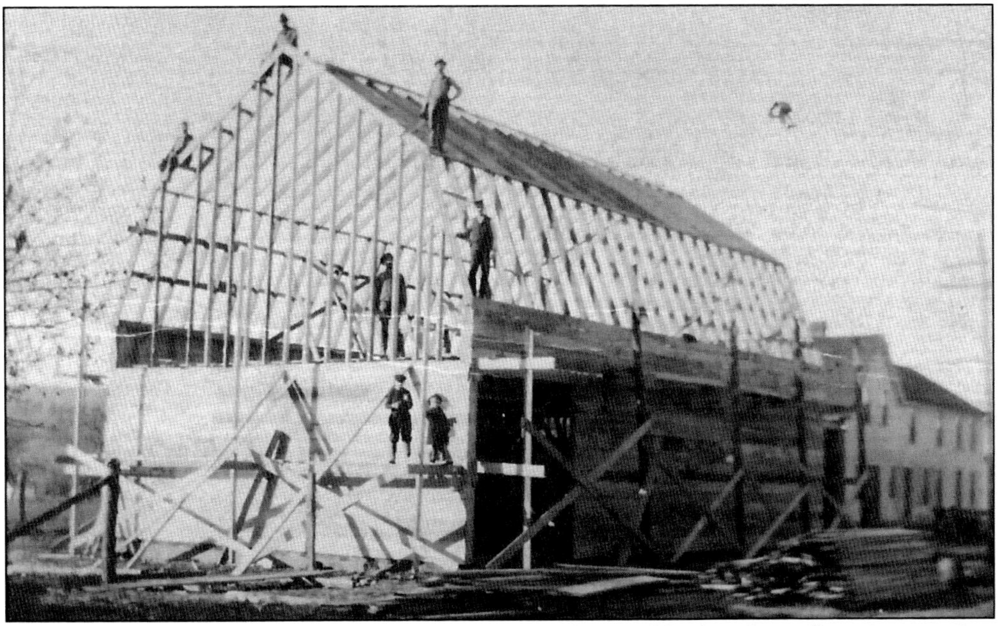

When it was time to build a new barn, everyone in the neighborhood usually volunteered to help. This *c.* 1907 photograph shows that these gentlemen were certainly not afraid of heights. With many neighbors helping, they are well on their way to completing the wooden skeleton of the barn that would house all the farm equipment, and maybe even one of those new horseless carriages.

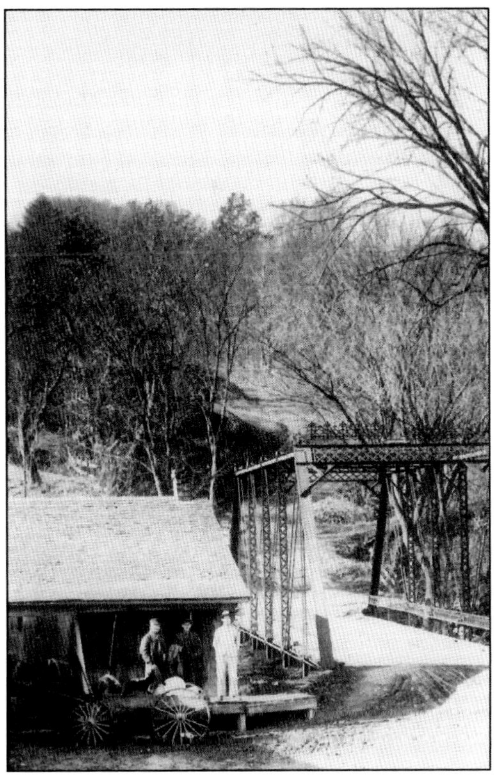

This handsome bridge is just one of many bridges built to allow travel across 18 Mile Creek. If listening carefully, one can hear the clip-clop of the horse's hooves as the wagon crosses the wooden planks. Unfortunately, the Victorian steel flourishes are now gone, but the bridge still exists on Mill Street in Boston.

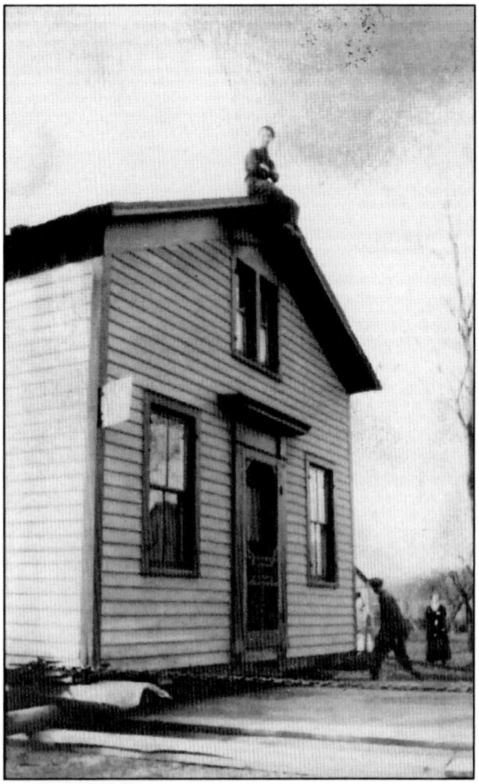

Fred Frank, who lived in North Boston, decided one day that he did not like where his house stood. He owned some property just down the street and decided to move the house to that lot. So he jacked it up, set logs under it, attached a chain to several teams of horses, and moved the house, its frame creaking with every inch. The house made it undamaged and still stands as the residence of the Carr family.

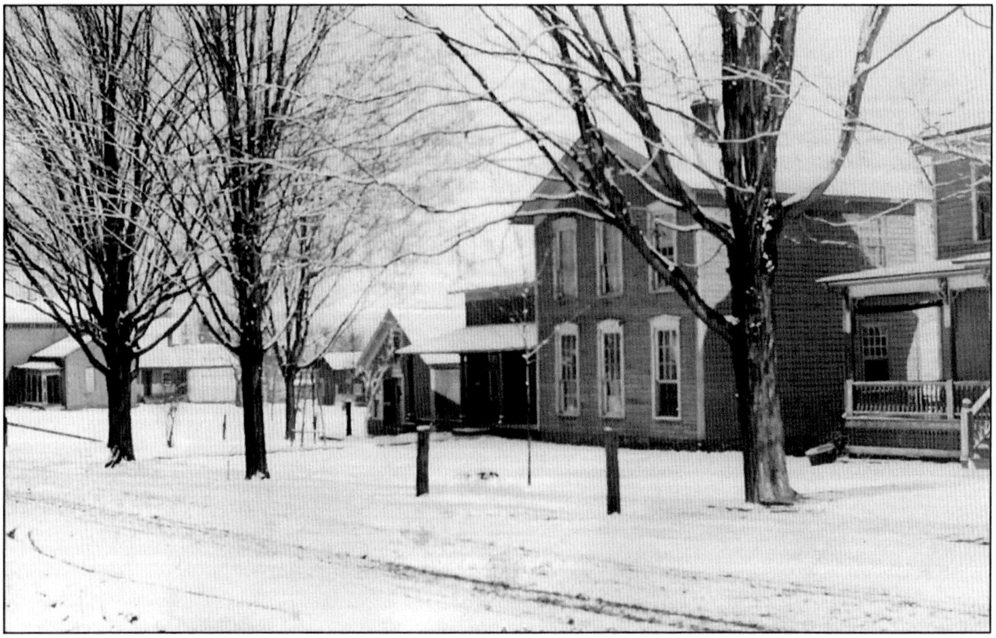

This house on Boston State Road in Boston was once the home of the Ashcraft family. Smith Ashcraft was an expert photographer, and he had his studio here, next to the house. His large volume of work is contained at the Boston Historical Museum and has provided most of the photographs for this book. Unfortunately the house burned down and no longer exists.

In 1877, the Boston Oil Company formed for the purpose of testing the ground to see if oil might be discovered. This well was discovered and still stood when the new Boston Fire Hall was built and can be seen in the middle of the picture. Way in the distance, on the east hill, the train station and hotel across the street from it can be seen.

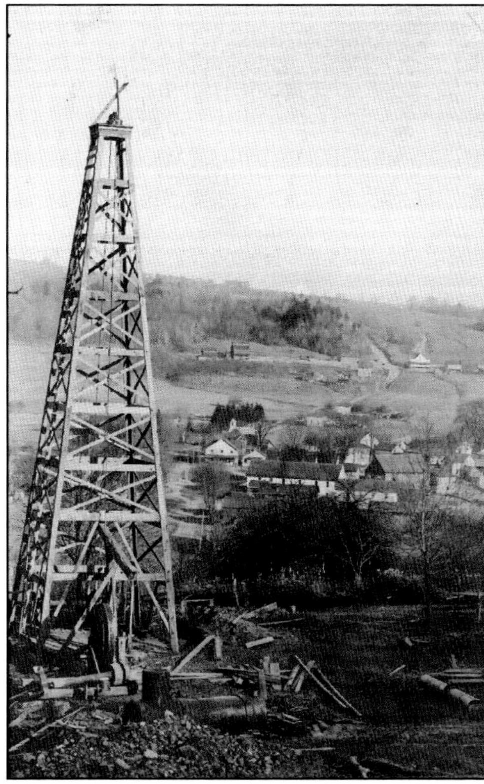

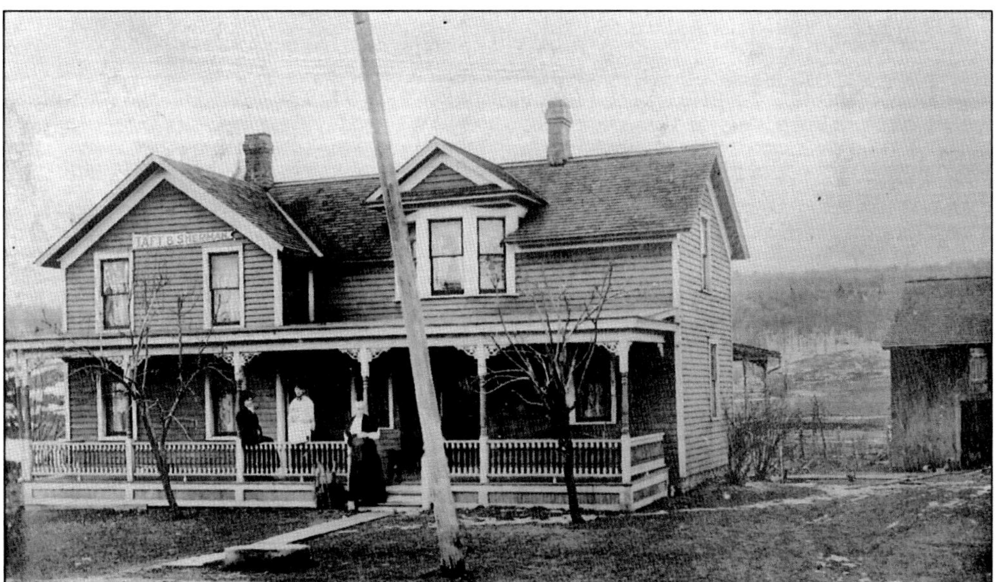

Political signs are one way to show the neighborhood who one supports. The banner on this house in North Boston proclaims the owner's support of the Taft/Sherman race for the White House in 1908. North Boston was a prominent gathering place for many political conventions of the southern district of Erie County at one time because of its central location.

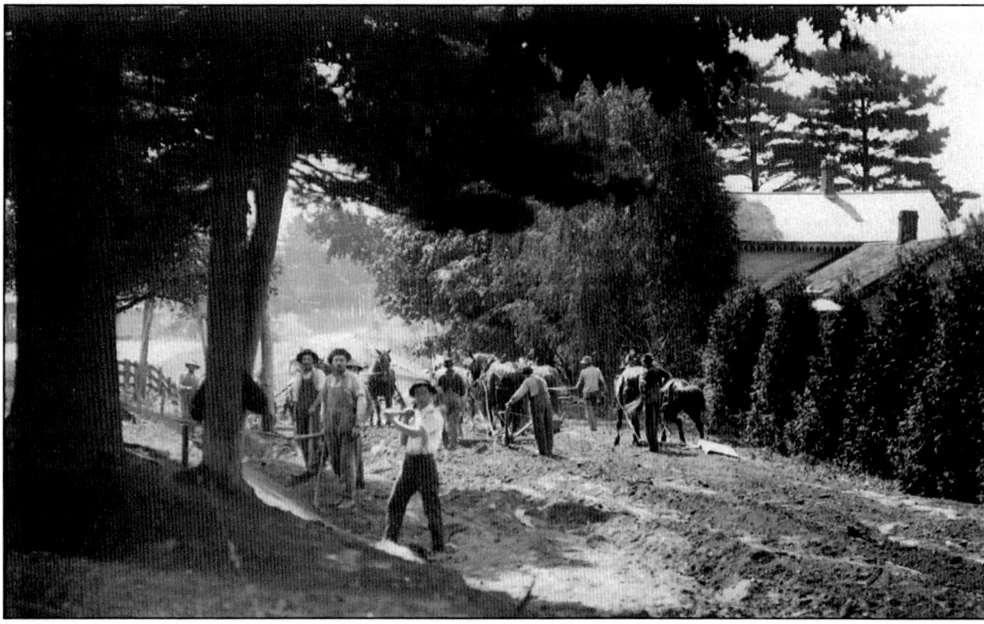

Winter snow and ice tended to make a mess out of the roads in the 19th century. At that time, men worked out their property taxes by working in teams to fix the roads and bridges, a job that required many hands. Everyone had to work together to make the roads passable. This group has put its horse teams to work plowing up the clumps from wagon wheel ruts so it could all be smoothed out once again.

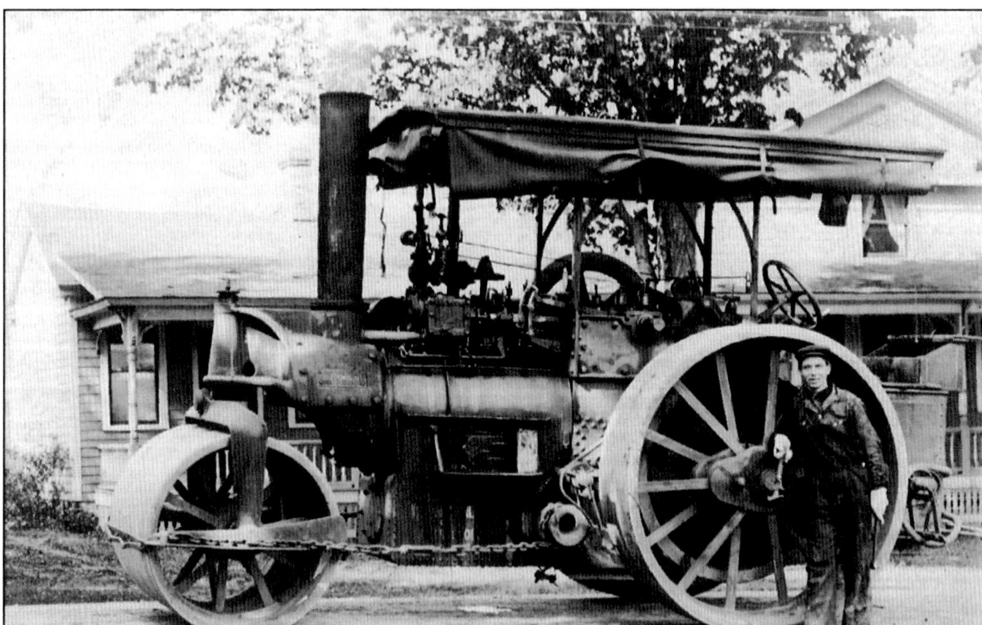

In 1909, giant steam tractors and steamrollers took over the job of road maintenance. The technology was such that roads could now be paved with hot asphalt. The asphalt was deposited over the dirt and stones, and this roller did the job of evenly spreading the sticky mess out to cool off and form a hard surface that would not wash away in the rain.

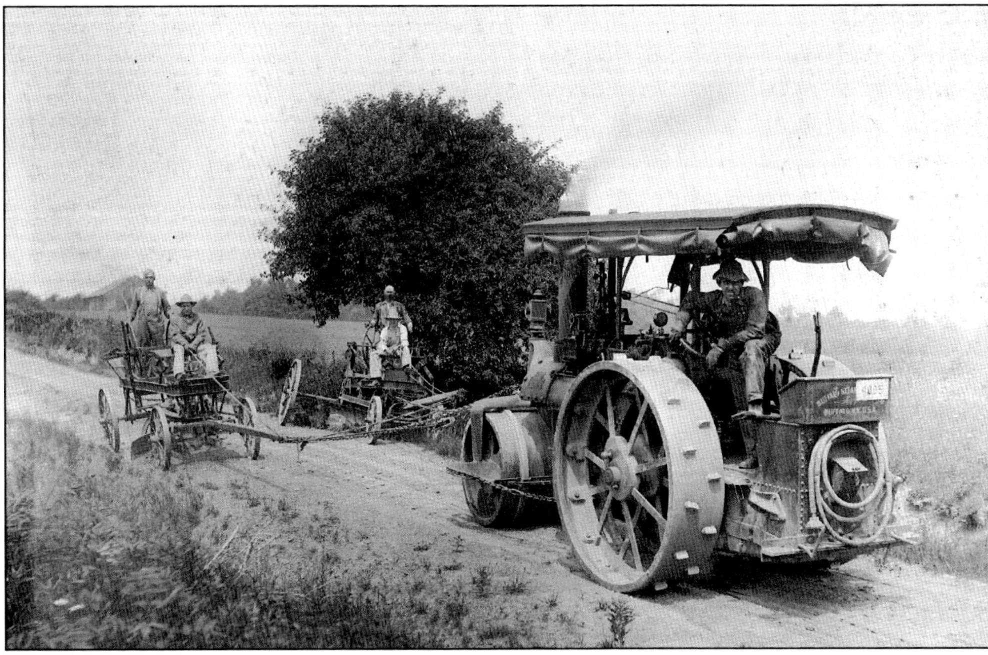

While contractors from New York City were paving the main road in the valley, the Boston Highway Department kept busy trying to keep the dirt roads up on the hill from falling into disrepair. This *c.* 1910 photograph shows, from left to right, Frank Bond, Fred Blanchard, Jake Hauck, Clarence Klein, and Charlie Klein.

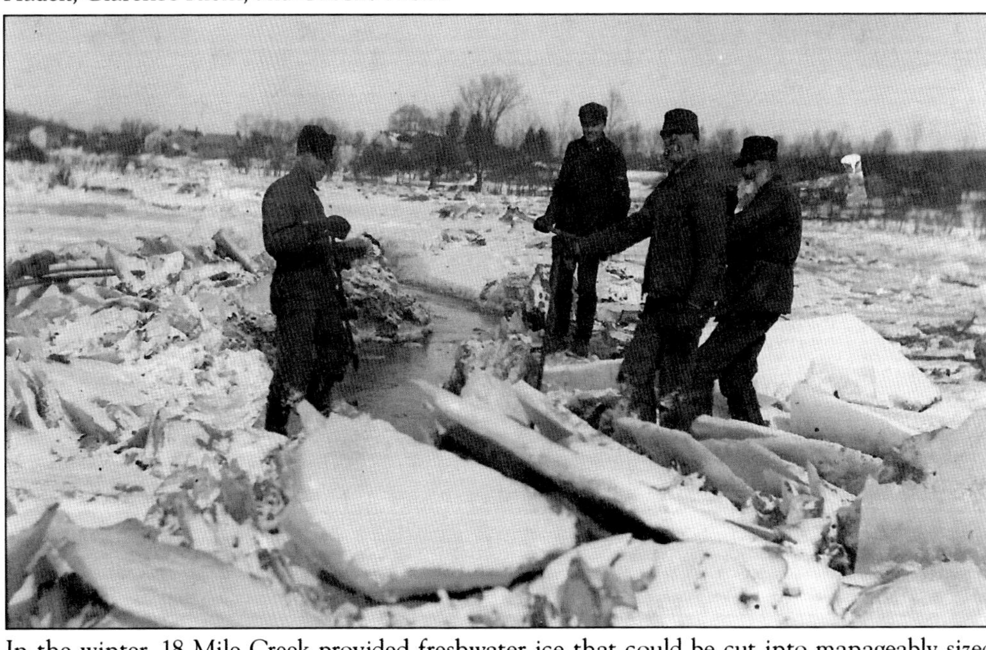

In the winter, 18 Mile Creek provided freshwater ice that could be cut into manageably sized pieces and stored in icehouses. This *c.* 1904 photograph shows men cutting thick ice so it could be transported on a wagon to icehouses where the pieces would be stacked using sawdust as an insulator. Stored in this way, ice could be kept cold for many months after the sun brought the spring flowers.

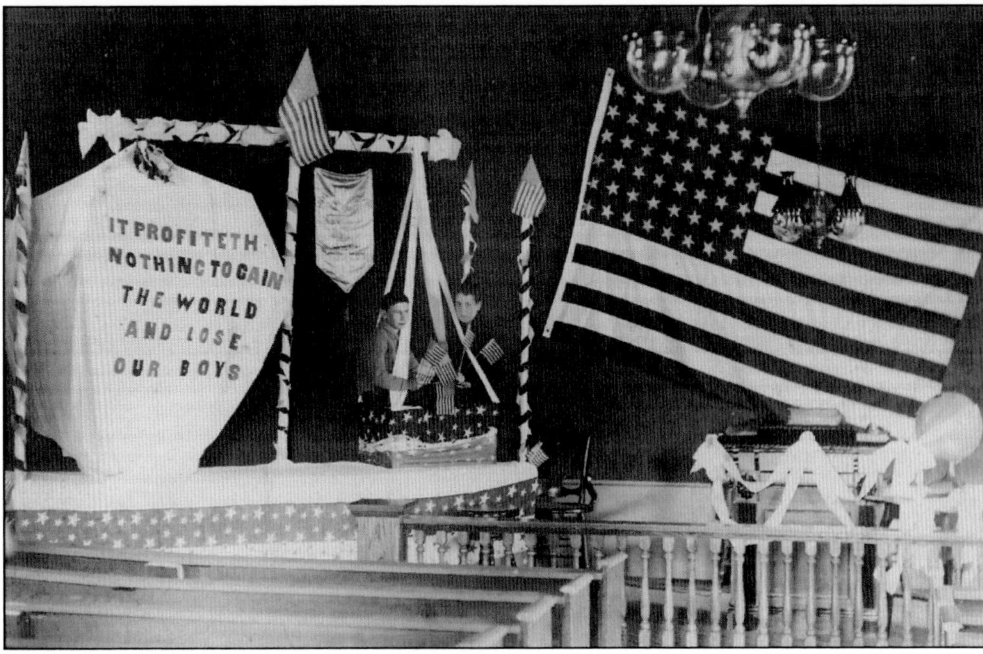

These boys are preparing for a meeting of the Women's Christian Temperance Union. The 48-star flag on the right helps identify the time period this photograph was taken in, which would make it between 1912 and 1959. The scales weigh the difference between the good allegedly done by war and the lives of two young men. The young men in the middle are Franklin Ashcraft (left) and Harland Williams.

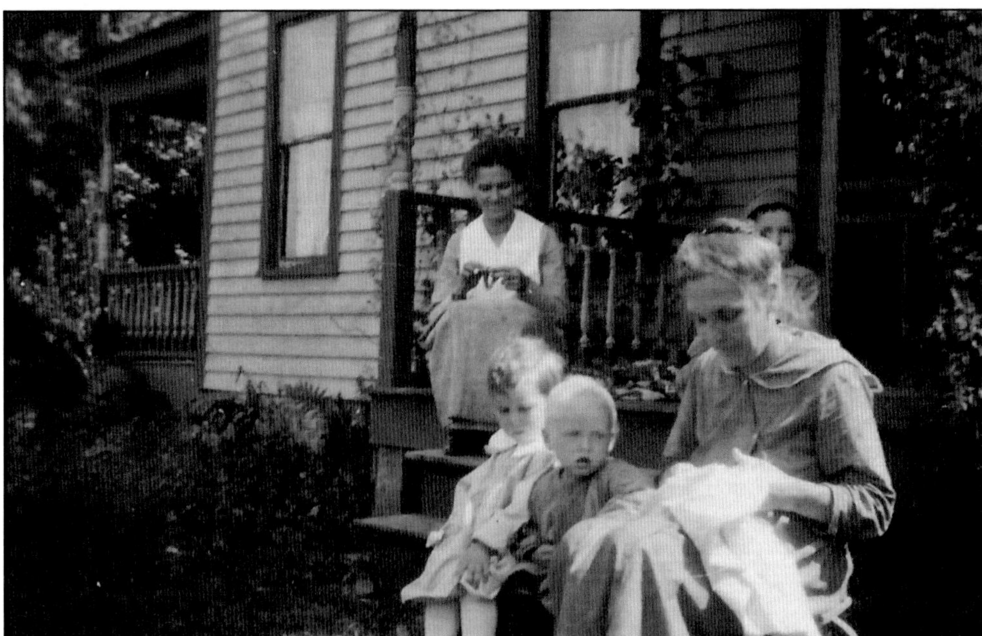

On the nicer days when the chores had to be done, sometimes mothers would take their children outside to sit so they could enjoy the sunshine while they did their sewing and mending. It was never too early in a child's life to learn the duties of a wife and mother.

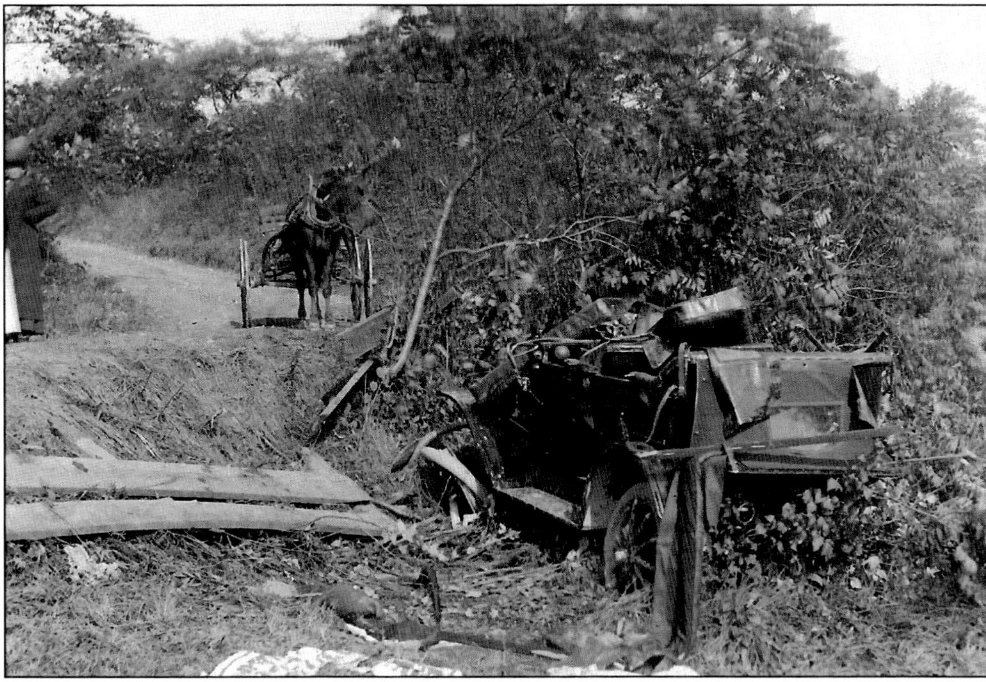

The automobile was a tricky contraption, when one was just learning to drive it. It did not work like a tractor, and it did not work like a horse. It did not work at all after it was driven off the road and into a bush. The horse looking on this scene is quite probably snickering!

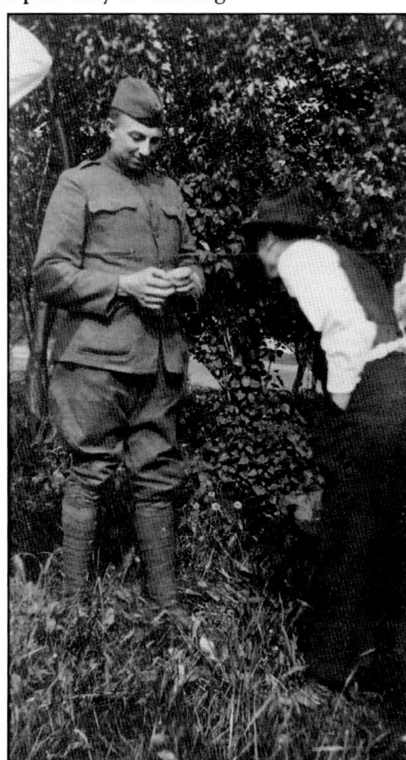

Leon Armbruster was just one of the many Boston residents who were called to serve their country during a time of war. He served bravely during World War I, alongside other well-known Boston citizens: Howard Cary, Clifford Drake, Glenn J. Koelmel, Burnell Dye, Leroy Pfarner, Michael Rucker, and Frank X. Weber, to name but a few.

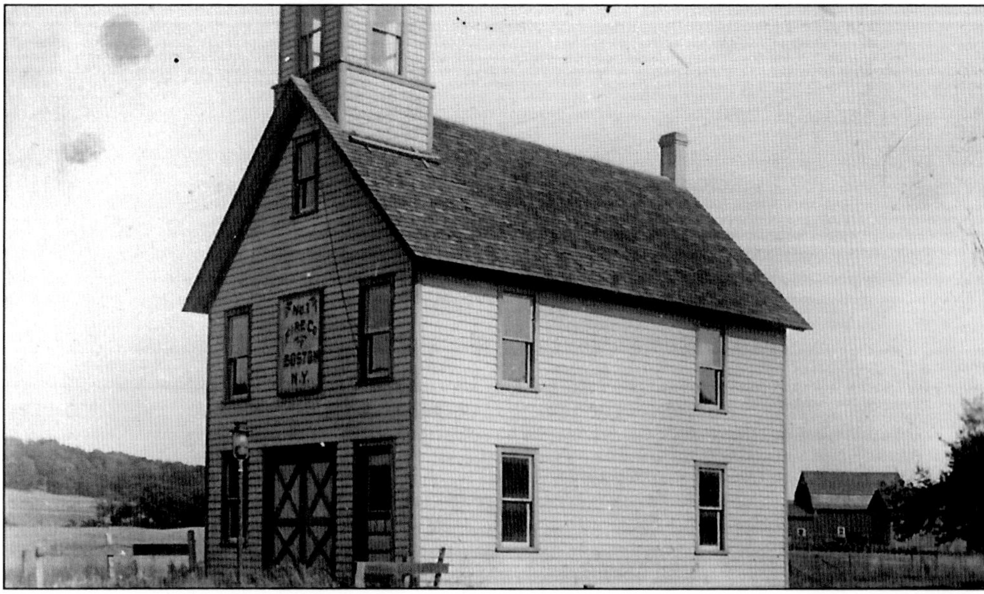

In 1908, a group of men in the area originally called Torrey's Corners got together and decided to form the Boston Fire Company. They built this hall in 1909 and it was used as a meeting hall and garage for their firefighting equipment for the next 30 years. The building still stands on Boston Cross Road and has been restored to its original appearance, sign included, by Clive "Tom" Rucker.

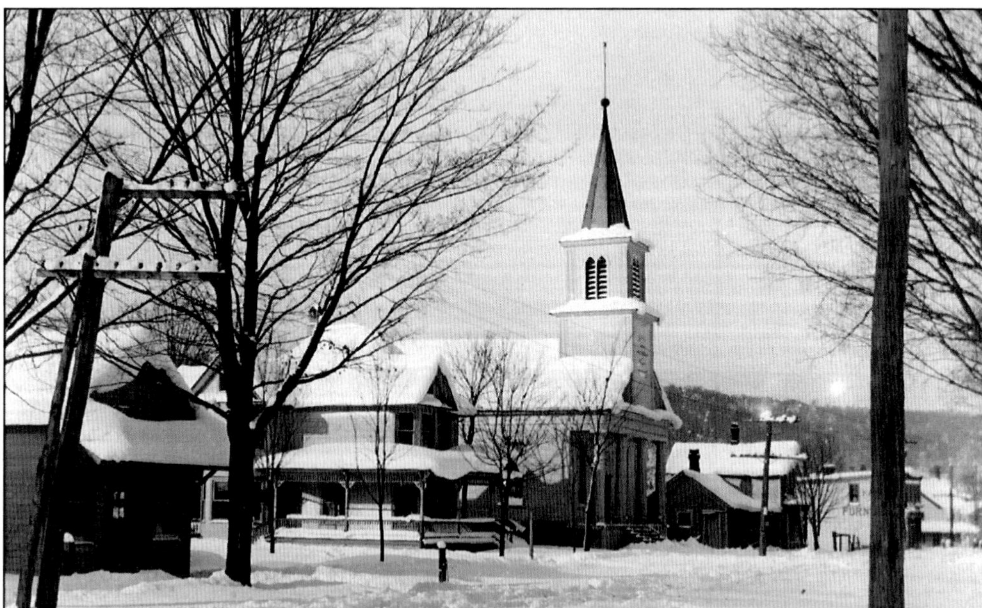

This winter scene was shot facing north on the state road in Boston. The church is one of the oldest in town, built in 1811. It was first a Dutch church, and then became known as St. Peter's. It later housed Faith United Church of Christ and now houses the Boston Historical Museum. The house on the left of the church stands on the ground where the Baptist church was built and eventually torn down.

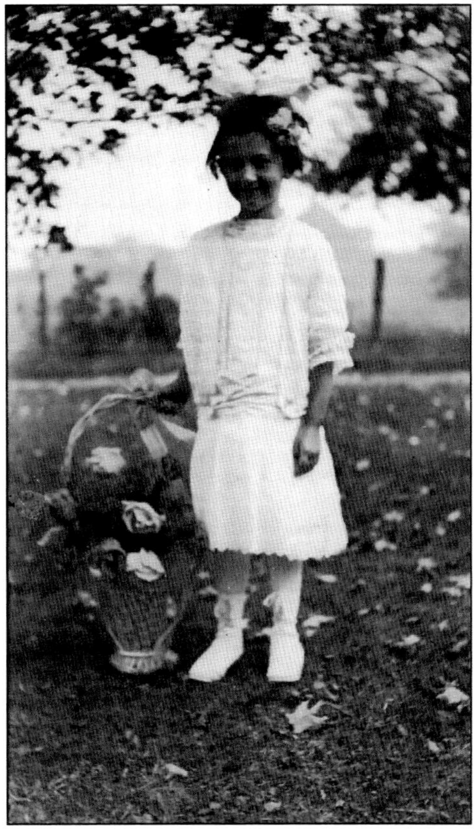

Florence Winkelman and her family lived on a west hill farm between Boston and Eden. She's all dressed up with a huge basket of flowers getting ready to stand up as a flower girl for the wedding of Andrew Mammoser III and Frances Rebman on September 16, 1919. In 1924, Boston's west hill fell victim to a tornado. Florence Winkelman remembered it and described it on an audiotape before she died. "It was dark out. I don't know just what time, but we were scared. It was just lightning continuously and thunder and wind and rain. It was so noisy, and besides that the dinner bell was ringing! We thought it was the end of the world. But we were lucky—we didn't get hurt." This photograph below shows what was left of the Thiel family's barn on Rice Road after the tornado hit it. (Courtesy of Bessie Enser.)

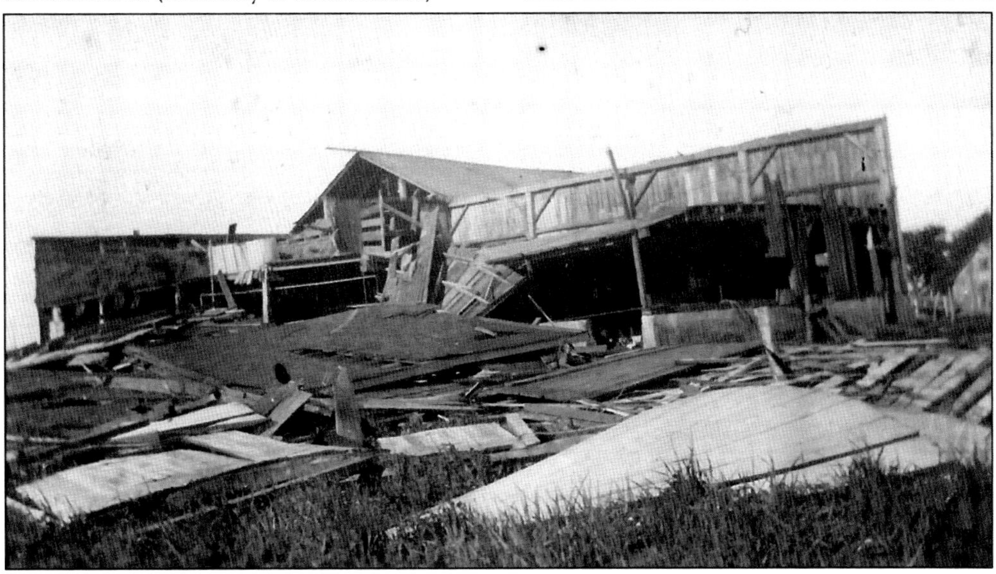

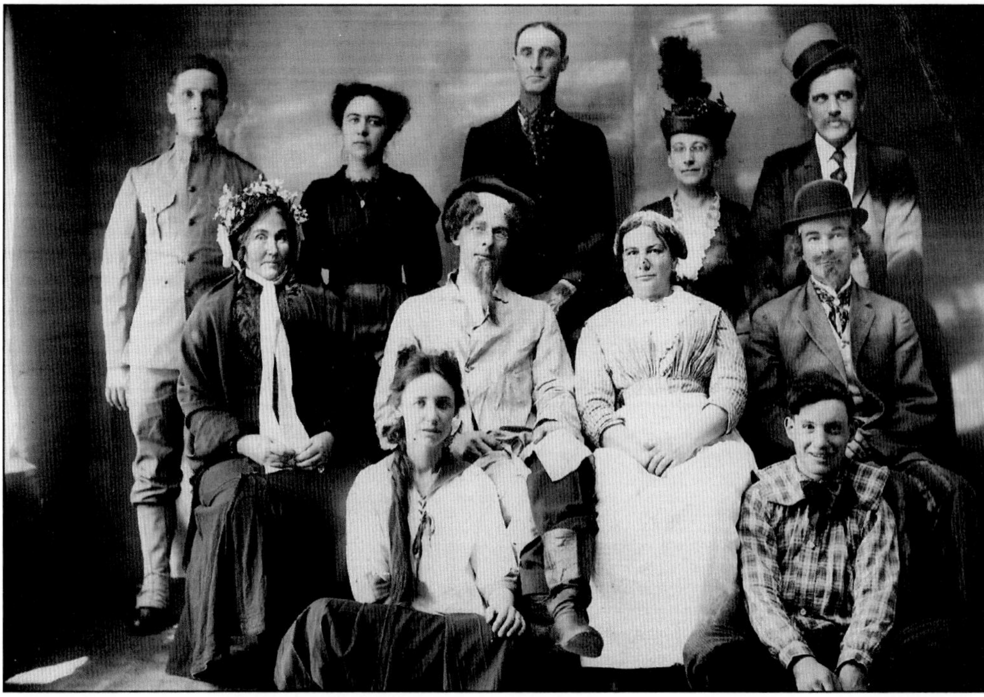

After the work was done during the day, people needed to be entertained. Sitting around playing cards and drinking cider lost its attraction after awhile. So a group of people decided to put together a theater group and perform plays for the public to come and watch. They called themselves the Boston Dramatic Club and they performed at the Boston Fireman's Hall.

Telephone Boston 162
BOSTON
HOTEL and RESTAURANT
Jacob M. Micherdzinski, Prop.

Telephone Boston 15-M
BOSTON GARAGE
C. J. THURBER, Proprietor
Special Prices on Overhaul Jobs for the Months of February and March

101 Main Street HAMBURG, N. Y.
SIPPRELL & CO.
Real Estate
Better Homes at Lower Cost

D. B. CHURCHILL
Dry Goods and Groceries
Telephone 247 PATCHIN, N. Y.

FARMERS—For the Land's Sake use G. L. F.
QUALITY FERTILIZERS
Pay Cash and Save From $3.00 to $7.00 per Ton
Carl N. Emerling, Distributor

Telephone Boston 156
F. A. WURTZ
Furniture and Undertaking

Diamonds & Hearts

A Three Act Comedy Drama
By Effie W. Merriman

1926

Presented by
THE BOSTON DRAMATIC CLUB
for the benefit of and at
THE BOSTON FIREMEN'S HALL,
Boston, New York
February Eleventh and Twelfth
February Twelfth Dancing until Two

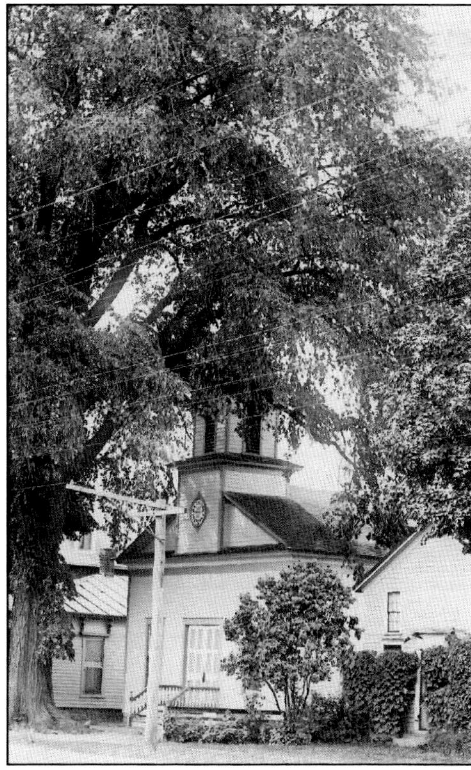

The Methodist Church in Boston was formed in 1824, but they had to meet in homes until they built this building in 1852. It still stands as a private residence on the east side of the state road in Boston, across the street from the Boston Historical Museum. The church was built originally without a steeple, as seen in the photograph below. An elm tree was planted in front of the building that outlived every resident in Boston. It succumbed at 200 years old and when it was cut down, a section of the tree's trunk was saved and is currently on display in the Historical Museum.

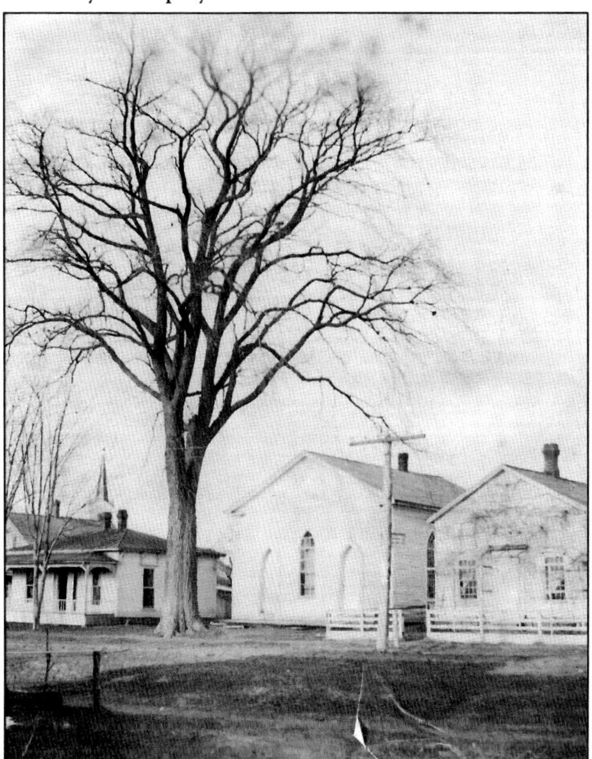

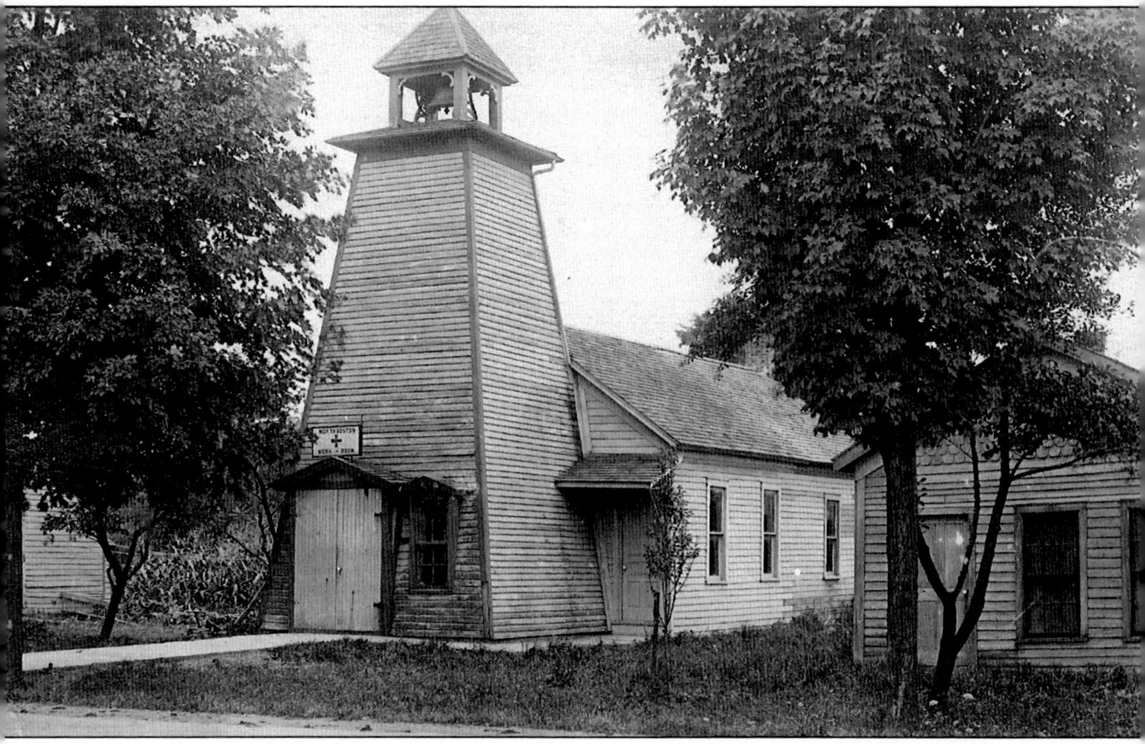

After the Shunk Hotel in Patchin burned down on Valentine's Day in 1904, Fred Frank donated some of his land in North Boston to build a fire tower. Later a lease was drawn up that allowed a newly formed fire company to use the land for free as long as it was used as a firehouse. They built a tower that was 14 feet long by 14 feet wide by 20 feet 6 inches high. During that era, when there was a fire somewhere in town, the church bells would be rung to warn the neighbors and to call the men together to fight the fire. There was no church in North Boston, so it was necessary to buy a bell. A bell was purchased for $14.60 that was 28 inches in diameter and weighed 450 pounds. When the bell was rung, the sound would echo across the whole valley. In 1959, the tower was torn down and a new building built in its place. The bell was saved and mounted on a display in front of the current fire hall, where it still stands today.

RECEPTION COMMITTEE.

—o—

DR. and MRS. H. P. JEHLE.
MR. and MRS. E. A. LAMM.
MR. and MRS. OSCAR HAUTH.
MR. and MRS. HOWARD OWENS.

FLOOR COMMITTEE.

—o—

FERD. FAULRING, LEE KUMMER,
GEORGE GASPER, LEE DEMMERLEY,
FRANK BRUNNER.

BOSTON FIRE COMPANY

WILL GIVE A

DANCE AND OYSTER SUPPER

AT HUND'S HALL, BOSTON, N. Y.

FRIDAY EVENING, FEBRUARY 9, 1912

And request the presence of yourself and ladies

MUSIC, THURBER'S ORCHESTRA

DANCE AND SUPPER, $1.00

On January 16, 1909, the first oyster supper and dance, sponsored by the newly formed Boston Fire Company, was held in Hund's Hall. The admission price was $1 per person, and that first dance made $197.62. The event was so popular that at least 15 more were held in the next three years. This pamphlet is from the February 9, 1912, dance and oyster supper. Thurber's Orchestra (most likely members of the cornet band) provided the music. It took the work of over 13 people to plan the event. The inside of the program lists all the dances and where the intermissions were, so people could plan their dance cards.

ORDER OF DANCES.

1—Waltz
2—Quadrille
3—Opera Reel
5—Two Step
5—Crooked S
6—Lanciers
7—Waltz

Intermission.

8—Waltz
9—Quadrille
10—McDonald's Reel
11—Two Step
12—Monie Musk
13—Quadrille
14—Double Lancers

Intermission.

15—Two Step
16—Opera Reel
17—Eight Hand Reel
18—Portland Fancy
I9—Waltz
20—Lanciers
21 Waltz

Intermission.

22—Waltz
23 - Flowers of Edinboro
24 Waltz
25—Crooked S
26—Quadrille
27—Two Step
28—McDonald's Reel

Intermission.

29—Waltz and Quadrille
30—Double Lancers
31—Two Step
32—Opera Reel
33—March Quadrille
34—Waltz
35—Double Quadrille

Intermission.

36—Three Step
37—Firemen's Dance
38—Crooked S
39—Waltz
40—Sweet Home Waltz

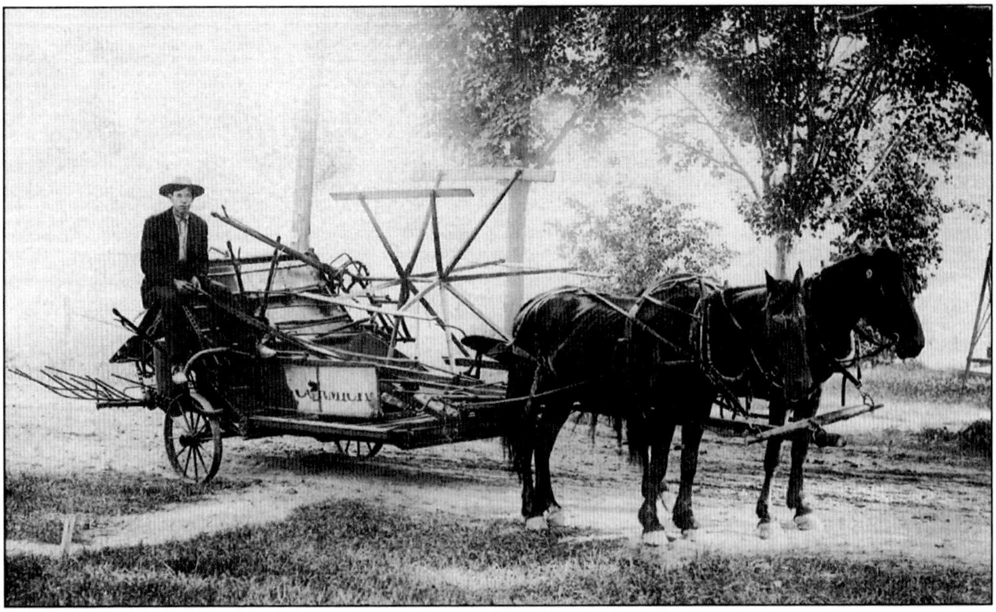

John Kader was a Boston farmer who grew mostly wheat. When the grain reached maturity in late summer, he would take this grain binder into the field and it would cut the stalks and tie bundles of it together. The bundles would then drop off the tines on the back of the machine to lay in the field a little longer to dry and then would be picked up later.

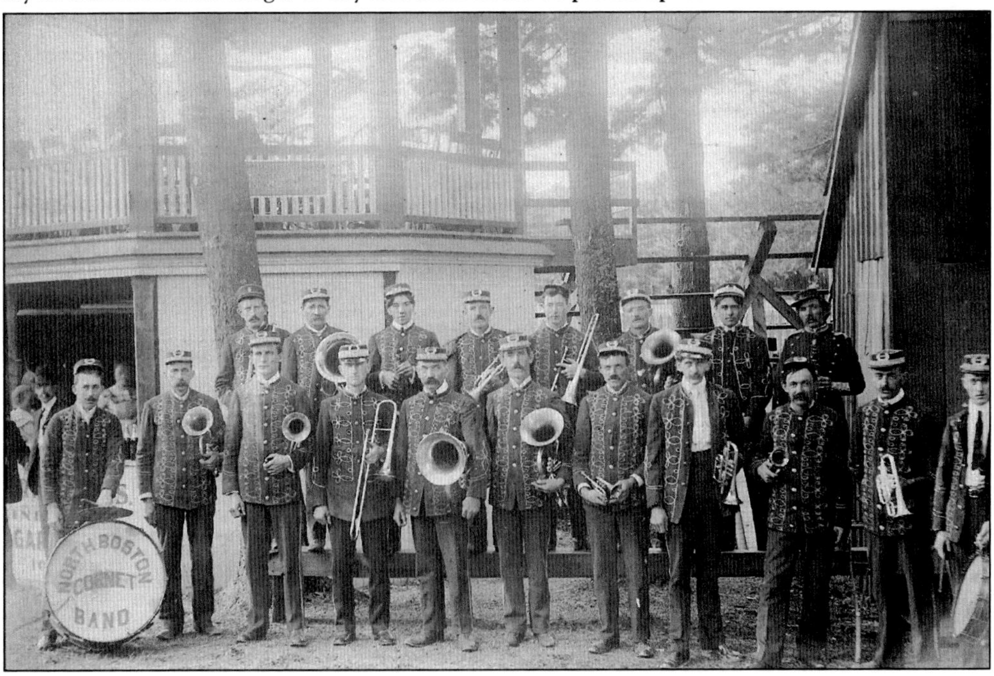

The North Boston Cornet Band bought uniforms and entered competitions at the Erie County Fair. This 1904 photograph includes, from left to right, (first row) Will Klein, John Eiss, Charles Endres, J. Broadbeck, Nick Liebler, Fred Herman, George Gaecker, Art Titus, Jake Frank, Frank Liebler, and Louren Klein; (second row) Ed Kaufmann, Doc Stitzel, Ed Radel, Fred Frank, Al Gisman, N. Von Gerchten, Henry Frank, and Mr. Radel.

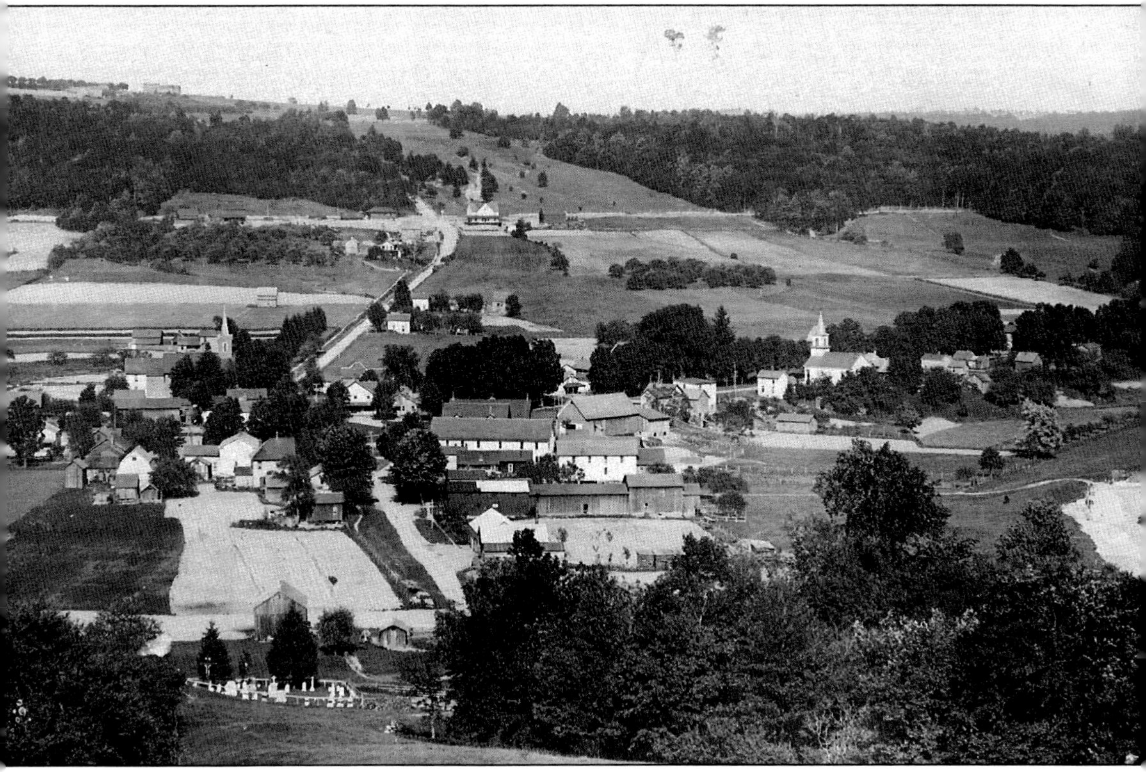

This photograph shows excellent detail of how the Boston "village" looked in the early 1900s. Starting at the bottom, St. John's Cemetery is surrounded by a grassy area. Follow the road down the hill, across the valley and back up the east hill and notice many landmarks—the sawmill, the wagon shop, both the Boston and the Iroquois Hotels, and Boston Commons, where Perry Dye owned a store. Then on the left is the steeple of St. John's Church (the Boston Fire Hall, across the street from the church has not been built yet) and further up Boston Cross Road is the train depot and the hotel. If one turned right at Dye's Store in the valley, one could see the flat roof of the Wurtz Furniture Store (which now houses a veterinarian's office) and finally the tall bell tower of St. Paul's Church. The 18 Mile Creek is seen on the extreme right, resembling the letter C.

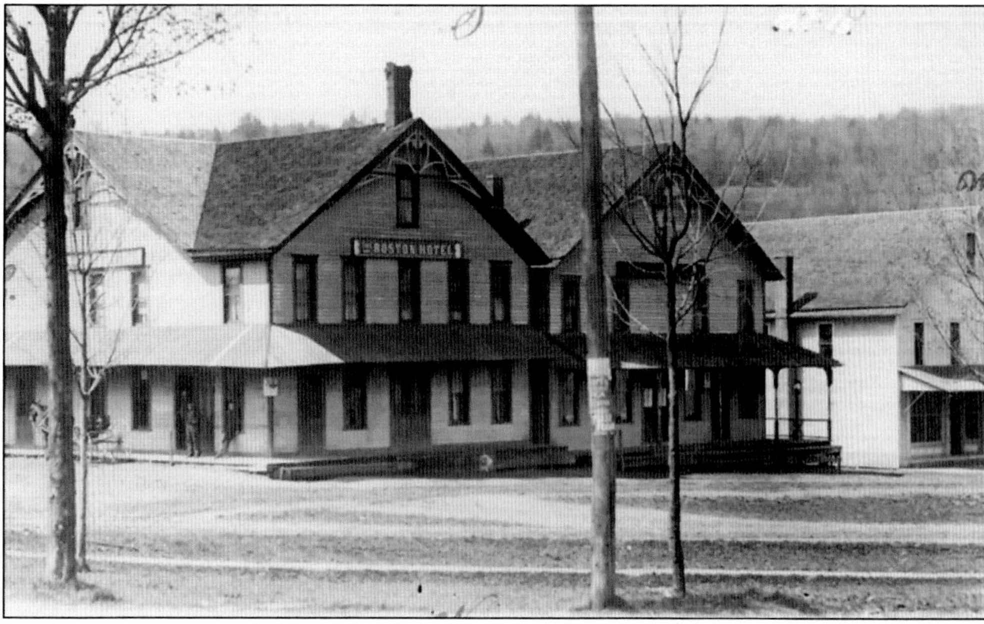

In 1911, a meeting was held in Hund's Hall to consider the possibility of organizing a Boston chapter of the National Grange. (Hund's Hall may be the building on the right next to the Boston Hotel and the Iroquois Hotel.) The purpose of the Grange was to unite the farmers to work for "the good of the Order, the country, and for mankind." Men and women alike were encouraged to join. At the beginning, their meetings took place in many locations and eventually they bought Hund's Hall. Their membership increased to over 100, and when Hund's Hall burned down in the great fire of 1920, they decided to build their own meeting place. In the photograph below, the work is beginning on digging the foundation for the new hall in 1933.

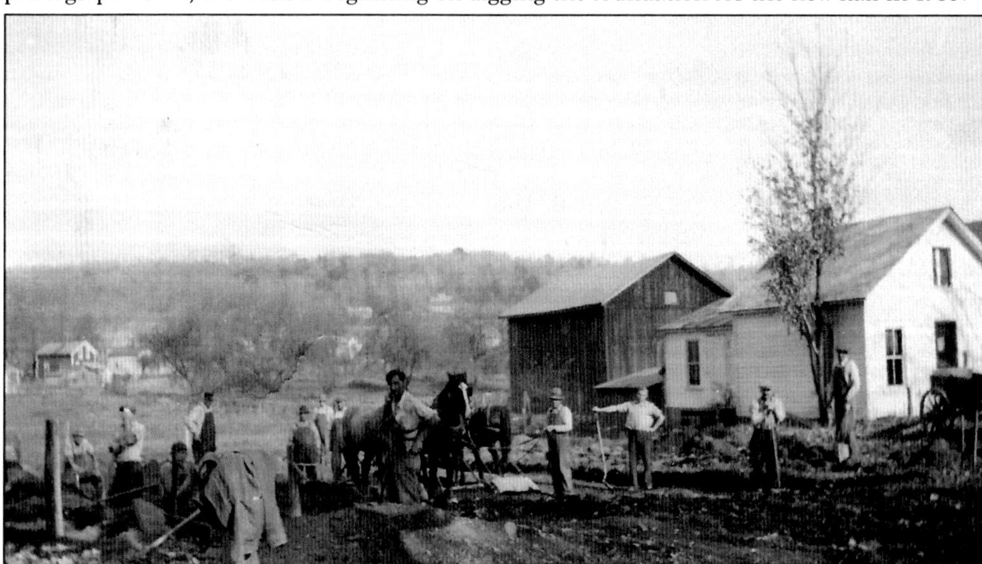

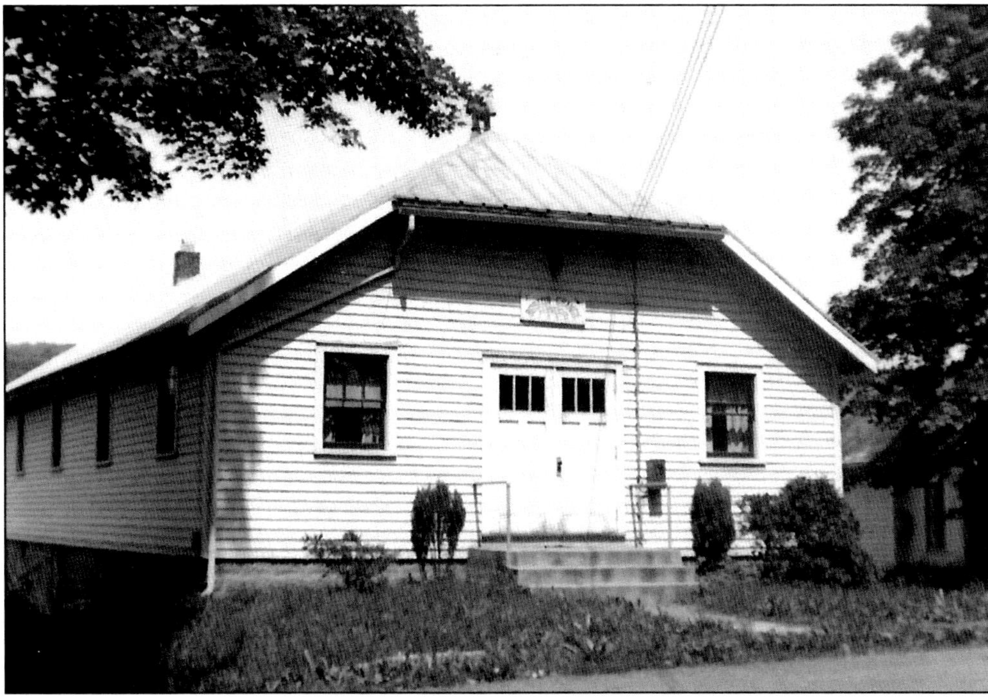

Earl Rockwood was elected in the first meeting in 1911 as the master of Chapter 1256, and most of the members that joined came from the following families: Rockwood, Trevett, Rauch, Thiel, Thurber, and Pfarner. The new hall was completed in 1935 and was dedicated on October 14 by Fred J. Truestone, who was at that time the state master. Membership in 1937 had reached 153. The organization exhibited at the Erie County Fair every year since its inception in 1911, winning many awards. The Grange sponsored many dances, card parties, dramas, auctions, and picnics like the one seen below. Over the years, it raised enough money to pay off the mortgage on the new hall in 1946. The Grange building still stands on Boston State Road across and down the street from the Boston Historical Museum, where it has been remodeled as a private residence.

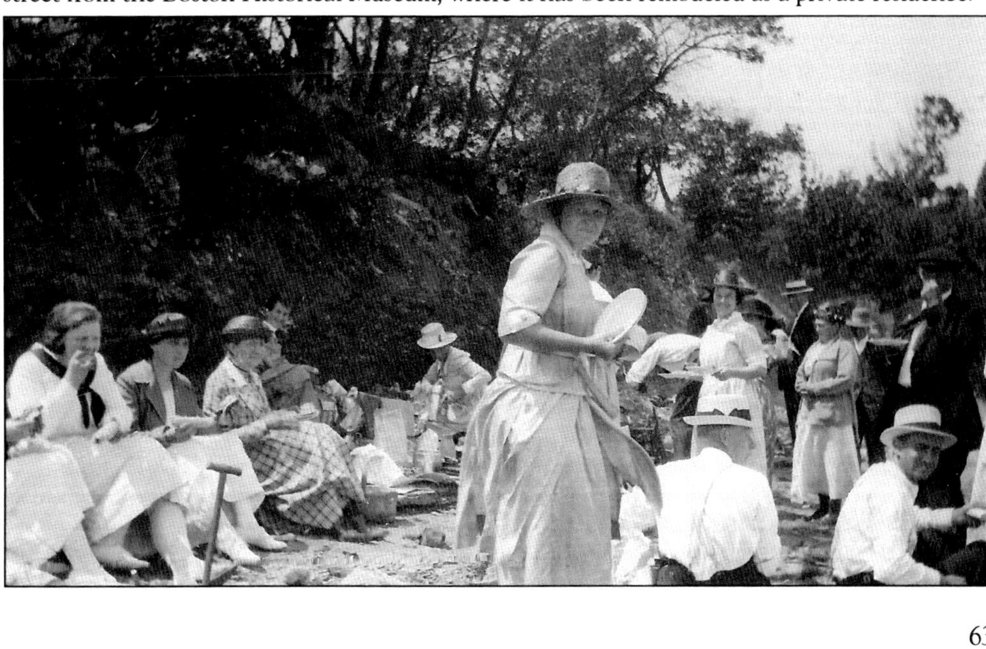

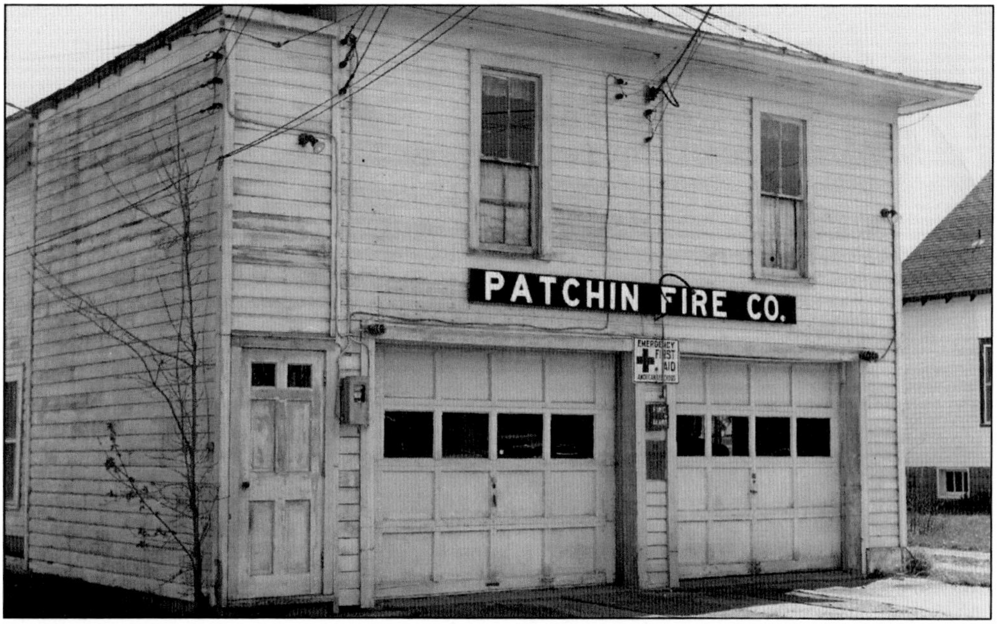

The Patchin Fire Company was first organized in 1908 when the loss of the Shunk Hotel in 1904 determined the need for a fire company in the center of town. The first fire apparatus was a hand cart pulled by a team of horses. The property was donated by Fred Kummer, and Lee Kummer was appointed the first fire chief. The original building still stands and has been remodeled as a private residence.

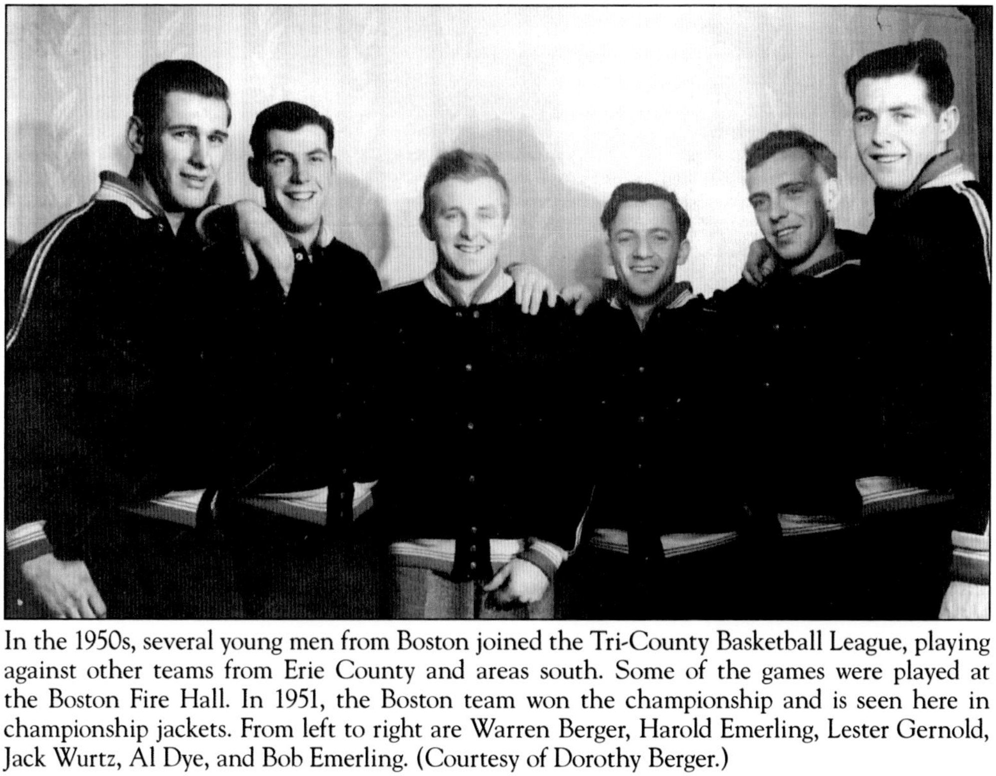

In the 1950s, several young men from Boston joined the Tri-County Basketball League, playing against other teams from Erie County and areas south. Some of the games were played at the Boston Fire Hall. In 1951, the Boston team won the championship and is seen here in championship jackets. From left to right are Warren Berger, Harold Emerling, Lester Gernold, Jack Wurtz, Al Dye, and Bob Emerling. (Courtesy of Dorothy Berger.)

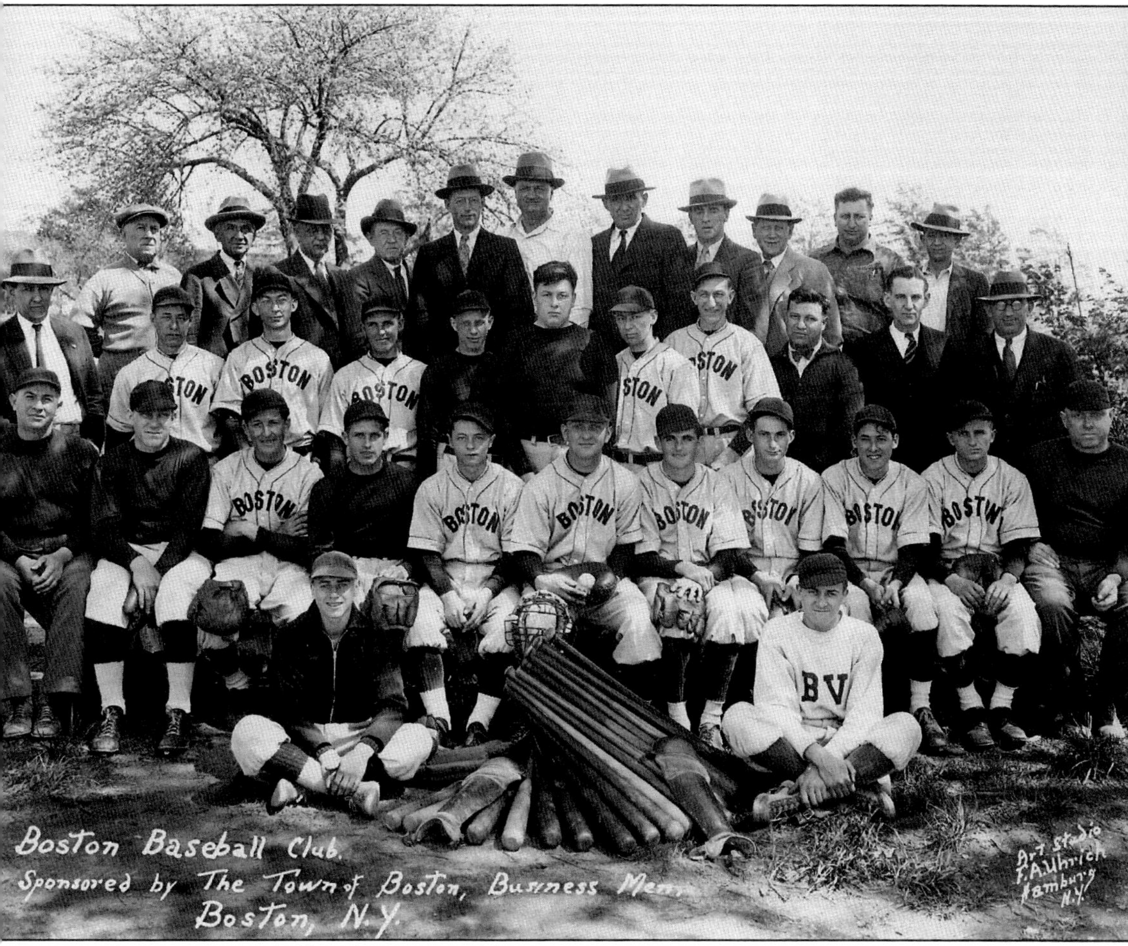

Here the Boston Baseball Club, sponsored by the businessmen of the town, gathers together for a group photograph in 1933. The team belonged to the Buffalo News Suburban Baseball League. From left to right are (first row) Edwin Pohle and Elery Heinrich; (second row) coach Irwin Heinrich, Howard Wittmeyer, William Stelmach, John Perrin, Walter Smolinski, Henry Bradl, Harold Rockwood, Carl Endress, Fred Seufert, John Smolinski, and coach Roy Smith; (third row) Bob Owen, Charles Pohle, Albert Wurtz, Bob Perrin, Kenneth Pohle, Vernon Massing, Jack Seufert, Clarence Wittmeyer, unidentified, Gardner Debo, and Buffalo News League representative Joseph Wittmeyer; (fourth row) George Colin, Otto Bradl, George Weber, Fred Frank, Carl Emerling, Fred Burkhardt, Charles Armbruster, Henry Rucker, Frank Weber, Leroy Pfarner, and Julius "Jack" Seufert.

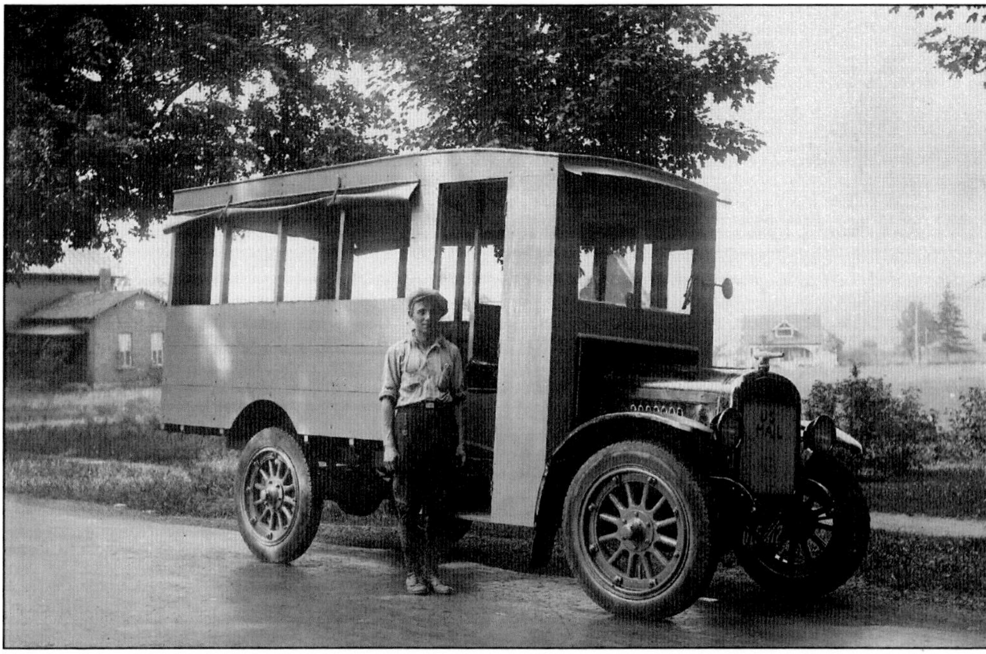

Once the automobile became the transportation of choice for the majority of people, the mail stage was no longer needed. This custom-made U.S. mail truck is parked on Boston State Road not far from the Grange hall. In the background on the right, the Zahler residence and the beginning of the line of giant pine trees can be seen.

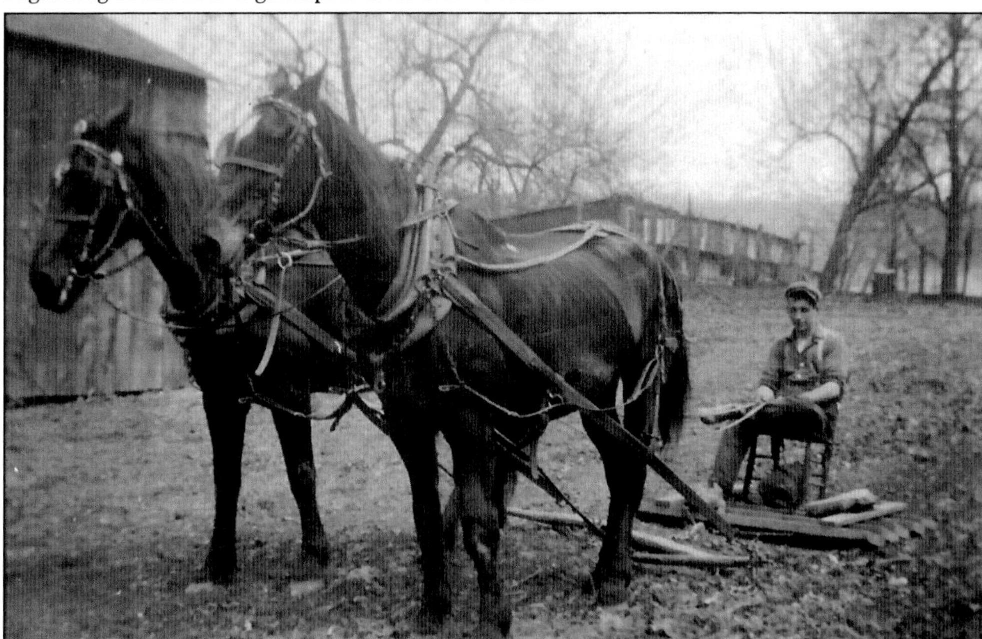

Before tractors came out with nice comfy seats, a farmer had to use brainpower to get the job done. This fellow took one of his mother's broken-down chairs, set it on top of a piece of corrugated steel, and added weight to the contraption with several large fieldstones. It did a fine job of breaking up clumps of soil as it drove over them, but it was probably a bumpy ride.

Three

THE RAILROAD

The history of the Buffalo and Susquehanna Railroad (B&S) encompasses a lot more than just its extension through the town in 1903, so this chapter is just going to focus on how it affected Boston. As the lumber, coal, and iron industries grew exponentially in western New York, the transportation of those valuable resources became not only necessary but profitable. Frank H. Goodyear and his brother Charles W. Goodyear were the biggest lumber and fuel dealers in the area and had their eyes set on expanding their reach and their profits. The hemlock forests between Boston and Pennsylvania were ripe fodder for the lumber business and very attractive to the railroad because tracks could be built through the middle of this natural resource. Construction began in 1903 to extend the B&S line from Buffalo to Wellsville by purchasing easements of land across the area now known as the "power line." The image on the last page of this chapter is from the *New Century Atlas of Erie County*, published in 1909, and clearly shows the path that the new railroad would take. It would cut though the valley to the east of and parallel to 18 Mile Creek. Valleys and streams had to be traversed, and hills had to be cut through. The task was so labor intensive and expensive the history books place the blame for the Goodyear brothers' eventual downfall on the three years it took to complete the extension. The biggest part of the project was to lay tracks across a tributary of 18 Mile Creek called Landon Brook in the southernmost part of Boston. Over the centuries, Landon Brook had cut a sizeable valley through the hills, and the decision had to be made to build a concrete tunnel for the brook to flow through and then backfill the whole valley and lay the tracks on top. All the photographs in this chapter were taken by Smith Ashcraft, Boston's resident photographer in the early 1900s. Residents are thankful to him for preserving this important part of the town's history.

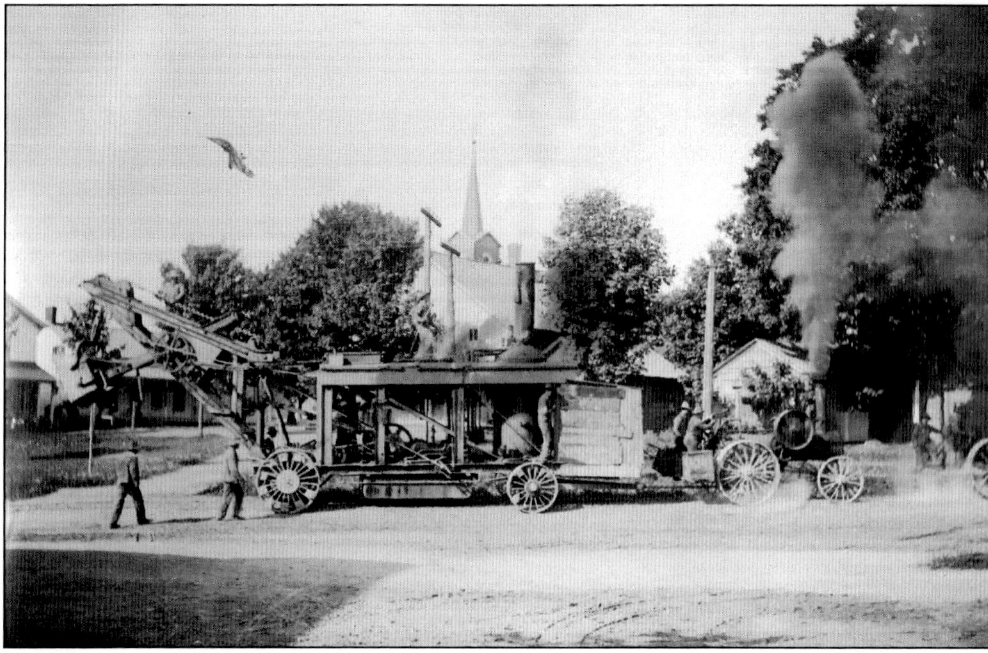

In order to build something as extensive as a railroad through town, the contractor had to bring in the big machinery. Here is a giant steam shovel making its way past Boston Commons, hitched to a steam tractor. The steeple of St. John's Church can be seen behind it. The object hanging in midair is the American flag, strung on a wire across the street.

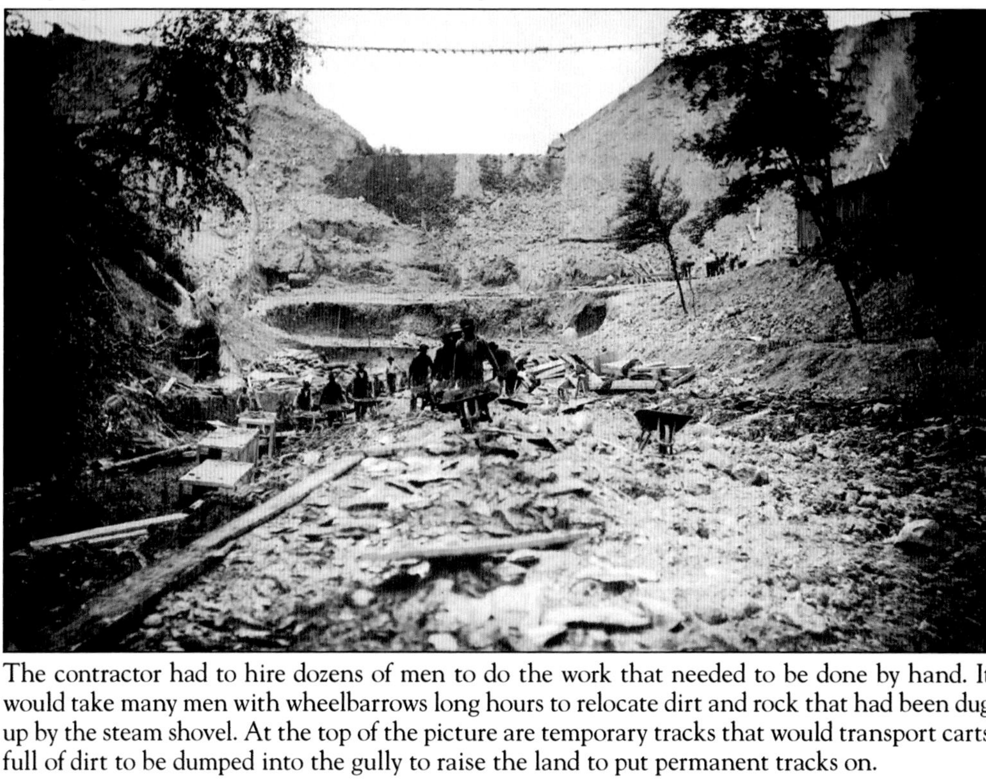

The contractor had to hire dozens of men to do the work that needed to be done by hand. It would take many men with wheelbarrows long hours to relocate dirt and rock that had been dug up by the steam shovel. At the top of the picture are temporary tracks that would transport carts full of dirt to be dumped into the gully to raise the land to put permanent tracks on.

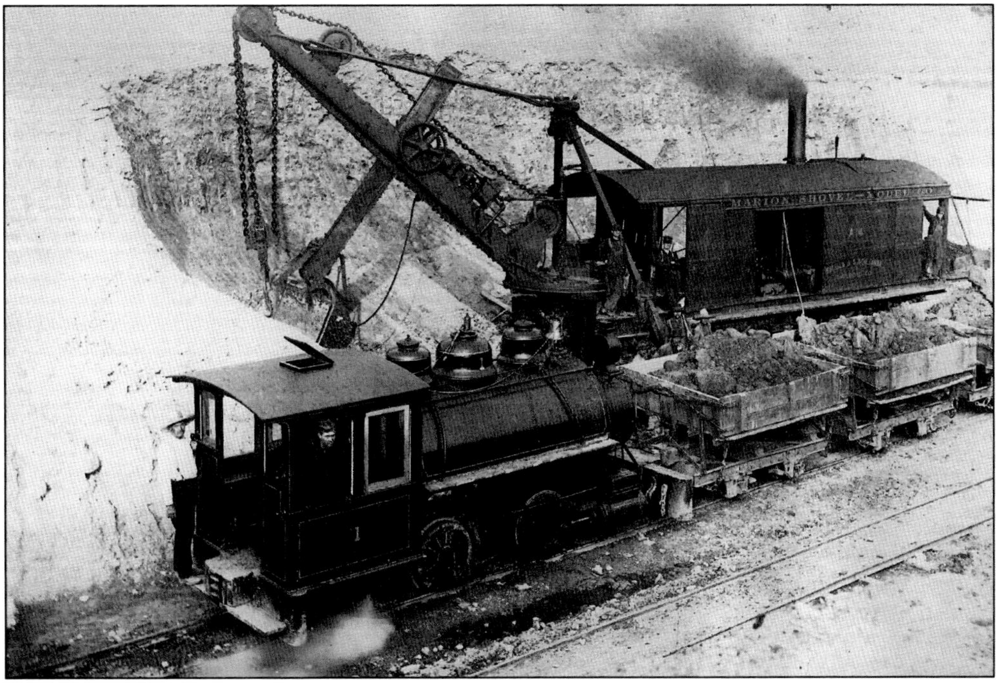

Here the steam shovel is in action. On the side of this leviathan it reads, "Marion Shovel—Model 60—A14—Buffalo & Susquehanna Railroad Co." After the shovel digs deep into the clay and shale rock earth, it dumps its load onto waiting railroad cars called "donkey carts."

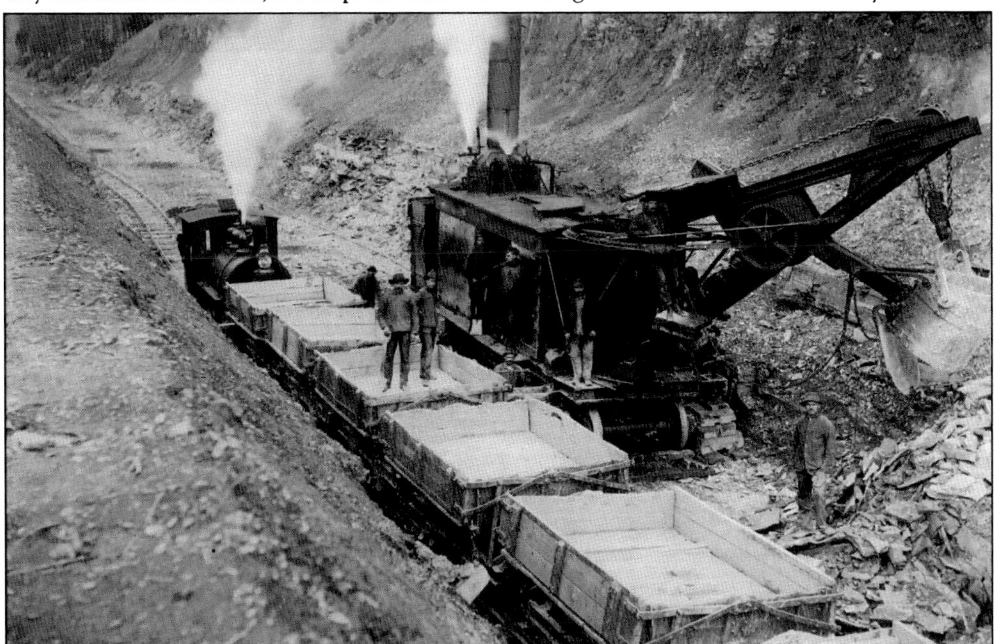

This photograph shows more of the shale rock the men had to contend with. In prehistoric times, about 280 million years ago, this whole area had been underwater. Then the hills and valleys were formed by huge glaciers that traveled south during the ice age some 100,000 years ago. The pressure of this glacier compressed the sand and clay in the soil to form shale.

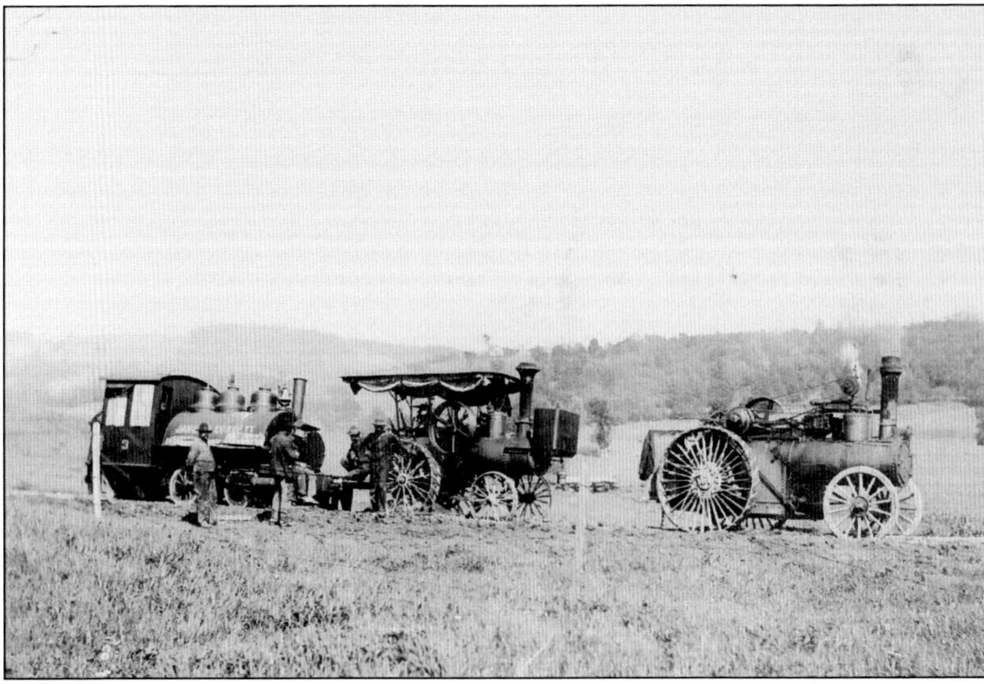

Many other large steam engines were used for other construction needs. These engines, called "donkey engines," are traveling along land roads toward their final destination. It must have been warm that day, as someone's jacket is seen hanging off the back of the lead engine.

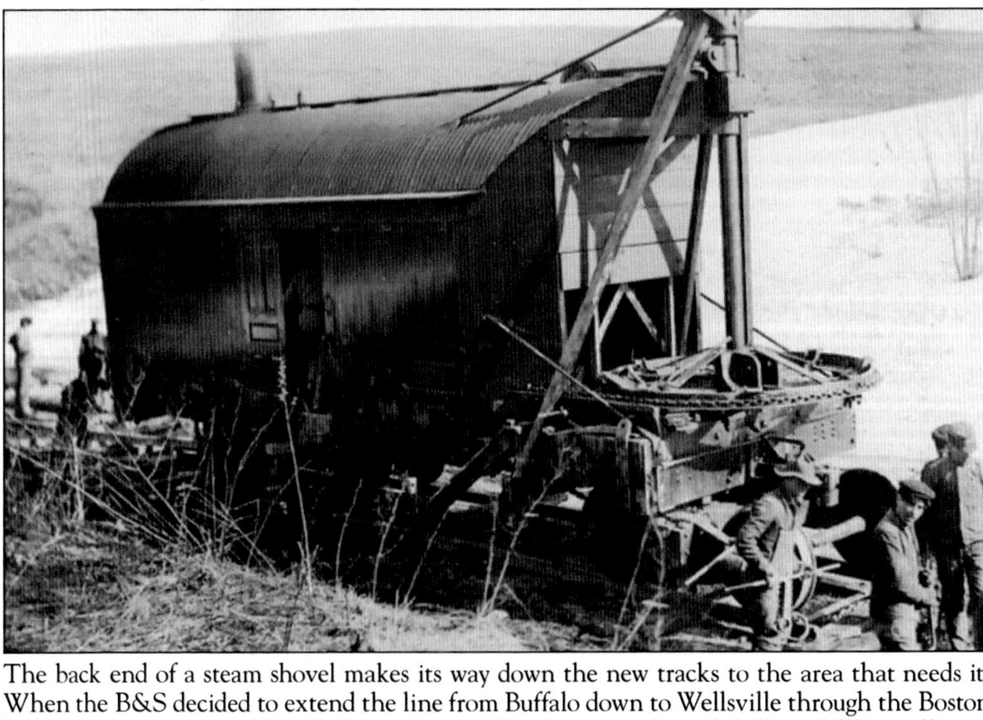

The back end of a steam shovel makes its way down the new tracks to the area that needs it. When the B&S decided to extend the line from Buffalo down to Wellsville through the Boston hills, it was not prepared for all the work it would take to cut through hills and fill in gullies. It was a very long process.

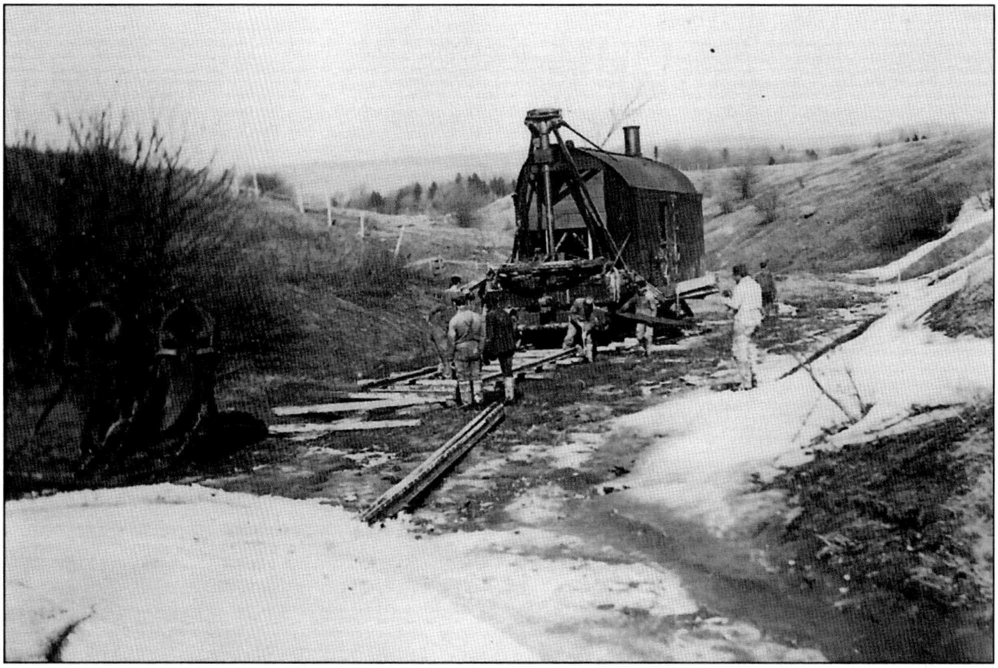

Here they are at a spot where the tracks end, and the men are laying the tracks as the machine moves forward. One man just to the right of the machine is carrying a railroad tie, and another man, just to the left of him, is pounding the previous tie into position.

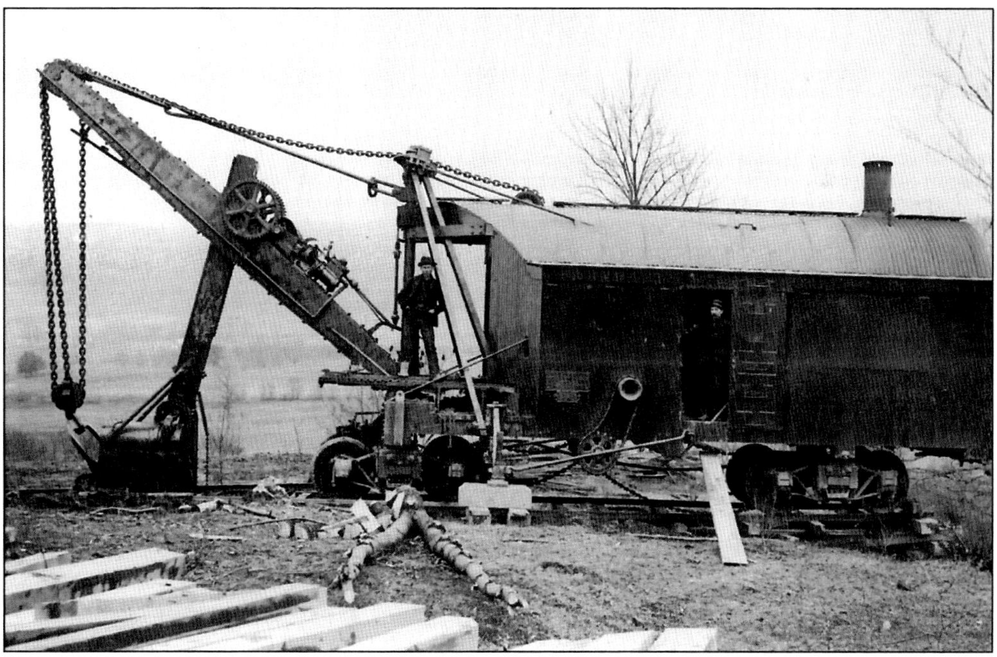

The steam shovel's back end, which they were transporting, is now connected to the actual shovel. The fulcrum of the shovel is on a chain-driven turntable so it can have a 180-degree swing and be accessible to both sides of the track. At the bottom of the picture is a pile of railroad ties ready to be placed on the new track.

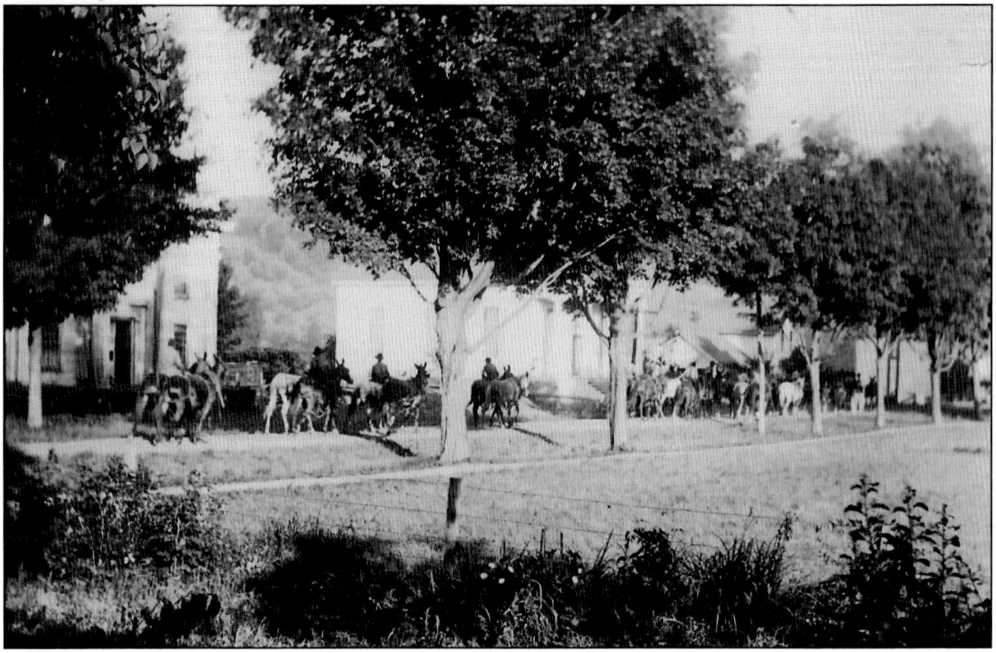

A dozen mule teams are traveling north on Boston State Road past the Baptist church (that no longer exists) and St. Paul's Church. The mule teams were used because they could get into narrow areas that the machines could not. They were used for everything from dragging heavy supplies to pulling wagons full of food and water for the workers.

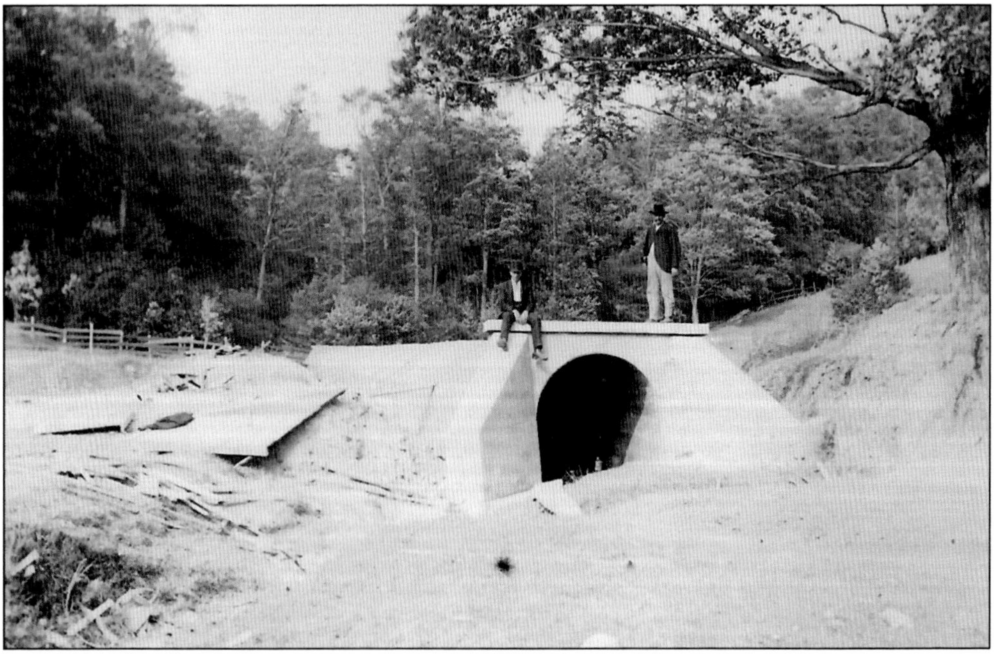

The railroad had to lay tracks over many tributaries of 18 Mile Creek. In those cases, concrete tunnels were built for the stream to run through, rather than diverting the path of the water. This tunnel was built just north of Omphalius Road and is still visible by anyone driving on Boston State Road.

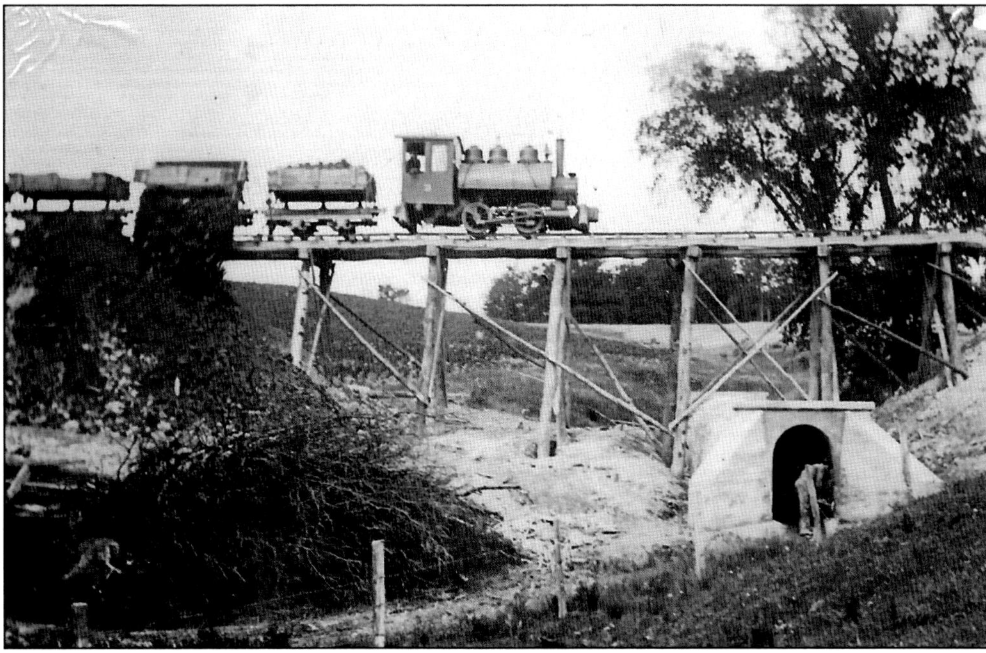

After the tunnel was completed, a temporary trestle was built for the donkey engine and donkey carts to travel on as they transported excavated dirt and other fill to where the Landon Brook tunnel was being built. It would be quite the scene and extremely dangerous if the trestle were to buckle or if one of the carts slipped off the track.

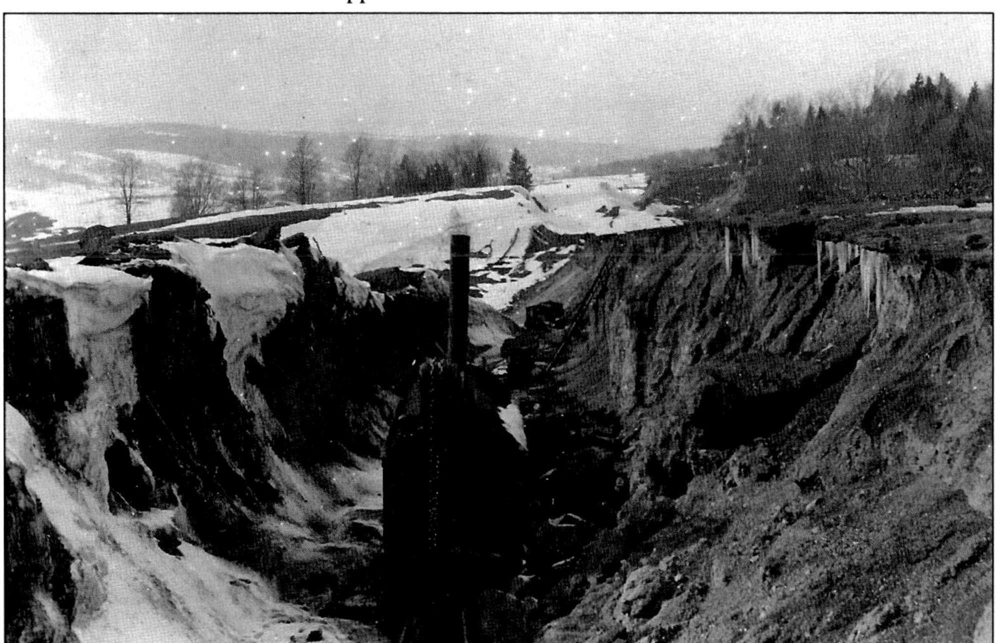

The work had to stop sometimes during the cold winter months. With temperatures below zero many times, it would be hard, if not impossible, to keep crews warm and fed and able to work efficiently in the cold. On the right side of the shovel, it looks like a cave-in has deposited huge rocks onto the track and possibly caused damage to the shovel.

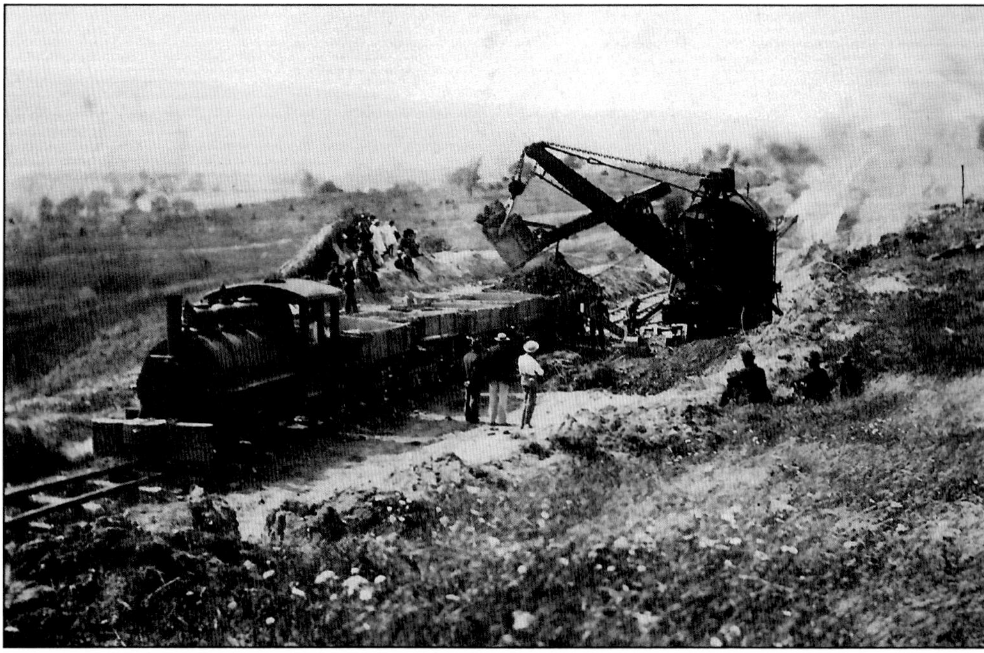

No one in Boston had ever seen the kind of construction that the railroad was completing. They had read about this kind of thing going on in the big cities, but here in Boston, it just did not exist. So on sunny days, the folks would come out and watch the big machines work. The hill on the left side of the shovel made a great natural seating area for people to watch.

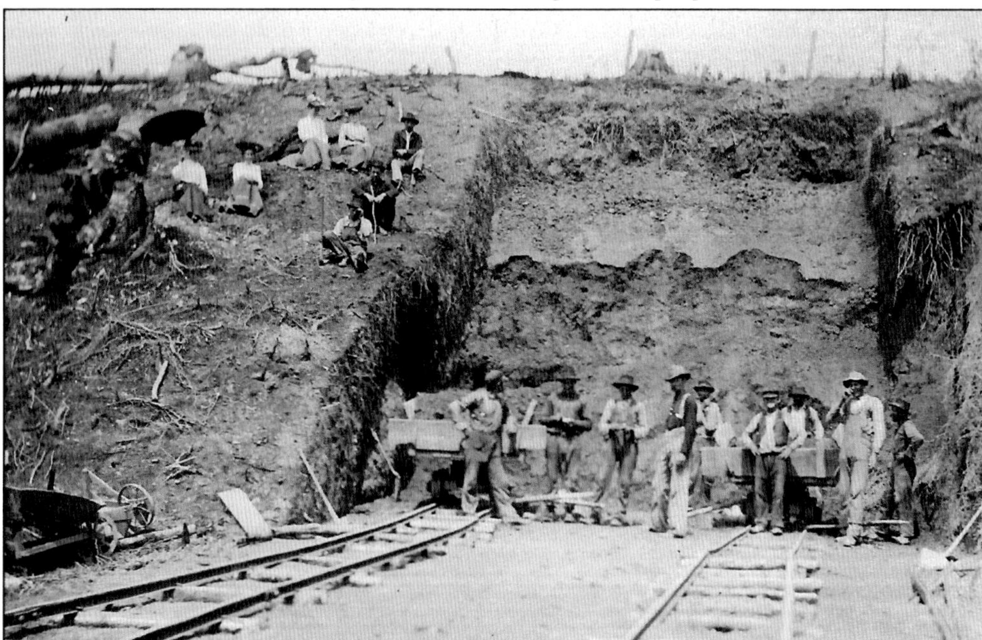

A hill is only as small as the work it takes to move it. The spectators were having great fun eating their picnic lunches and talking among themselves and wondering when the big shovel was going to come and take a bite out of the obstacle. One woman even brought her parasol to keep the sun at bay while she watched.

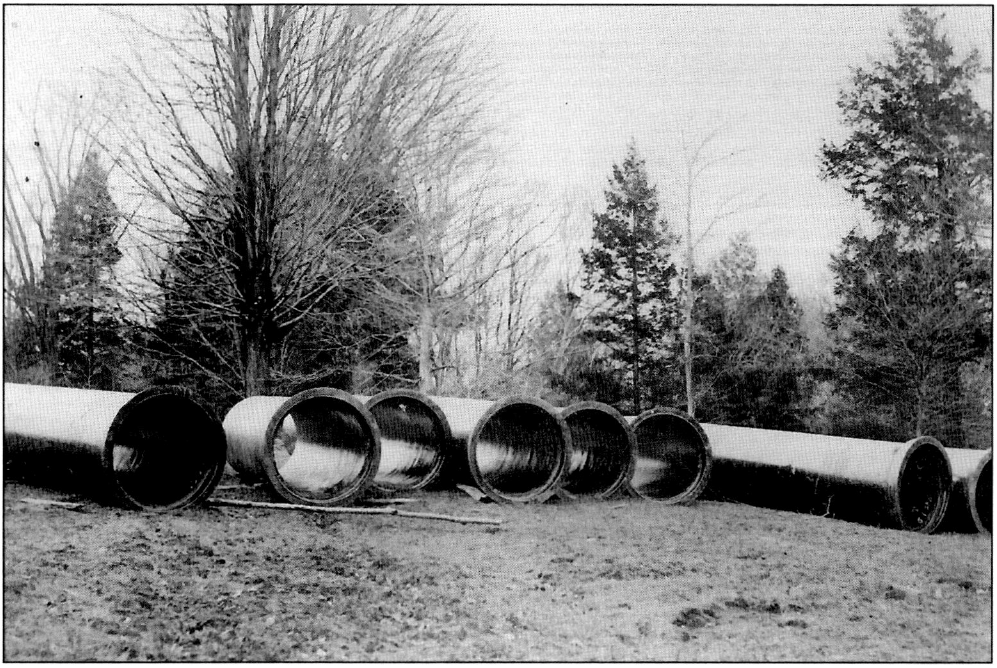

Smaller streams and areas that get washed out with excess rainwater in the spring were fitted with long pipes that would carry the water safely under the tracks. There was a real science that dictated how a track should be built in order to hold and last many years. Keeping water erosion from washing away supporting soil was something that was a big concern for the contractors. The pipe would be put into place and a temporary trestle built over it. Then the donkey carts would bring soil and rock to fill in the small gully around the pipe.

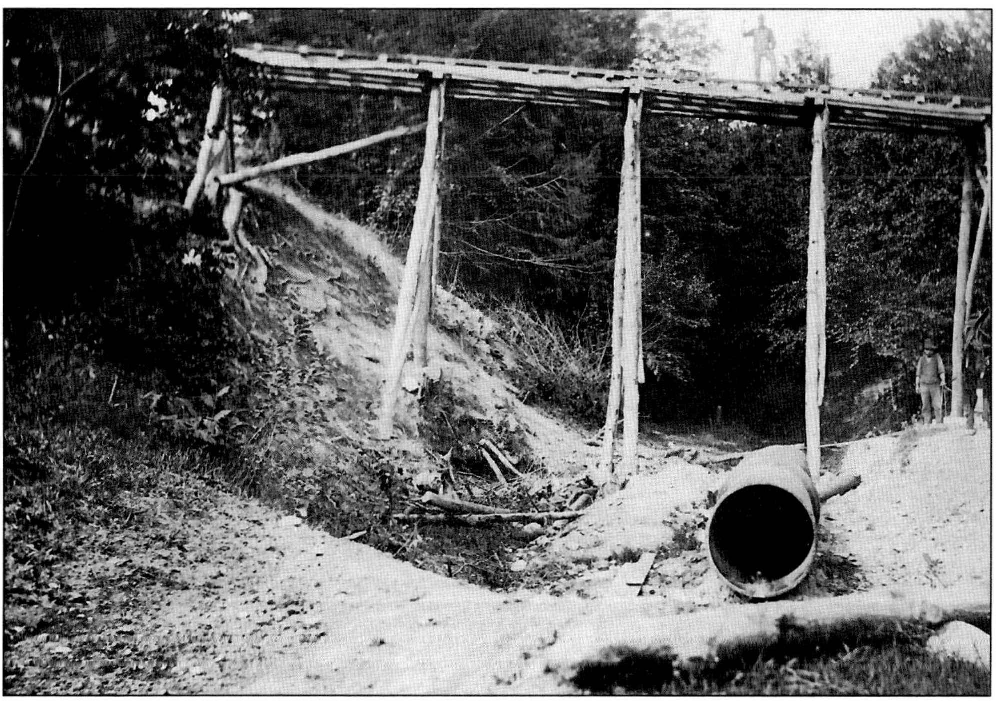

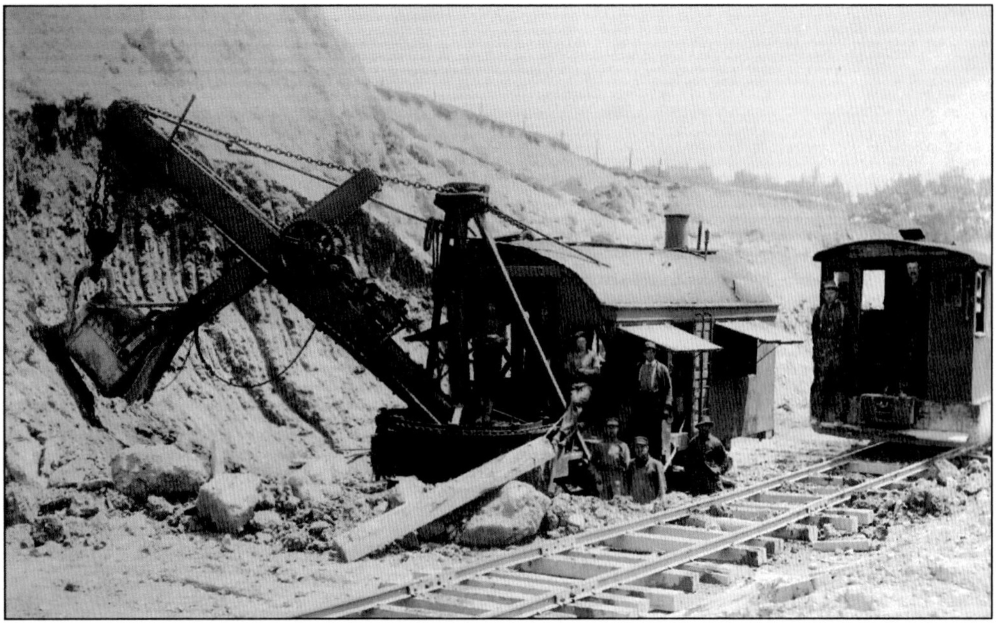

The rock and soil in this particular spot must have been exceedingly tough to get through. The crews decided to partially bury the shovel in the ground so it could exert more pressure to the cliffs. They also needed to cut away more of the cliff to protect the new track from rockslides. The large boulders in front of the shovel are rocks that were deposited by the glacier during the last ice age.

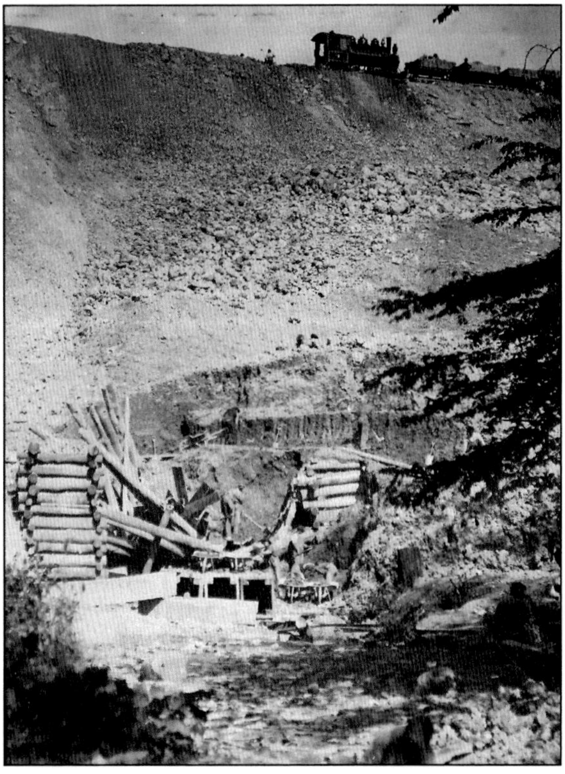

The construction of the tunnel over Landon Brook was a huge undertaking, much bigger than anyone imagined. Here is the framework of the tunnel being built over the brook. The logs used to support the concrete forms were stacked "Lincoln log" style. The idea is to fill in the whole gully between the locomotive down to where the men are working.

Here one can see how they were building the tunnel. It was a little like building a small barn and then covering it with concrete. At the top of the picture, one can see how the donkey carts full of dirt would be dumped onto the two chutes and then teams of men with wheelbarrows stood ready to distribute it.

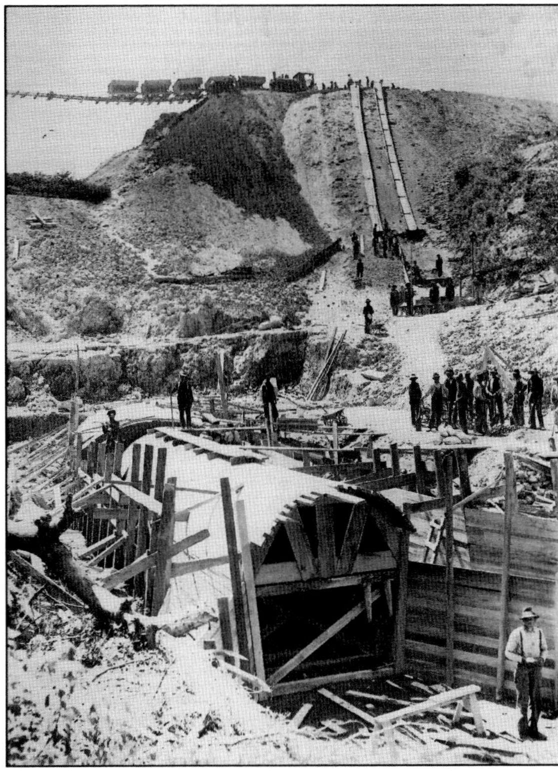

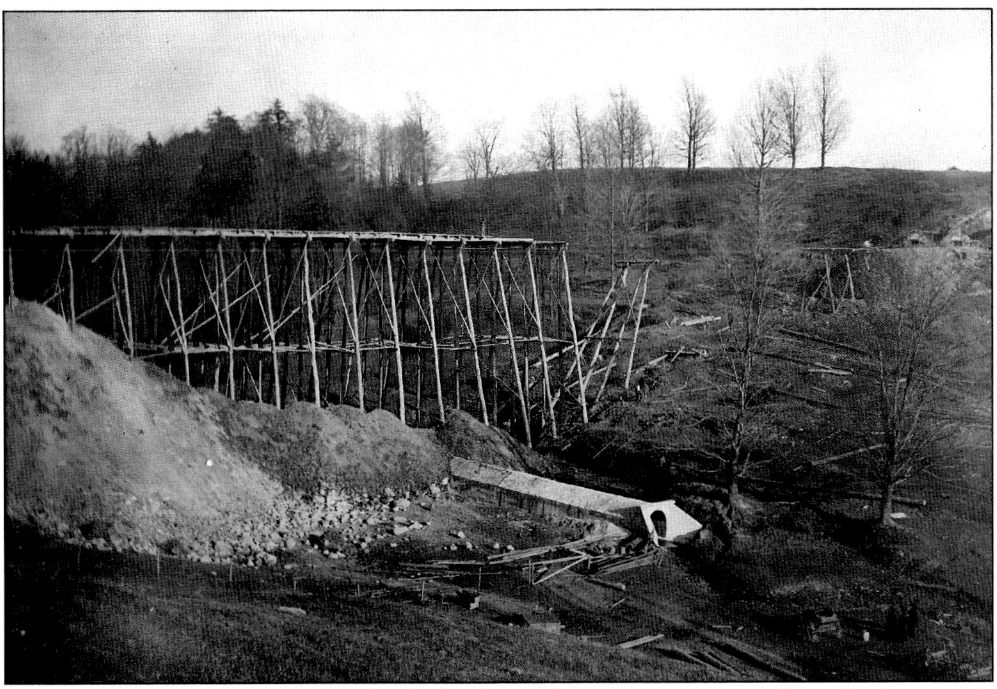

In this picture, the tunnel has been finished and now the temporary trestle is being built to stretch from one side of the hill to the other. The scope of the undertaking is enormous. How convenient it must have been to have all the tree trunks needed for the trestle growing right there.

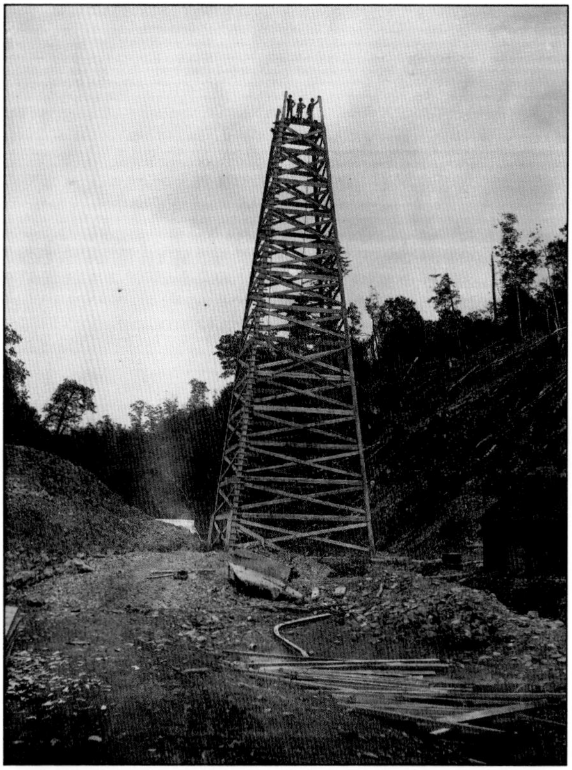

This huge freestanding support tower was built to string wires to the top of the trestle where the donkey carts would dump the fill onto the tunnel. This was done to steady the trestle so it would not swing from side to side. Notice the three men standing at the top to get some idea of how tall it really was.

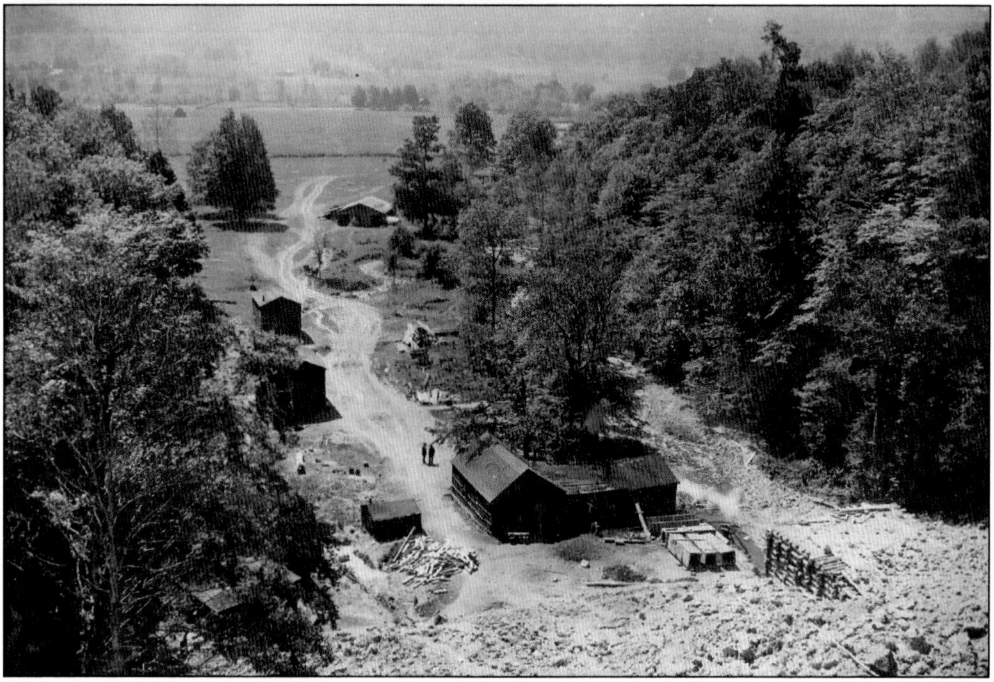

This view is from the top of the hill looking down where the crews were transported from the state road to work every day. The buildings held supplies, water, a mess hall, and a kitchen. The path of Landon Brook passes the largest building on the right side.

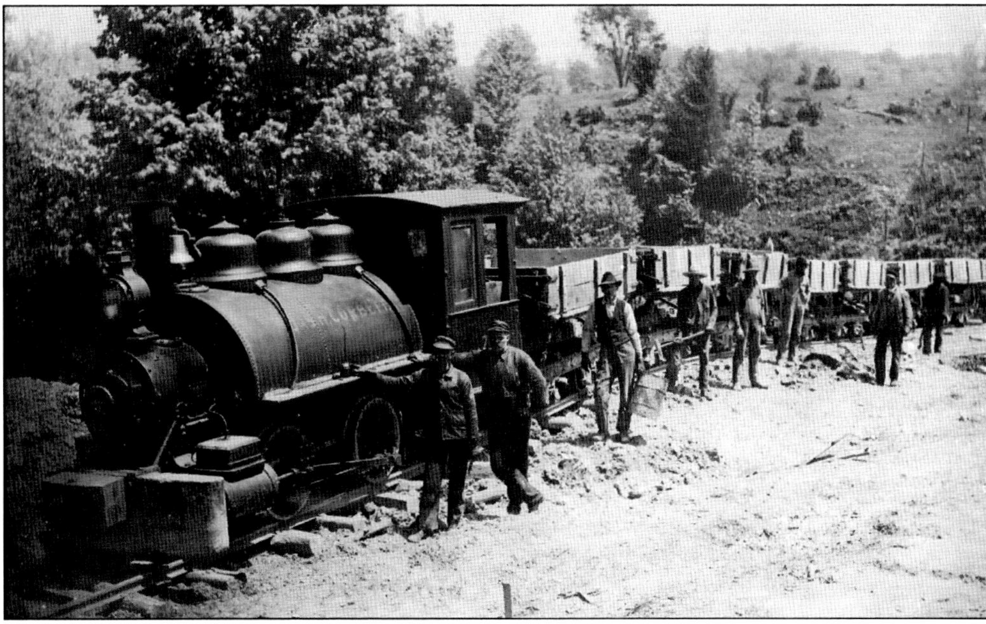

The conductors of the donkey engine and the fellows who kept the donkey carts in good repair are seen here next to the real workhorse of the project. Without these machines, the labor needed to get the railroad through would have been prohibitive. The record does not mention if there were any deaths or bad accidents that occurred because of the construction. Perhaps no news is good news.

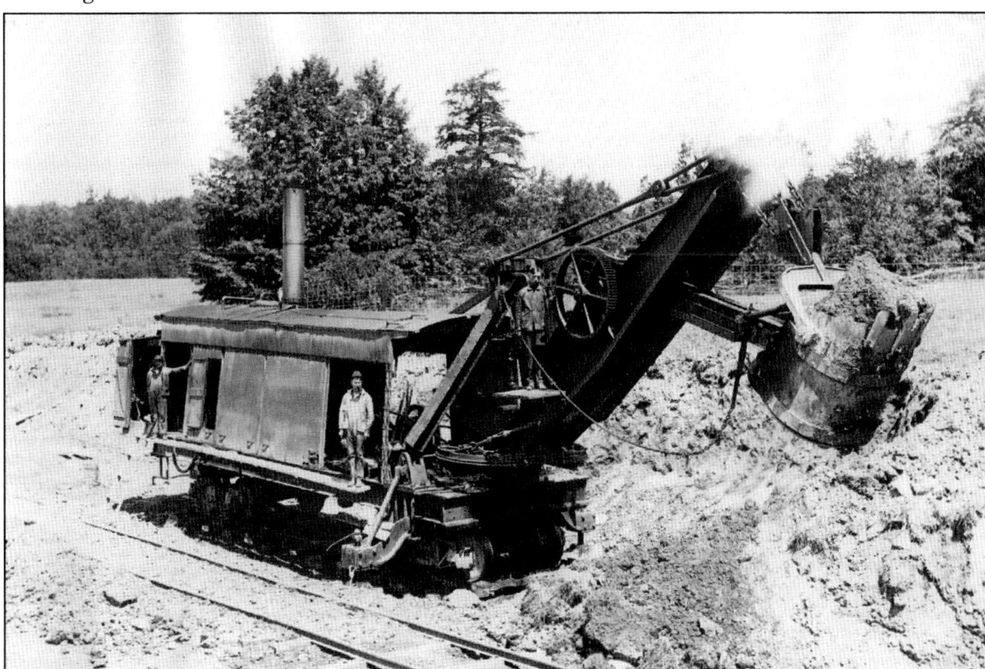

One can see here what a behemoth the steam shovel was. Standing on the ledge above the turntable must have been a loud and dangerous job, being just inches away from that giant gear. It looks like it might be time to replace the bucket, as the digging edge is getting pretty ragged.

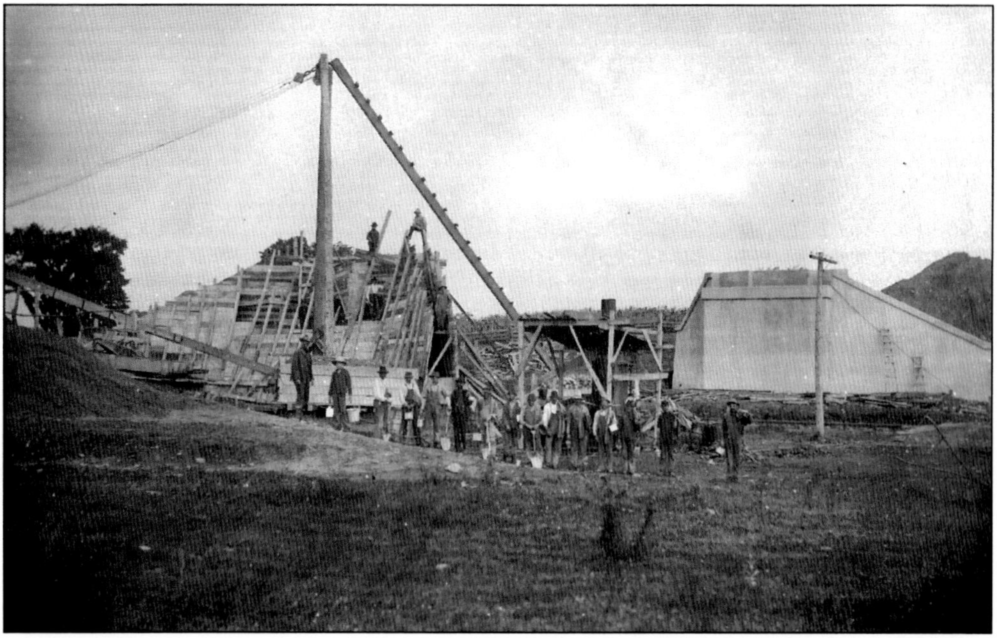

Building bridge abutments was also part of the job of getting the railroad through. Here one can see how the men are building the form to pour the concrete into to make the matching abutment. Right in the middle of the picture is a steam engine protected by a lean-to for some unknown purpose.

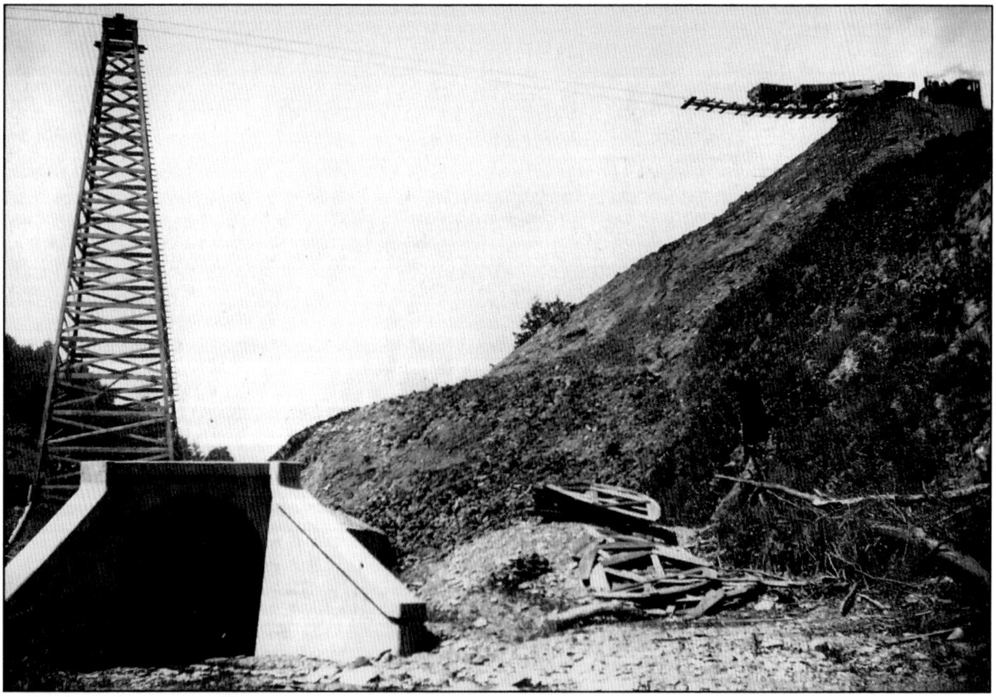

This is a great view of the Landon Brook tunnel with some of the donkey carts high above it, dumping fill off the side of the track. Some of the wooden forms used to pour the concrete lie on the ground like giant Tinkertoys. The tunnel is so long, one can peer into one end and not be able to see the light coming through the other end.

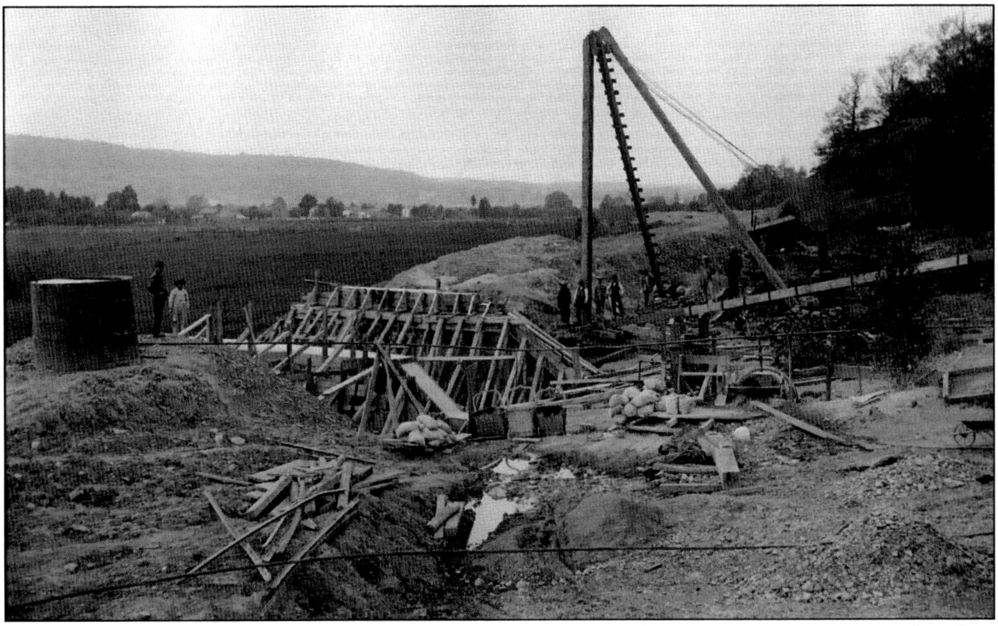

This photograph shows a lot of different things going on. The men are using a tripod with a giant pulley to lift a larger pole up to a vertical position. Canvas bags filled with cement lie next to huge buckets to mix with water to make the concrete. And finally, on the right side of the picture, way in the distance, laundry is hanging on a clothesline.

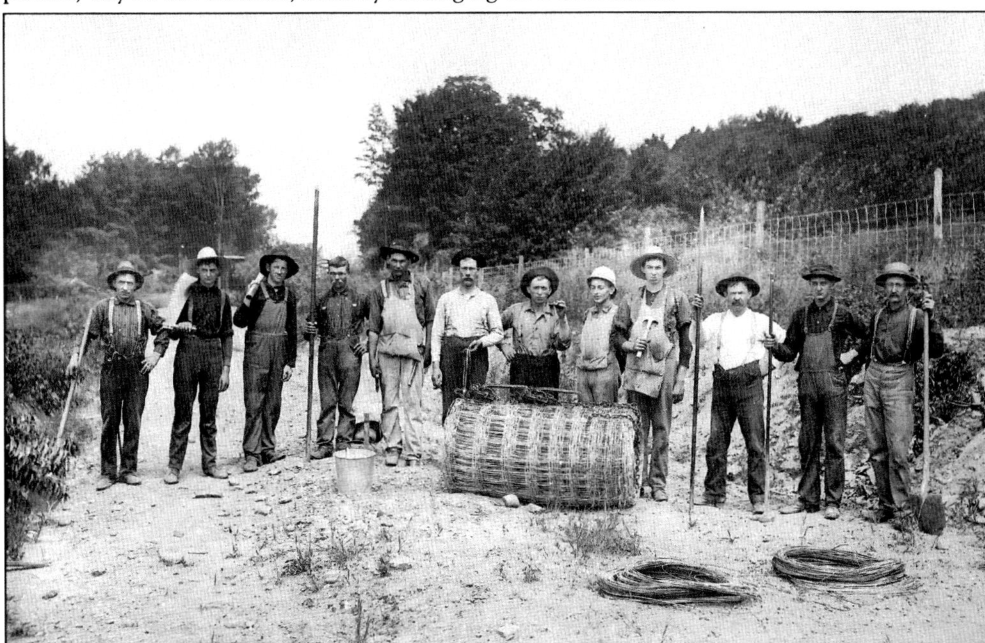

Part of getting the railroad through was putting up fences so wayward cows or people would not wander onto the tracks and get hurt. This crew from 1905 consisted mostly of Boston residents. From left to right they are John Eckert, Jacob Weis, Joe Bell, Steve Godlaska, Albert Weisser, Charles Parcels, superintendent Joe Nowak, Lee Blakley, Leon Armbruster, Jacob Frank, Peter Weis, and George Fay.

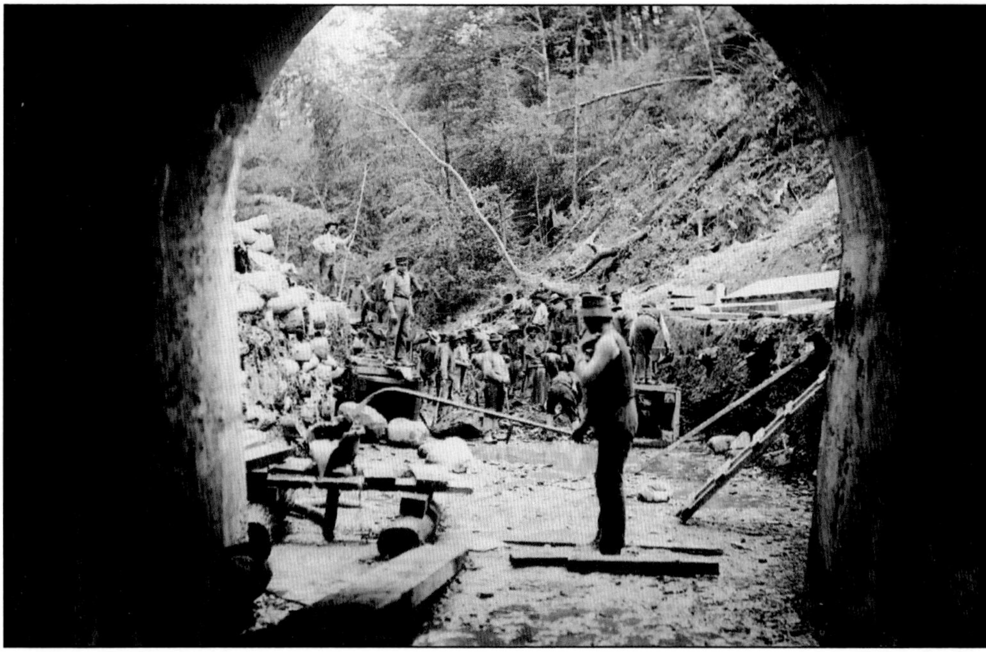

Smith Ashcraft was not just a photographer, he was a great photographer. Standing inside the tunnel and focusing his camera on the water globe scene outside was pure art. The man in the middle of the picture is standing on a couple of railroad ties so his feet will not get wet, and he is pouring something out of a large ladle attached to the long pole in his hand.

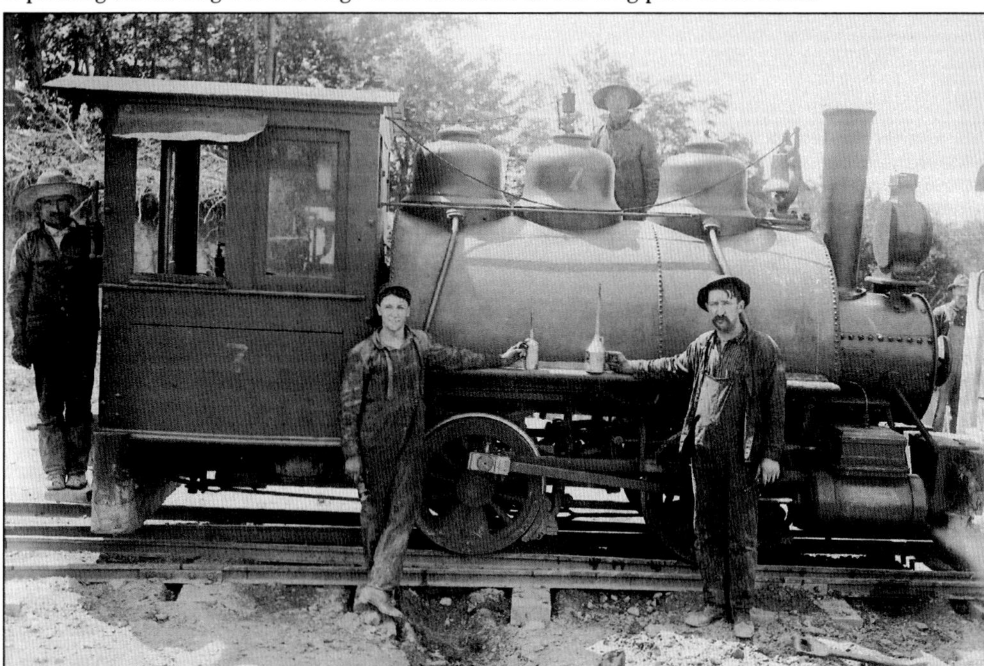

Here is a close-up view of donkey engine No. 7 and its crew. These little steam-driven workhorses were the backbone of the railroad crew. The guys with the tin-man-type oilcans are making sure that No. 7 is kept in peak condition.

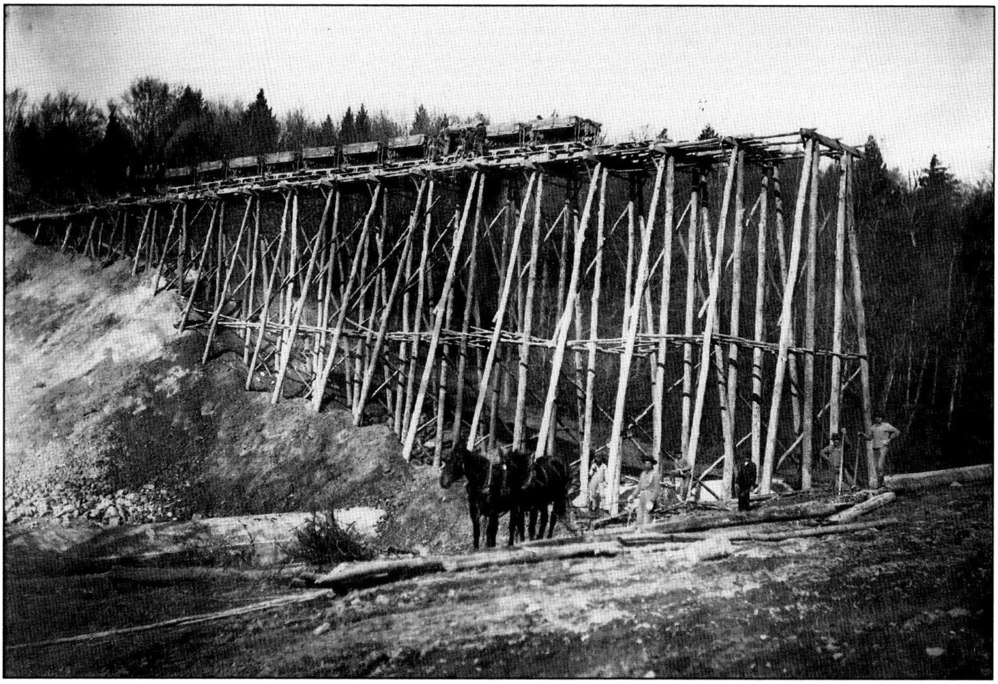

Building 50-foot-high trestles out of tree trunks with the branches cut off had to be a challenging job. There are no visible means of attaching the timbers together, just a lot of cross beams. The mule team was probably spooked more than once by the creaking that must have emanated from the structure as the donkey carts were pushed to the other end by the engine.

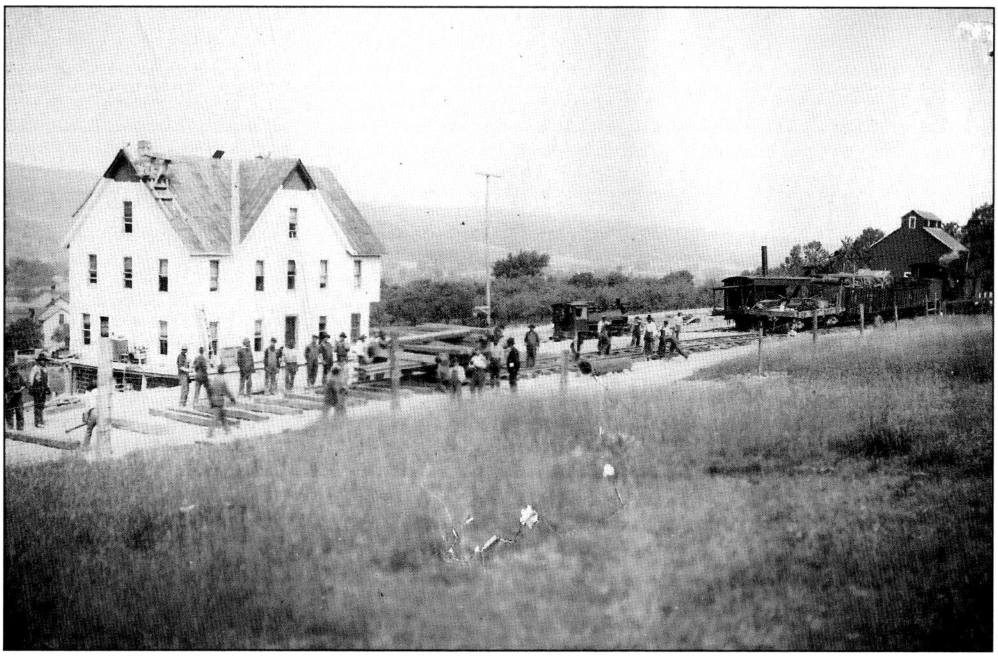

Thinking ahead was what prompted the building of a new hotel right next to the Boston depot. It was thought that many city people might want to get away from the hustle and bustle of city life by taking the train out to the Boston hills and staying a few days to enjoy the clean air.

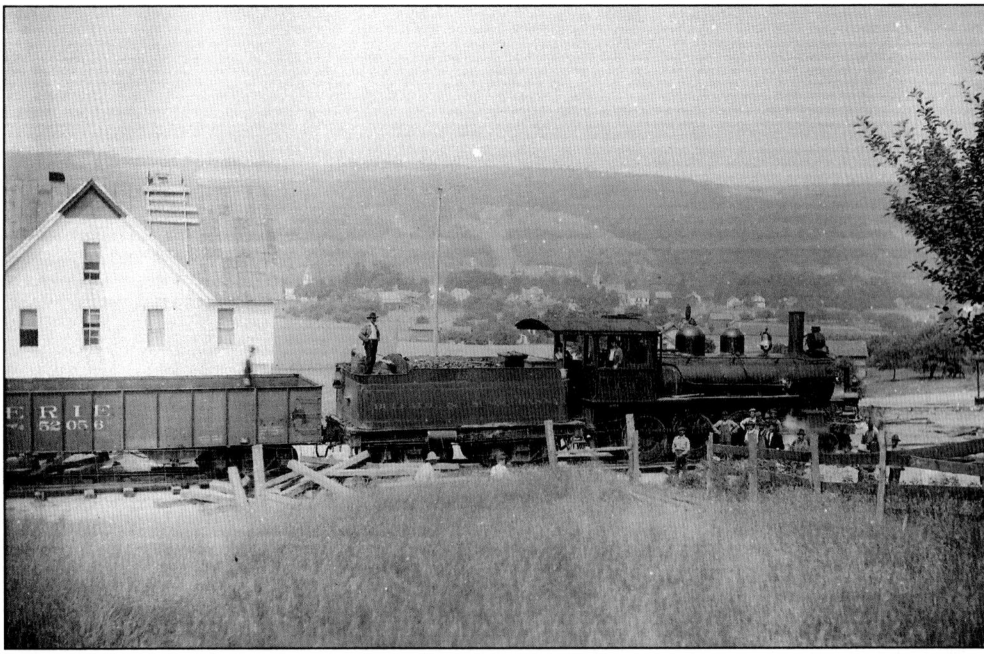

The track is finally completed after three long years. Engine 153 of the B&S makes some initial runs over the new path that will transport people from Buffalo all the way to Wellsville faster than they ever dreamed possible. In the distance, one can barely make out the steeple of St. John's Church just above where the engineer is standing.

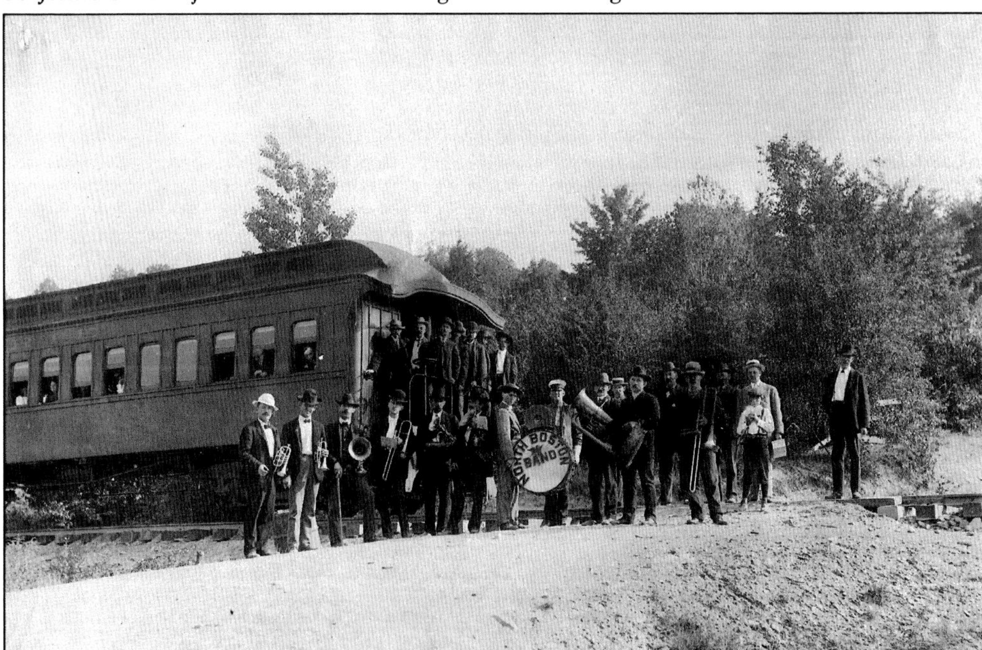

The first day of full service is finally here, and all the dignitaries in their Sunday suits have come out to celebrate. They all want to be the first ones to ride on the great iron horse. Of course, the North Boston Band is here to give the lucky riders a musical send-off.

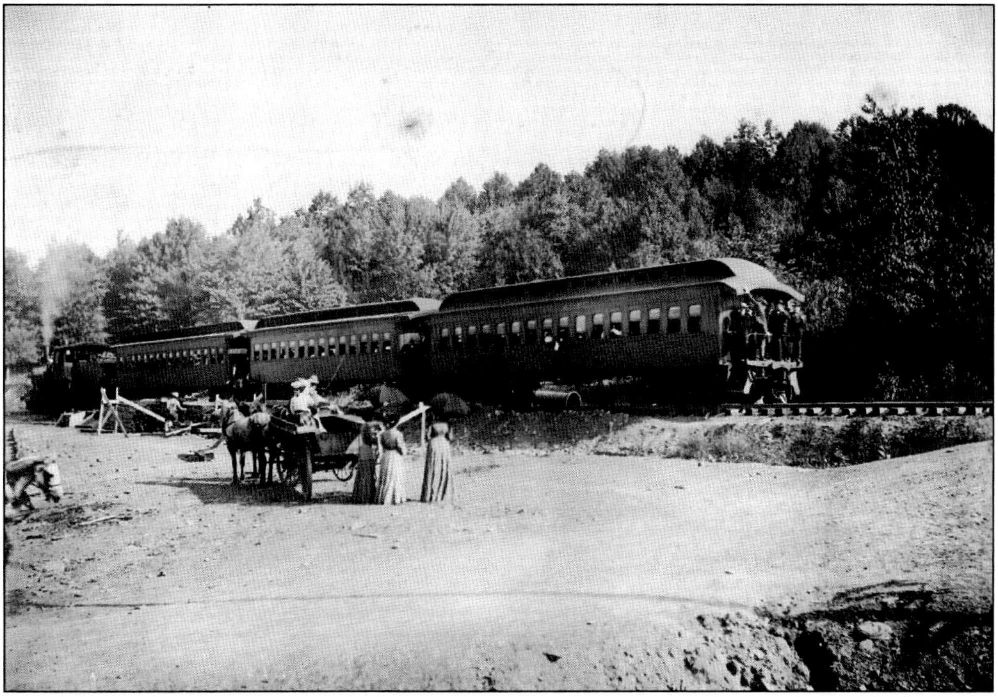

Above, the ladies in their long dresses and parasols wave to the riders as they embark on the first train ride from the Boston station. Every window is filled with a smiling face. Below, Boston residents wait for the train to take them to the Erie County Fair. Until the railroad came through town, families had to pile into their wagons and drive their team of horses 10 miles to the town of Hamburg, where the fair had been since 1841. With the train, one could sit on a cushioned bench protected from the sun and rain and enjoy the ride into town without getting all dusty. So everyone put on their Sunday best and waited at the station on Boston Cross Road for the train to come north out of Springville to take them to a fun-filled day at the fair.

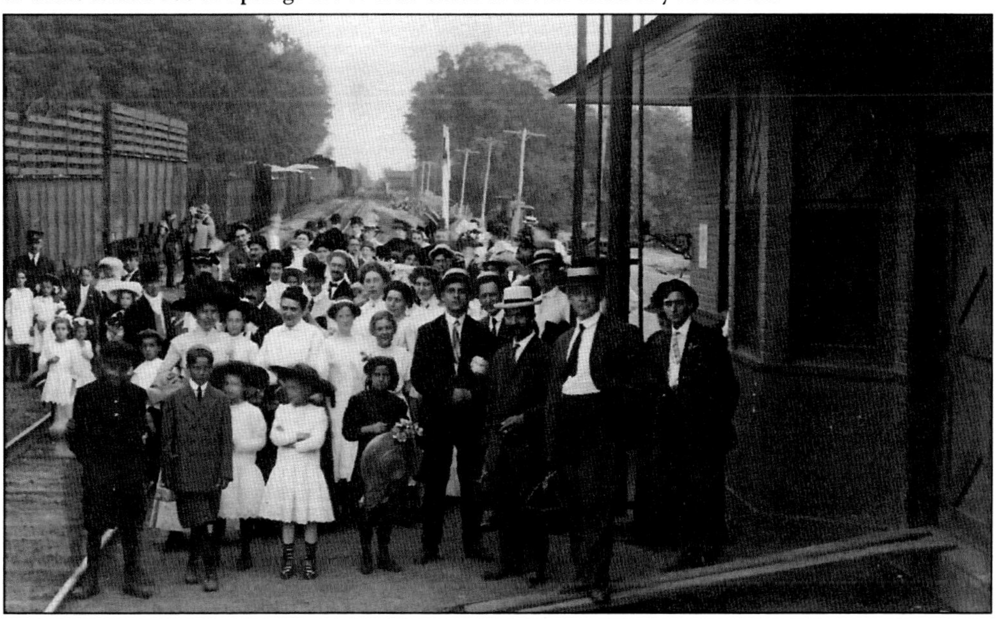

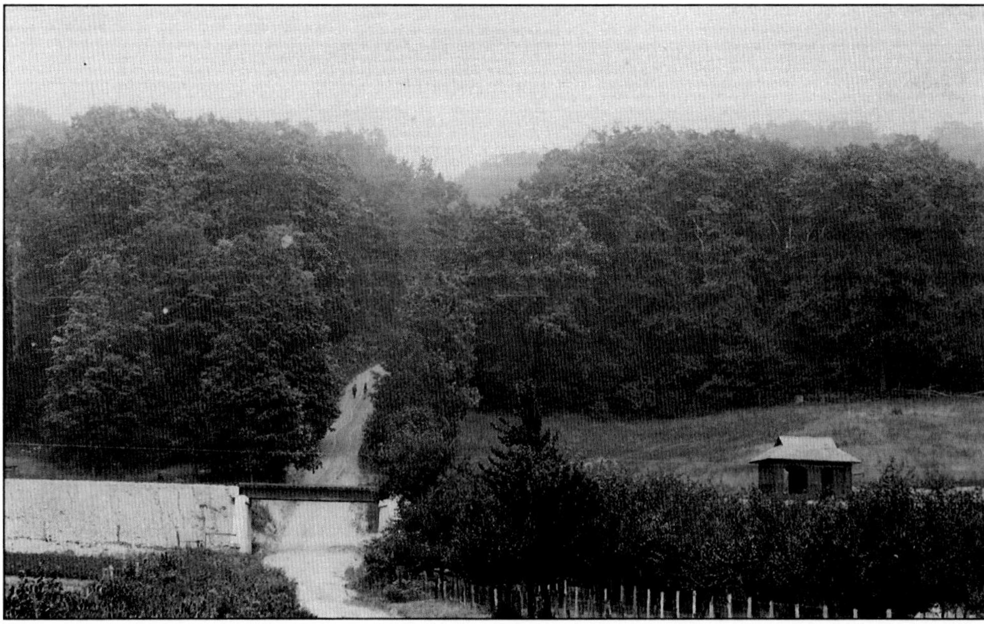

Not many people know that there were train stations in North Boston and Patchin as well as Boston. This photograph shows the Patchin depot just south of what is now called Liebler Road. It was much smaller than the Boston Station; it only offered shelter from the weather for half a dozen people. Years later, the bridge was removed as well as the station.

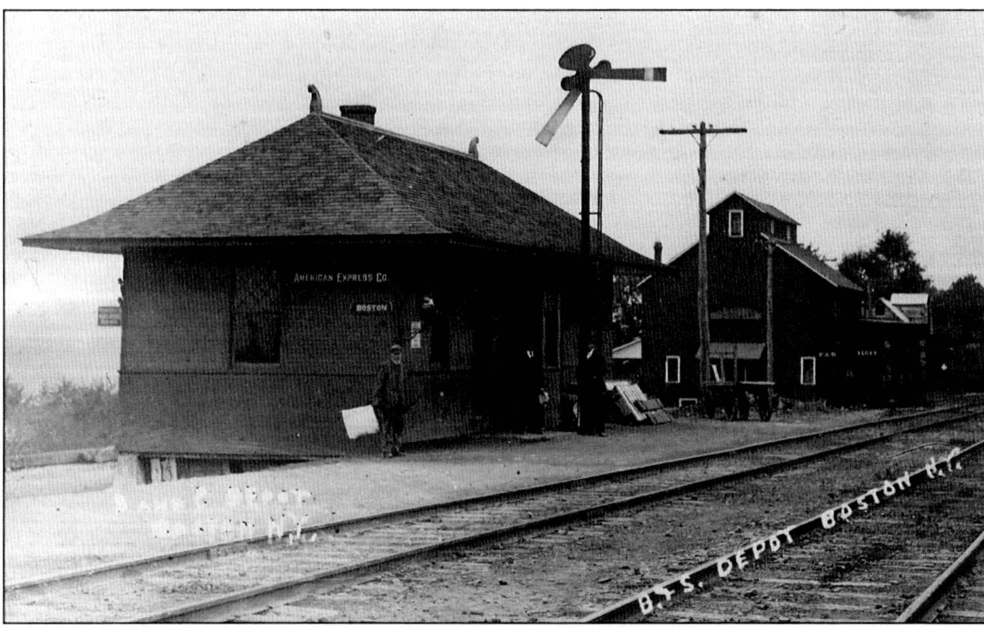

Here is the completed Boston depot in front of Faulring's Feed Mill. The railroad was certainly a boon for the mill, enabling it to send and receive product and supplies without having to hitch up the horses. The mill is now gone, but the Boston depot still stands, although it was remodeled and moved to private property on Boston Cross Road.

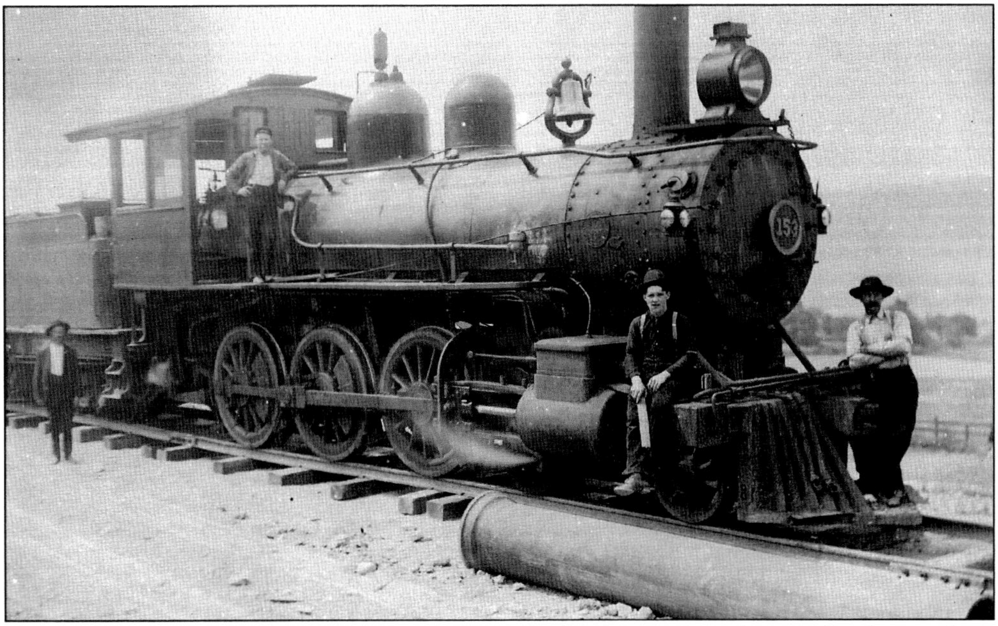

Now here is the real thing. Engine 153 is reporting for duty and ready to make the trip from Buffalo to Wellsville and back again. One can imagine how awestruck the farmers and their families must have been, seeing this massive machine coming down the tracks. Notice how the cowcatcher is attached to a 12-inch-by-12-inch railroad tie. This locomotive was a model 14017 made in Philadelphia.

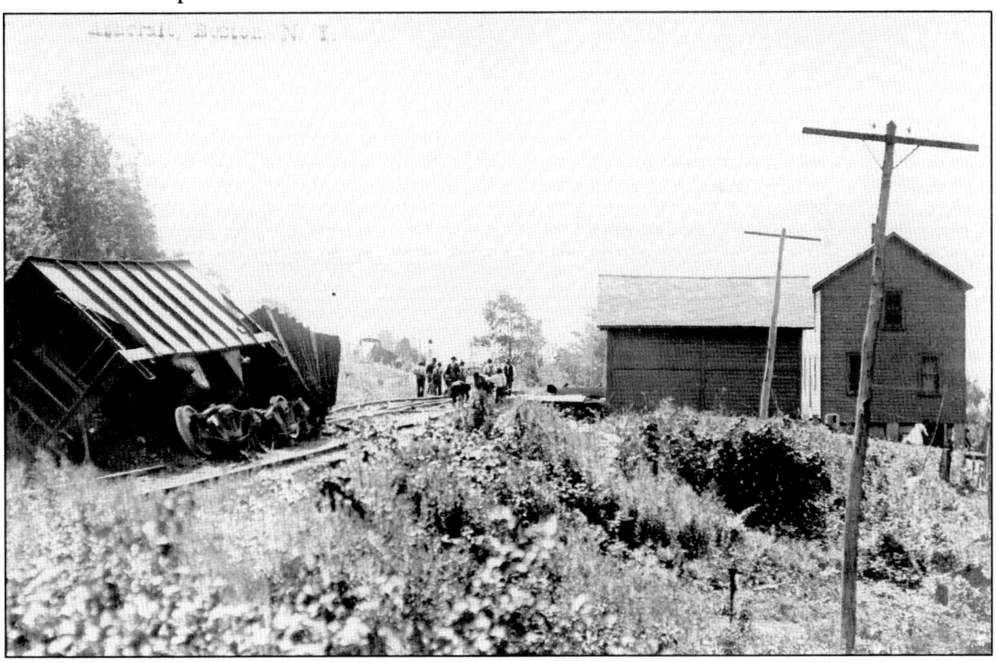

Not everything went smoothly with the extension. This derailment occurred just north of Faulring's Feed Mill on Boston Cross Road. Derailments were usually caused by a switch not working properly that was to direct the train to another track. They took a long time to clean up, so it is a good thing only two cars seem to have been affected.

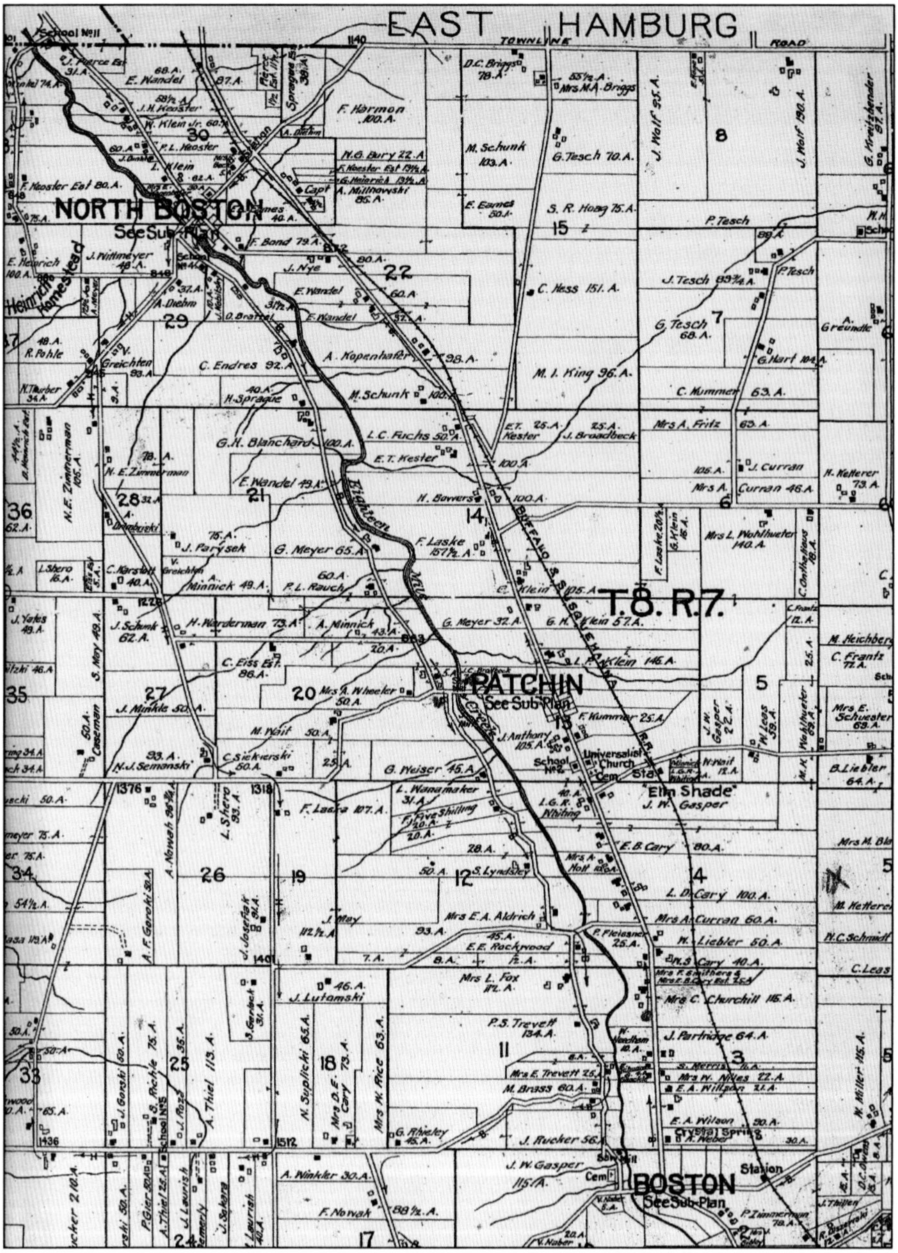

This map comes from the *New Century Atlas of Erie County*, published in 1909. It shows the exact route that the tracks took through Boston. It followed pretty closely the north–south route of 18 Mile Creek. After running for only 10 years, Frank Goodyear died and left his brother with a financial mess. It finally became necessary to make a hard decision. The railroad line through Boston was to be eliminated, and the Goodyears' business ended up in receivership. The tracks were torn up and sold, along with engine 153. The year was 1916, and steel was a highly priced commodity due to the war. So all the steel from the tracks, the bridges, and even the railroad spikes was sold to France as scrap. It is rumored that the ship was attacked and sank in the Atlantic Ocean. So after all the work, all the planning, all the hype of the future coming to Boston, it was all taken away and is lying at the bottom of the ocean, never to be seen again.

Four

THE CHILDREN

Children will always be children—curious, cheerful, and wondering. Life was simple in the 19th century. The family was the anchor that kept children's focus. Their world revolved around their mother, father, sisters, and brothers. It was not unusual for a family to consist of parents, grandparents, and a dozen children, all in the same house. Each day was spent working for the common good: the good of the family. So when the father spent his days planting crops, fixing machinery, and caring for the animals, it was all for the good of the family. Mothers spent each day cooking, mending, and keeping the house neat and clean—all for the good of the family. The children learned how to mimic their mother and father so they too would do everything for the good of the family. Grandparents were a great source of knowledge for the children. The stories of their childhood served to show children that life was hard but it was also good. The stories gave the children a goal that they could focus on for their lives. They knew that every day was a learning experience. They would learn how to sew, learn how to birth a calf, learn about God, and learn to read. Then in the evening, when the learning was done, the family would be together, making popcorn, sipping fresh cider, singing songs, and listening to more of their grandfather's stories. It was a good life.

The simplicity of children's lives in the 19th century is what makes memories of them so precious. The images of them from residents' collective past are fascinating, as people wish their own lives could be that simple once again.

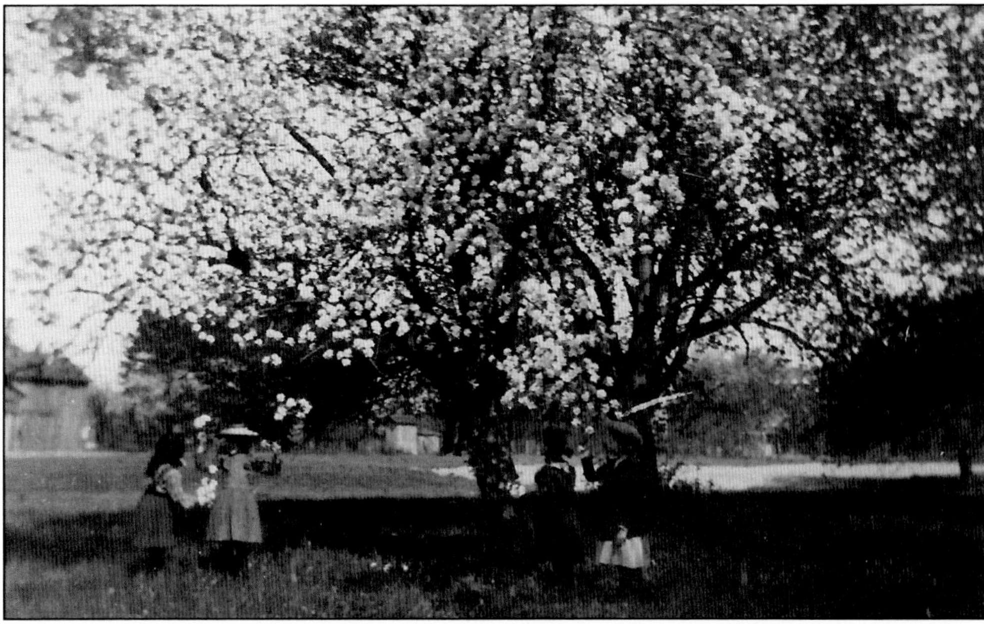

There is nothing that little girls like more than flowers. This beautiful flowering tree was a favorite spot for these four little ones in the spring. The fresh sweet smell of the blossoms would attract them like bees to honey. They could play and dance under the boughs all day long until their mother called out the front door for them. Then they would have to say good-bye to their imaginary world under the floral canopy.

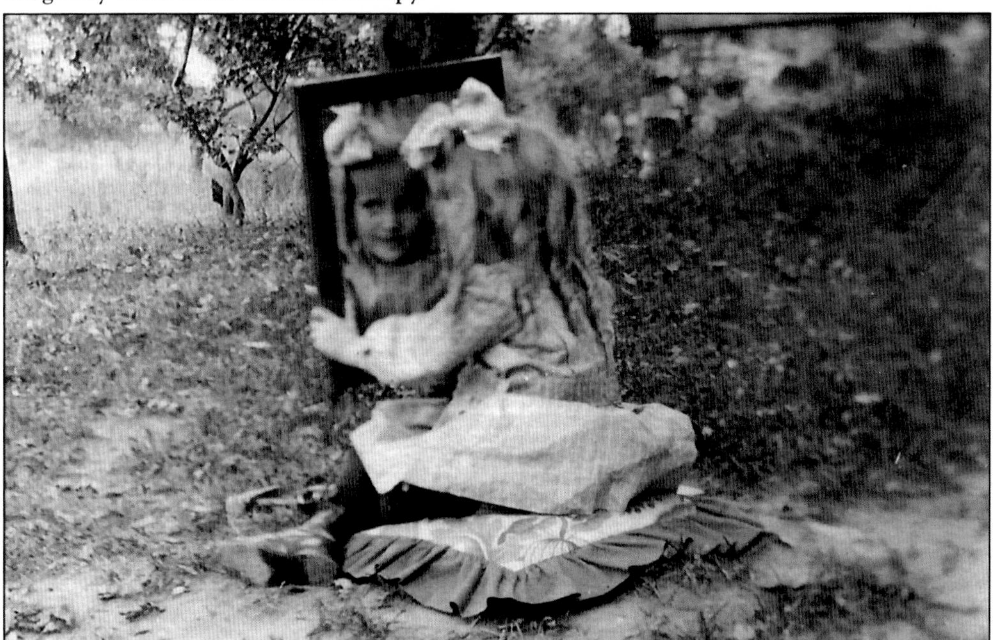

This little girl's name could have been Alice. Her father could have read to her at night about white rabbits and tea parties. Her wondering imagination could have led her to take a soft pillow to sit on and a looking glass to peer into in a very quiet place under the tree. If she was very quiet and very alert, she just might see the white rabbit behind her in mother's mirror.

Eleanore Williams was born in 1902. Her mother was Jennie Dye, who married Casper Williams in 1901. Her uncle Perry Dye owned a store for many years in Boston Commons. This was Eleanore's favorite doll, which was why she wanted to have her picture taken with it. Her descendants still have the doll and love it just as much as Eleanore did. (Courtesy of Jane Clarke.)

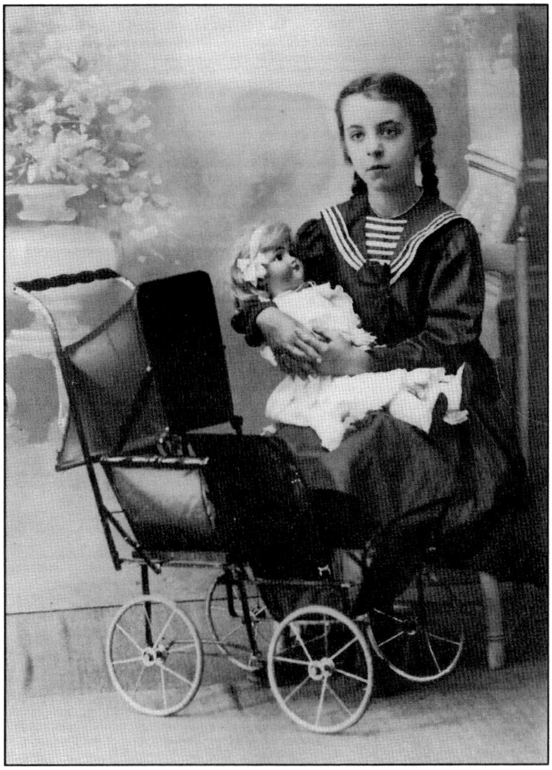

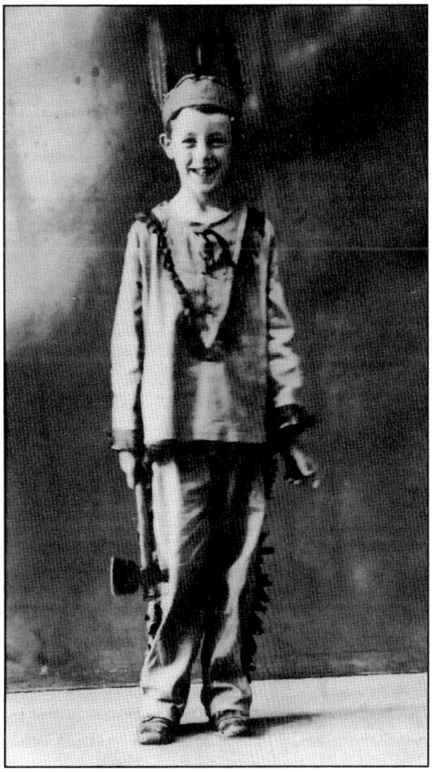

Eleanore's brother Harland was two years younger than she was. He was always teasing her, as little brothers are wont to do. When Halloween came along, he wanted to dress up like the American Indians that his grandpa Casper Williams would tell stories of. Unfortunately, Harland only lived to be 19 years of age, dying of pneumonia after a trip to California. (Courtesy of Jane Clarke.)

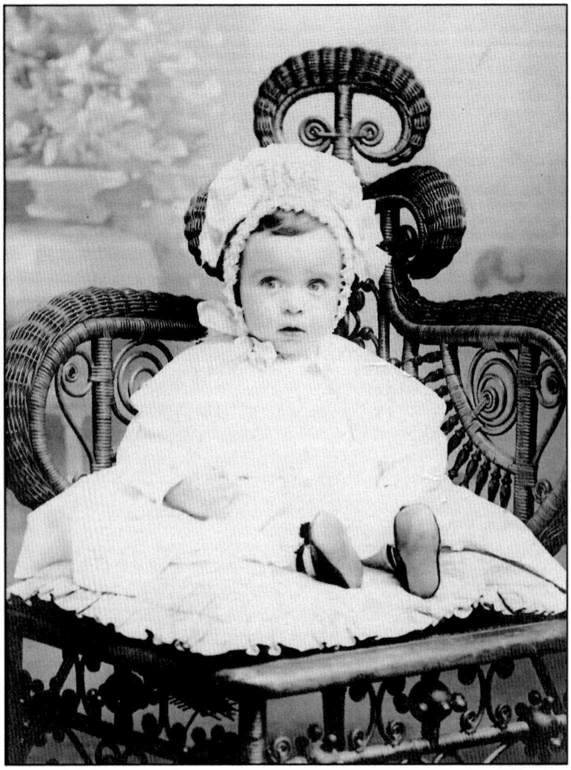

Baby Leland Dye is seen here posing for his first portrait in the Ashcraft studio. Smith Ashcraft posed many of his youngest clients in this wonderful corner wicker chair. It is seen in many of the portraits in the Boston Historical Museum's collection. Leland has a look on his face that seems to say, "Just take the picture so I can get down and start getting dirty again!"

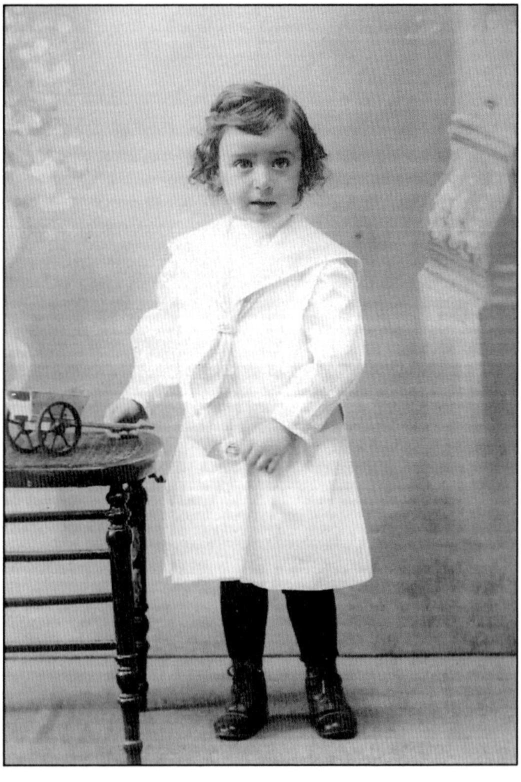

Leland Dye was Eleanore and Harland Williams' cousin. He was born a few years after them. Here he is a little older and posing in an outfit not unusual for a boy in the early 1900s. Clothing for boys and girls was virtually the same style until a boy reached the age of five, when he would start wearing short pants. (Courtesy of Jane Clarke.)

Dora Pfarner is beautiful in this lovely white dress. She was born in 1894 to George Pfarner and Mary Faulring Pfarner. The look on her face shows pride and a self-awareness beyond her tender years. Her mother, Mary, must have spent a long time with the hair crimper to make her hair look as lovely as it does.

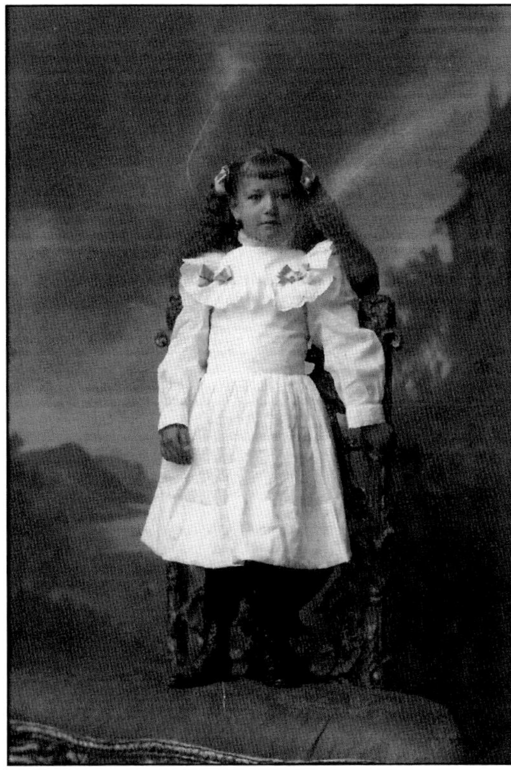

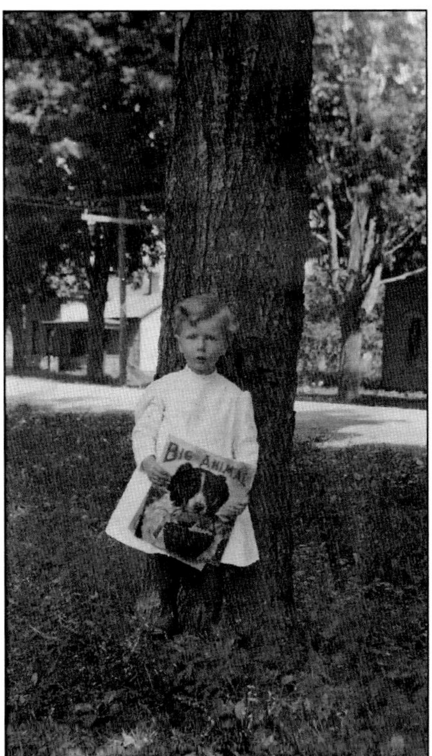

Two-and-a-half-year-old Raymond Hauth liked big animals. His big animal book proves it. His outfit was made only for Sundays so he would not get it dirty. The book might have been his favorite or even brand new, as he is clutching it so it would not fall to the ground.

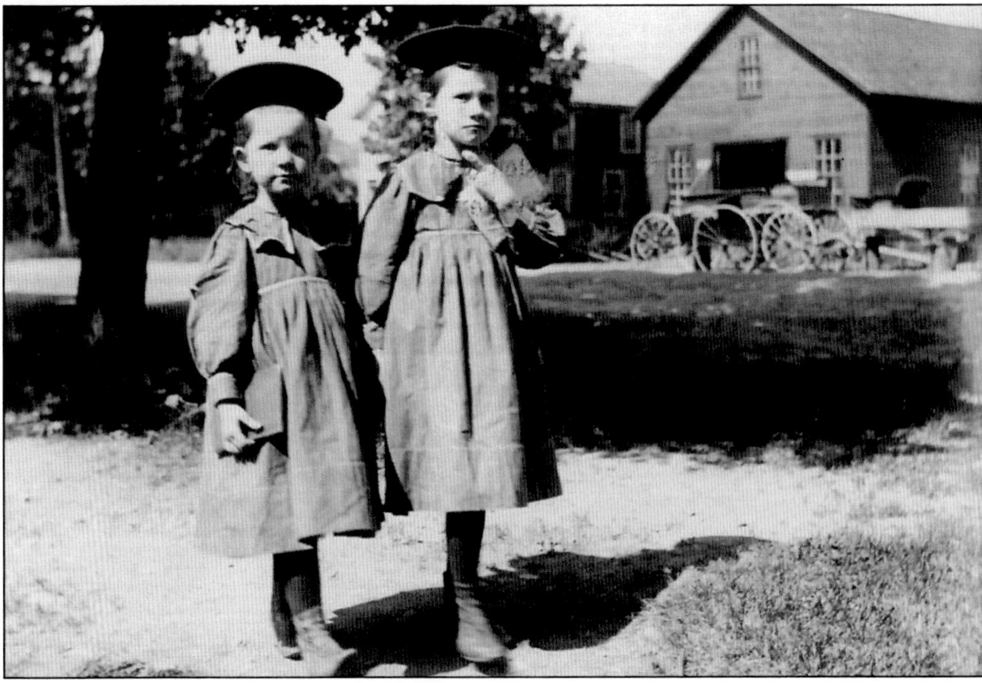

These sisters are on their way to school past the blacksmith shop. There were several blacksmith shops in Boston in the early 1900s. Sometimes on their way home from school, they would stop and watch the blacksmith put new shoes on someone's horse. And maybe, if they were lucky, they would get a ride home in someone's wagon.

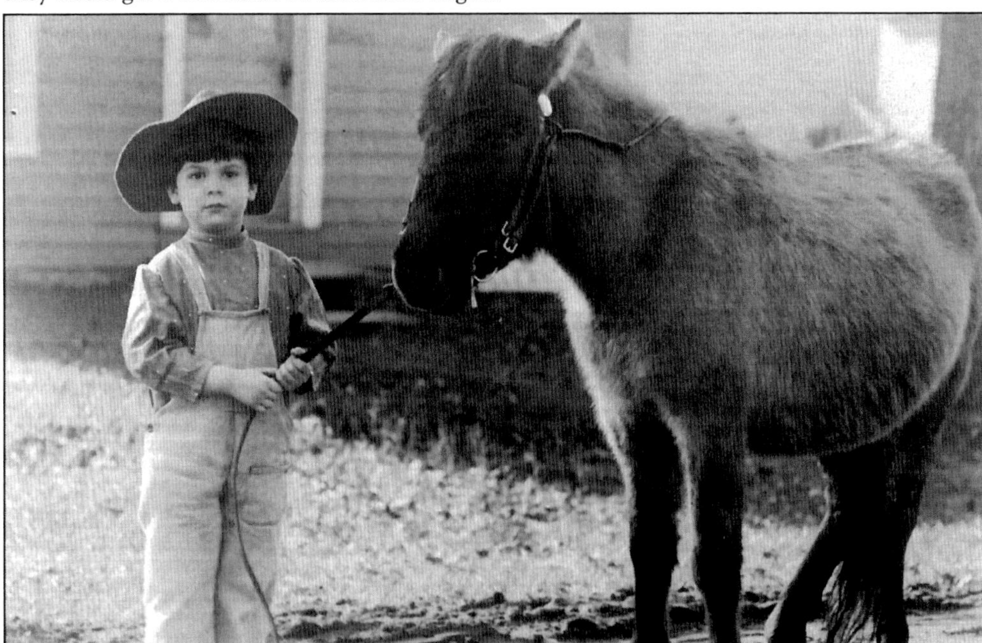

Jack Corbett was always asking P. J. Griffith if he could play with his pony, Onlee. Corbett and Onlee were great friends. Corbett felt like a big boy, being able to put Onlee's harness on without any help. He would lead Onlee around by the reins, and they would have great adventures together.

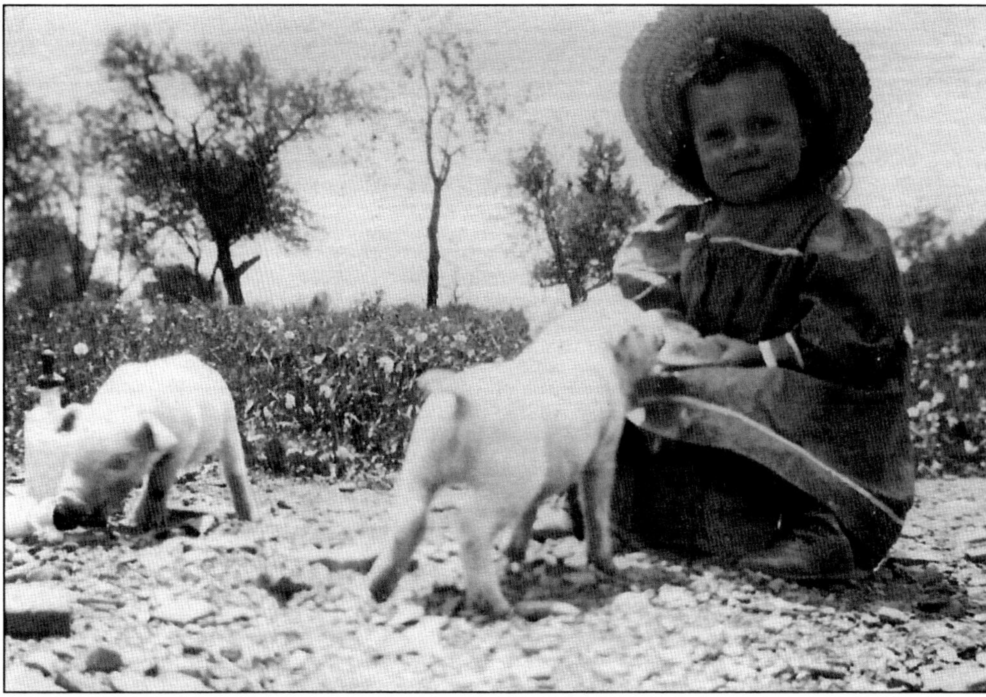

Livestock was the most important thing to have on a farm. Each family would have owned several horses, a dozen or more cows, a team of oxen, and chickens and pigs by the score. Everyone had their chores to do, and it looks like this little one's job was to feed the piglets. She does look like she's having a good time.

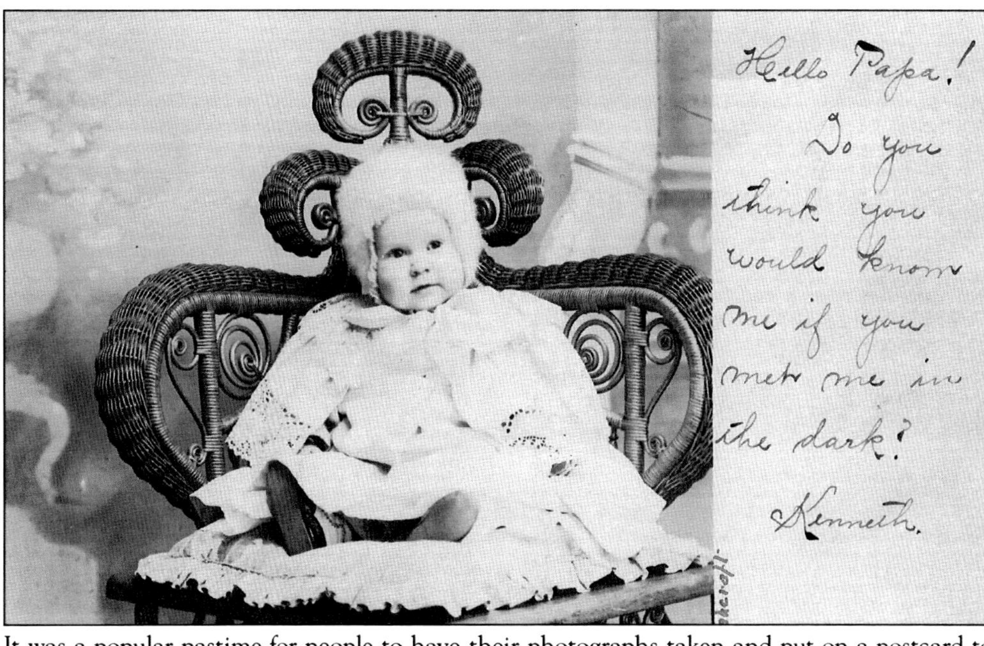

It was a popular pastime for people to have their photographs taken and put on a postcard to send to a loved one. Here is Kenneth Rice seated atop Smith Ashcraft's famous corner wicker chair. His outfit is no doubt made of hand-crocheted lace at the edges of his coat.

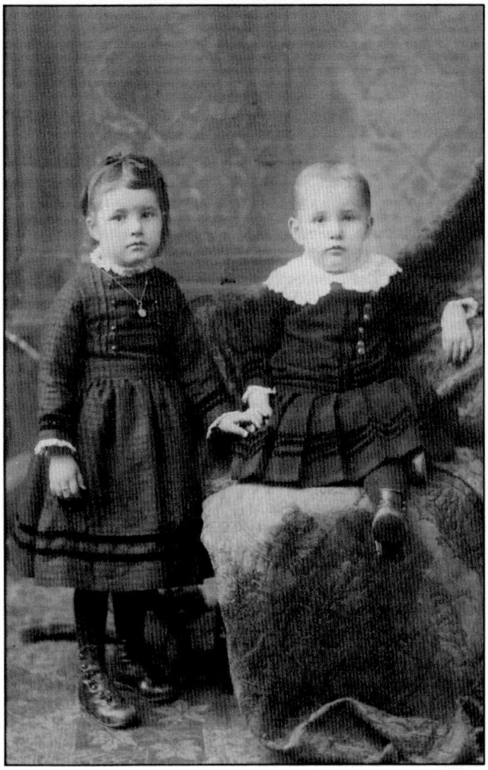

Here is further evidence that young boys were dressed the same way as young girls. These adorable outfits were handmade by a mother or grandmother in very exacting detail. Both have velvet stripes sewn around the bottom hem and around the cuffs. Both have brass buttons sewn around pleats of fabric on the bodice, and both have crocheted lace around the collars and cuffs.

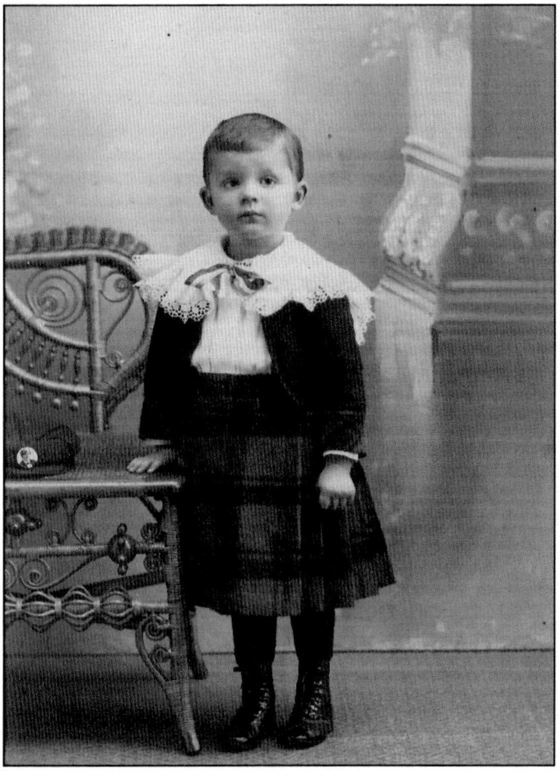

This adorable young man is wearing a wool plaid skirt, hand-pleated white starched shirt, and a short jacket finished at the cuff with the same wool plaid as the skirt. The hand-crocheted lace collar finished with a tricolored satin ribbon at the neck completes his ensemble. He is a very sharp young man.

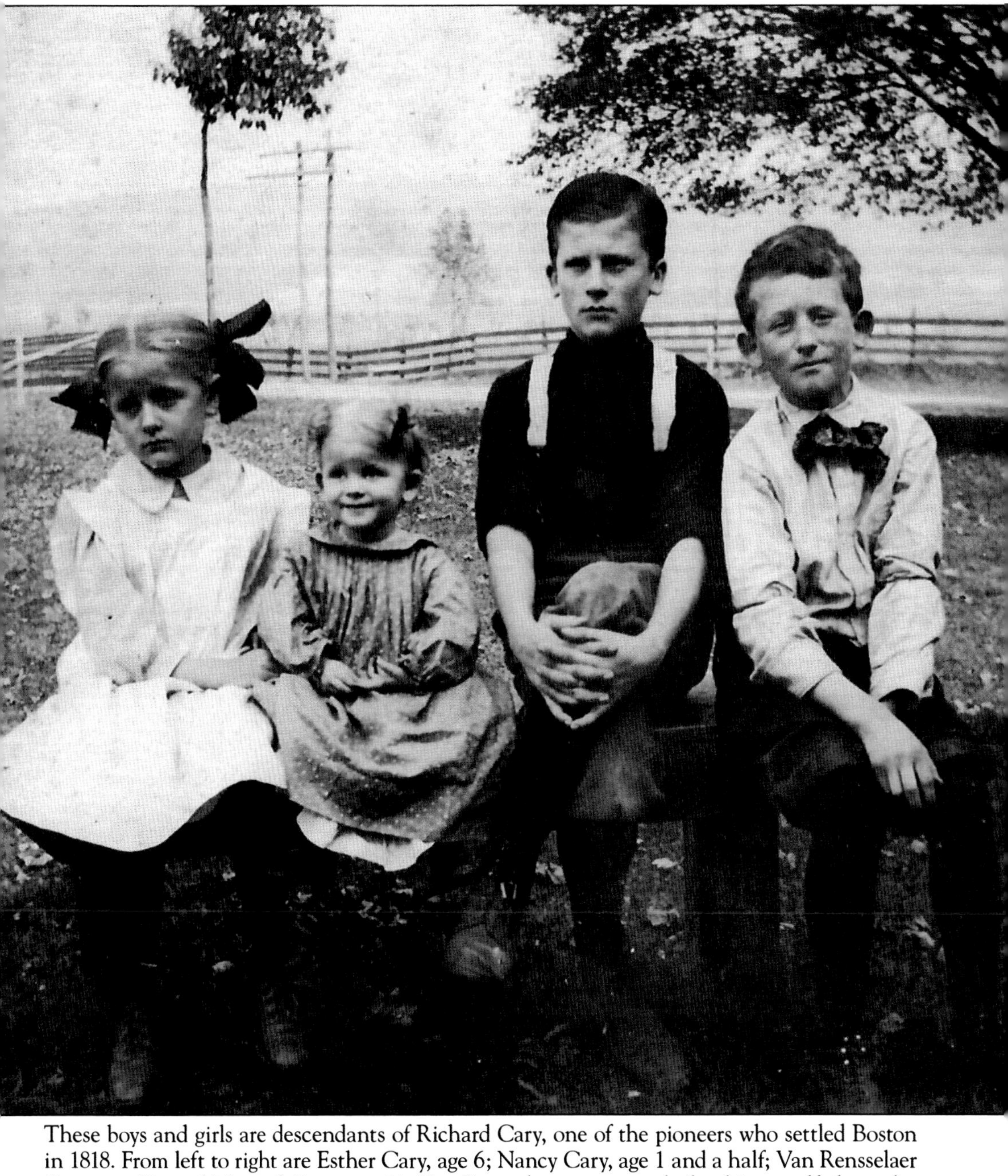

These boys and girls are descendants of Richard Cary, one of the pioneers who settled Boston in 1818. From left to right are Esther Cary, age 6; Nancy Cary, age 1 and a half; Van Rensselaer Cary, age 12; and Howard Cary, age 11. Van Rensselaer was named after his grandfather, who was quite the upstanding citizen in his day. His grandfather taught school in a log schoolhouse with slab seats in Sardinia at the age of 17. Two years later, he taught school in Armor to a student body of 100 pupils. He became a seaman for a time and sailed up and down the coast of the United States and Canada. He returned to Boston where he built a house (which still stands today), got married, and had three children. He was appointed postmaster of the Patchin Post Office in 1869. Little Van Rensselaer had some big shoes to fill.

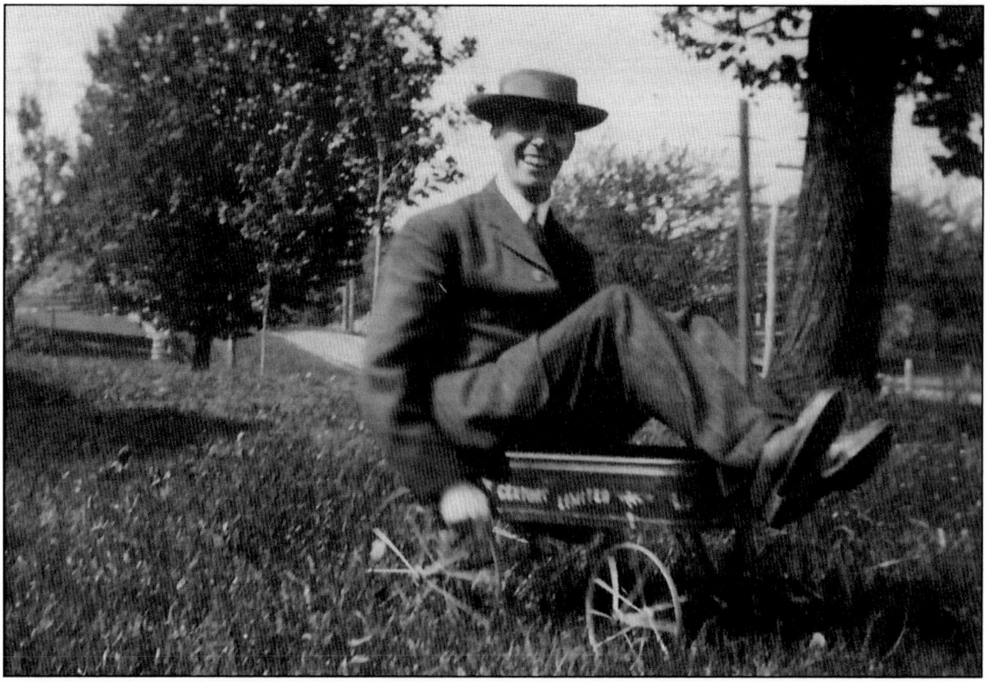

Who let these guys in here? Oh, sure, all this talk of the simple life spent playing, dressing up, taking the pony for a walk, reading about big animals, and seeing white rabbits out of the corner of one's eye. Who would not want to go back to simpler times? So go ahead, it is ok to go through a second childhood. But what is the goat's excuse?

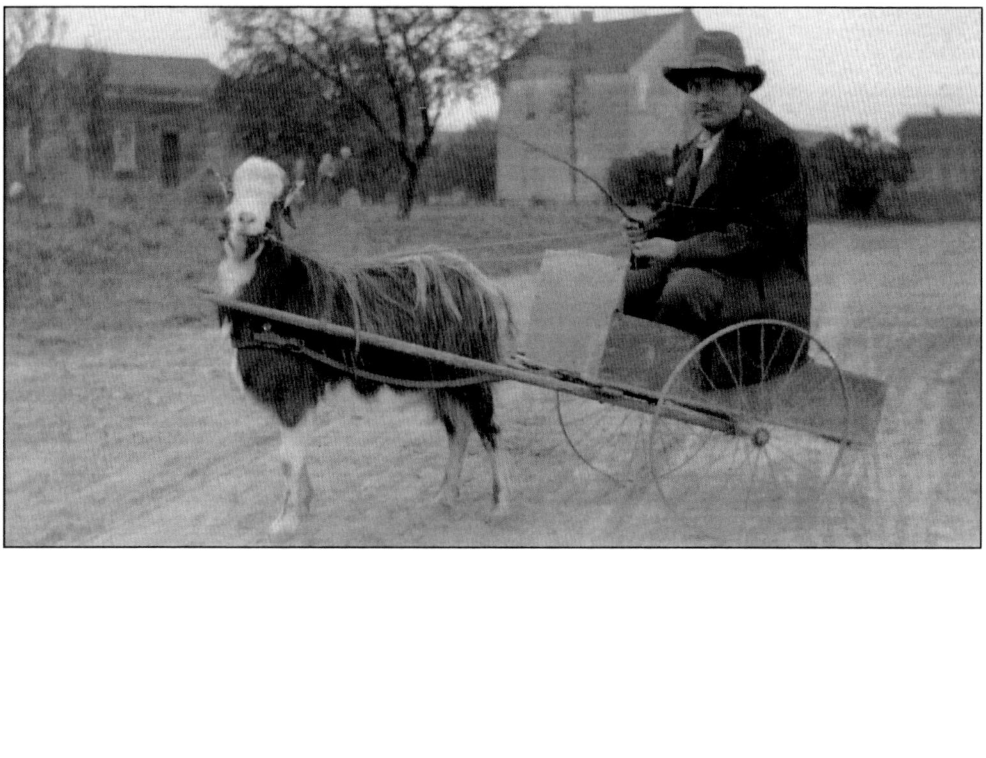

Five

SCHOOLS

When Samuel Abbott was elected the first town supervisor in 1818, he knew that in addition to making sure there were new laws for their town, they would have to make plans for the education of the children. That is why at the very first town meeting, several commissioners of common schools were elected and the building of the schools was begun. Due to the fact that the farms were so far apart and the town encompassed homesteads popping up on both hills as well as the valley, the fact had to be considered that since there was no public transportation, the children could not come to the schools as much as the schools would have to go to the children. So a minimum of 10 school districts were planned, and 10 schoolhouses would have to be built. Three for the west hill, three for the valley, and three for the east hill, with another one thrown in where it was needed the most. From the records available, the following locations of each district have been determined. District No. 1 was at the corner of Boston Colden Road and Boston State Road. The original building burned down. District No. 2 was on Boston State Road across the street from Maplewood Cemetery and is now a private residence. District No. 4 was in North Boston on Back Creek Road next to Boston Valley Elementary and has since been demolished. District No. 5 was consolidated with District No. 9 in 1867 and was located on Rice Road, just west of Zimmerman Road. District No. 6 was on the corner of Feddick Road and Keller Road in North Boston and is now a private residence. District No. 7 was on Wohlhueter Road between Cole Road and Lower East Hill Road. The building is no longer there. District No. 8 was on Eddy Road just west of Cole Road. The building is no longer there. There was a District No. 11, which was in the valley at Boston's northernmost point, and the building is now part of the Zittel farm.

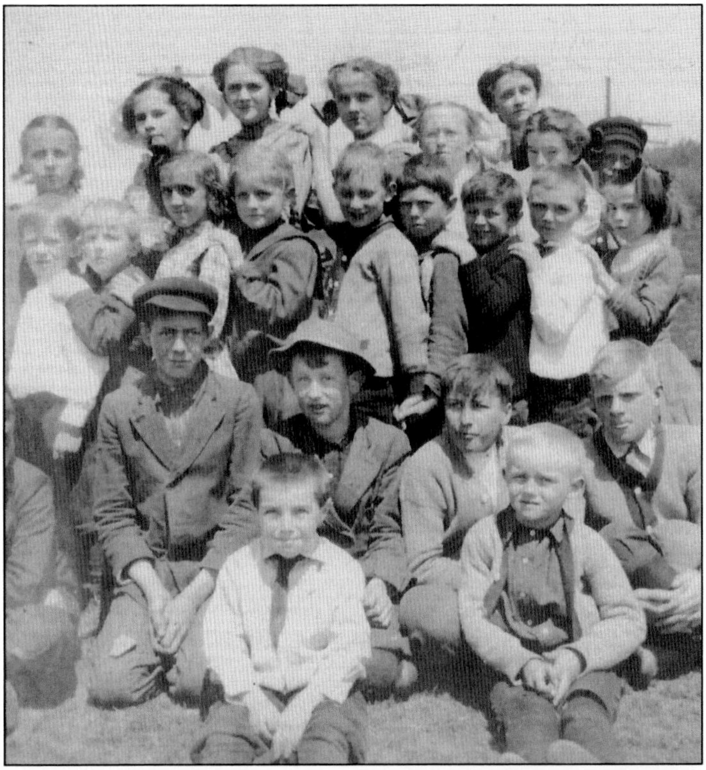

This was Nora Klein's classroom, district unknown. From left to right are (first row) George Kaufman, Howard Pfarner, Howard Cary, Glenn Trevett, Edward Gasper, and Alvin Klein; (second row) Edward Kaufman, Bill Minnick, Iva Rauch, Esther Cary, Lester Weisser, Howard Minnick, Leonard Liebler, Chas Geckle, and Z. Dye; (third row) Anna Rauch, Anna Kaufman, Ruth Trevett, Myrtle Rauch, Esther Kummer, teacher Nora Klein, Florence Dye, and George Pfarner.

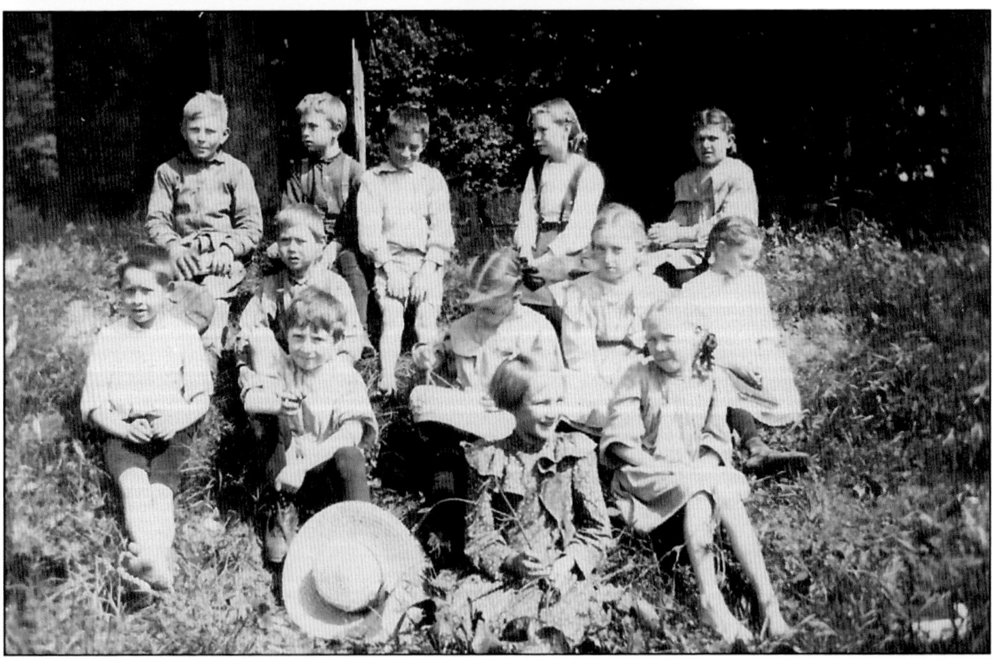

When school was done for the summer, it was good and bad news. The weather was warmer and children could take off their shoes and wiggle their toes in the grass. It was also time to work the farm. Every child who could walk had to help out. The girls had to help their mother with cooking and canning, and the boys had to help their father in the fields.

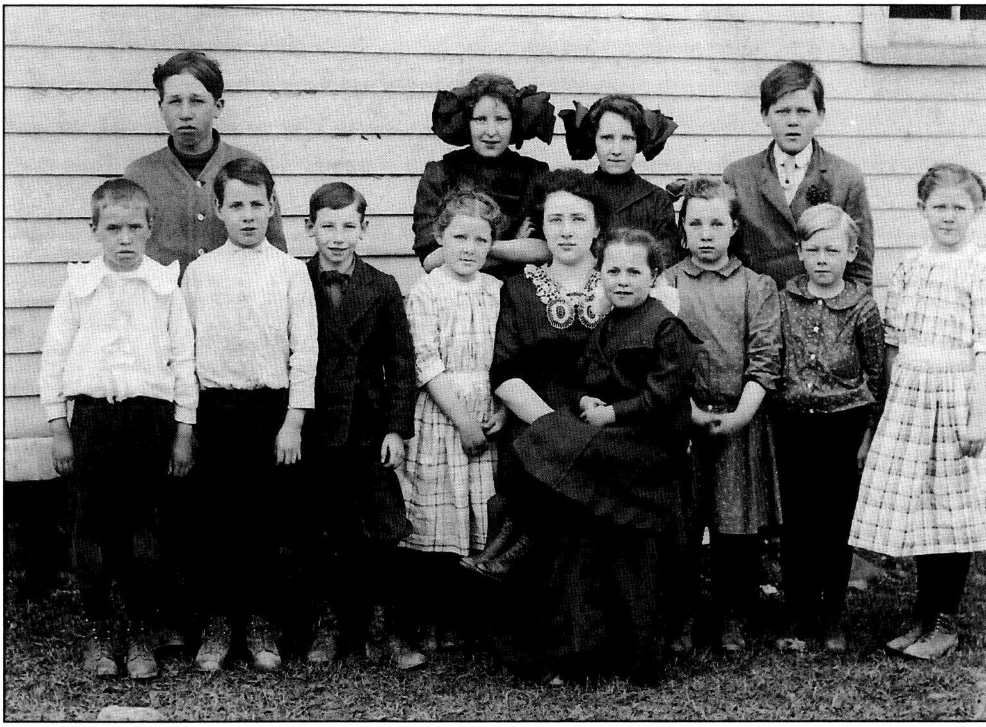

This group went to school in District No. 1 in 1910. From left to right are (first row) unidentified, unidentified, Franklin Ashcraft, Laura Koelmel, teacher Esther Koelmel, Loretta Hauth on her lap, Thelma Owen, Frank Sibley, and Doris Koelmel; (second row) Oliver Owen, the Lavin twins, and Hubert Koelmel.

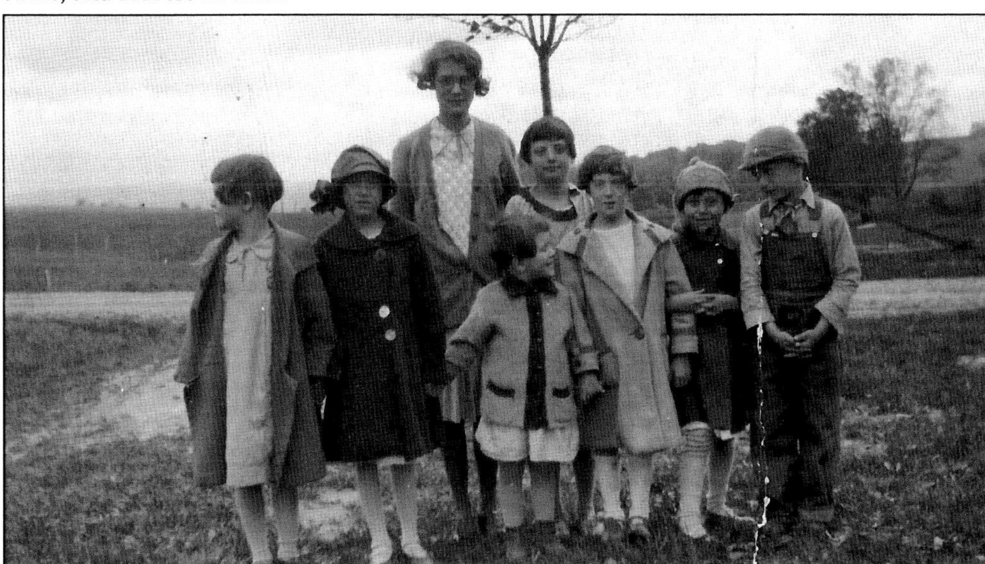

Up on Wohlheuter Road, the farms were far apart from one another, so it was a longer walk to get to District No. 7. This group was in school in the 1930s. From left to right are (first row) Esther Ketterer, Regina Niefergold, Dorothy Ketterer, and three unidentified students; (second row) teacher Reva Smith and Evelyn Lehning.

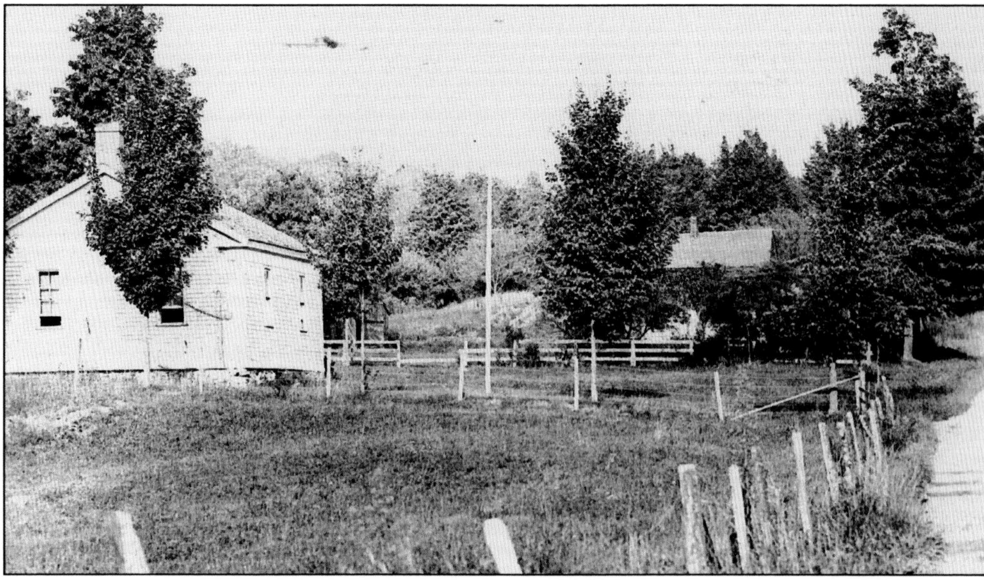

The schools were built with one large room and a large fireplace at one end to provide heat in the winter. There were no indoor bathrooms, just the outhouse in the back. Children had to cut through cornfields and across cow pastures to get there. Usually school was only in session for four months each year, so the children could help the family with the farmwork when there was no snow.

SCHOOL DISTRICT NO. 1

June 2, 1926

Teacher, OLGA L. HERREN

Board of Education

George Faulring, Trustee
May Blakely, Collector
C. Hauth, Clerk

PUPILS

Alice Broeneman	Ethel Faulring
Frances Mentlewska	Lenora Northey
Kathryn Owen	Lillian Owen
Lorain Owen	Marguerite Owen
Verna Owen	Lillian Sibley
Rosamond Schenk	Onnalee Trevette
Emma Weber	Frances Weber
Kenneth Bower	Kenneth Byerly
Raymond Byerly	William Broeneman
Donald Estabrook	George Estabrook
Delbert Follman	Herold Faulring
Lavern Hauth	George Northey
Arthur Mentlewska	Chester Mentlewska

In 1926, teacher Olga Herren had a program printed for the graduation ceremony. The program is filled with short essays on bidding farewell and wishes for enduring friendship. On the last page it reads, "A fond farewell I give to you, my wishes best extend. A love that springs from heart that's true, I give to you my friend."

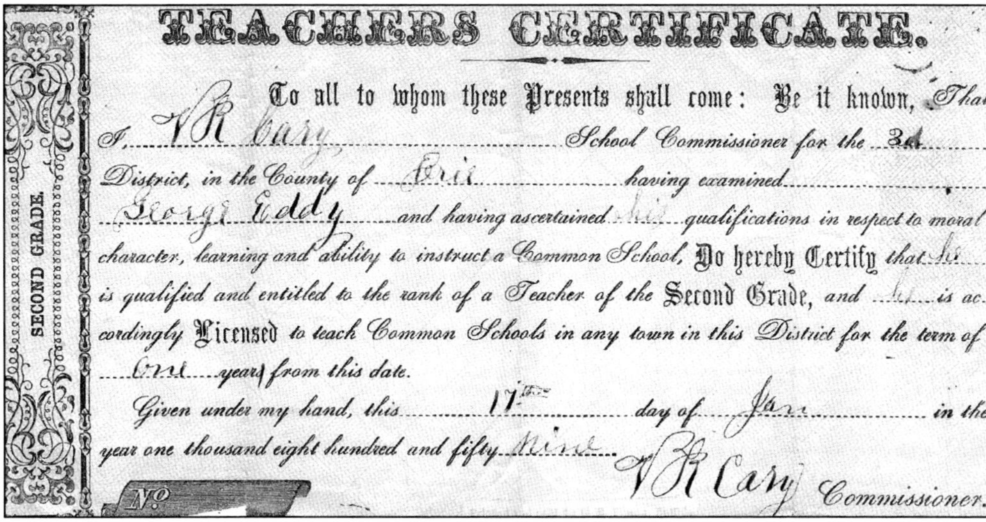

TEACHERS CERTIFICATE.

SECOND GRADE.

To all to whom these Presents shall come: Be it known, That I, V R Cary School Commissioner for the 3d District, in the County of Erie having examined George Eddy and having ascertained his qualifications in respect to moral character, learning and ability to instruct a Common School, Do hereby Certify that he is qualified and entitled to the rank of a Teacher of the Second Grade, and he is accordingly Licensed to teach Common Schools in any town in this District for the term of One year from this date.

Given under my hand, this 17th day of Jan in the year one thousand eight hundred and fifty nine.

V R Cary Commissioner.

No

All that was needed to be allowed to teach in the schools was a certificate signed by each district's commissioner of schools. Here commissioner Van Rensselaer Cary certifies that George Eddy is qualified to teach second grade in the town's third district for the following year, beginning January 17, 1859.

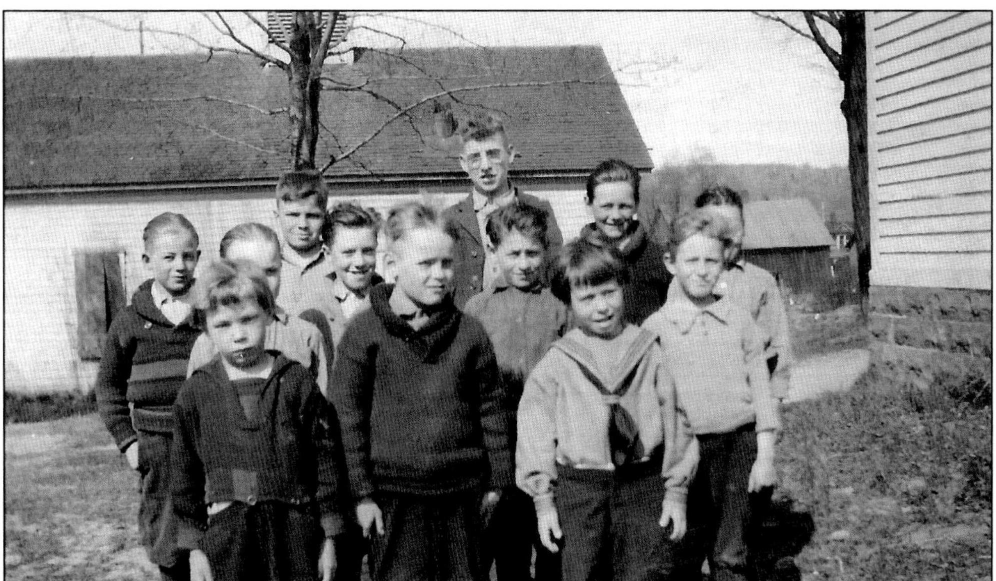

Here are just the boys of District No. 1 outside their school in 1925. From left to right are (first row) Bill Broeneman, A. Estabrook, and Delbert Follman; (second row) George Estabrook, Lavern Hauth, and two unidentified; (third row) two unidentified, Kenneth Bower, George Northey, and unidentified.

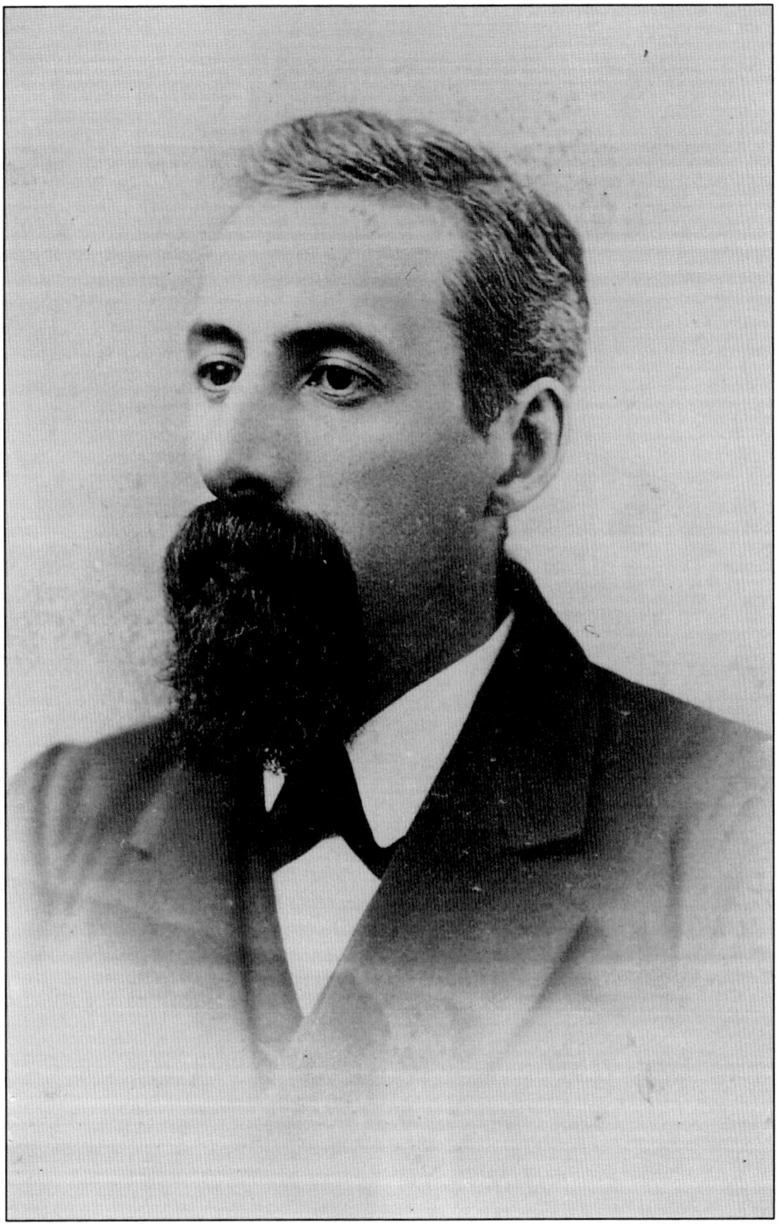

A. A. Underhill taught school all over the country and wrote of his experiences in a diary. "During these seasons of managing cheese factories in the summer, (this was near Buffalo, New York) I followed teaching in the winter, and about this time was employed as a teacher at West Falls, NY, just a few miles from the factory I managed for a few years. This school of approximately fifty scholars of all grades I taught for two winters in succession. This was in the years of 1875 and 1876. There it was friendships were formed lasting through a long period of years." Later he talks about how he was a student once at "the Academy at Springville, NY" when another student took him under her wing "and assisted me in my studies to the extent that I became a better student, and to look upon life as meaning something more than a mere existence . . . through her influence, a desire was implanted in me to increase in knowledge and to live in a higher plane of thought and purpose."

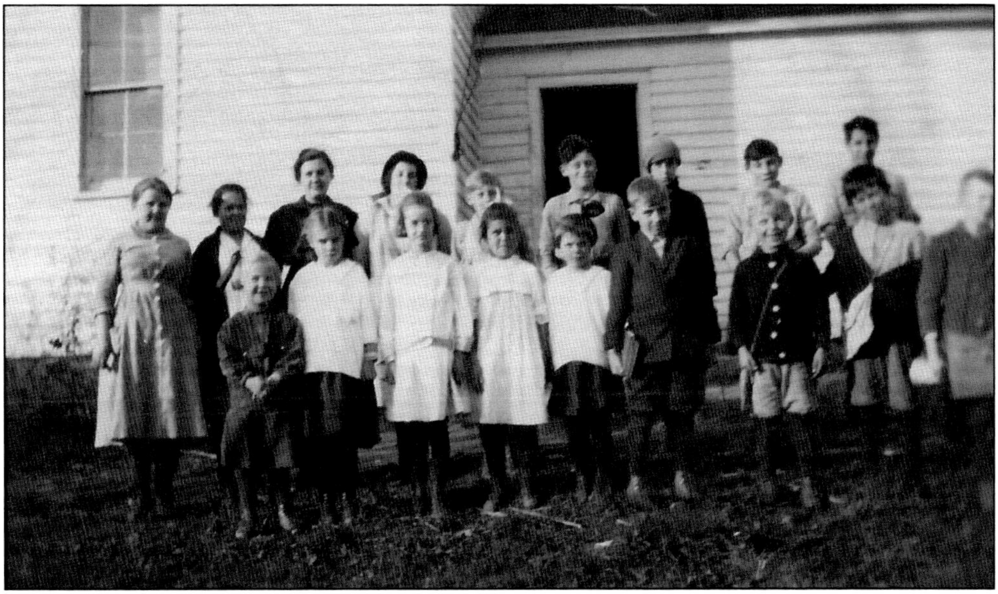

The students in Boston came in all shapes and sizes. Their clothes were almost always hand-me-downs. They lived in a time when children had to work almost as hard as the adults to keep the family afloat. But they gathered together during the winter months so they could learn the three Rs—reading, writing, and arithmetic. The weather was brutal in the winter; stories filter down in the families of children standing behind a barn for hours waiting for the icy blasts of snow to calm down enough to get home safely. Other stories tell of rubber boots being lost in the mud that was several inches deep. So when a grandfather says he had to walk three miles to school through floods, mud, and ice, believe him! It really happened.

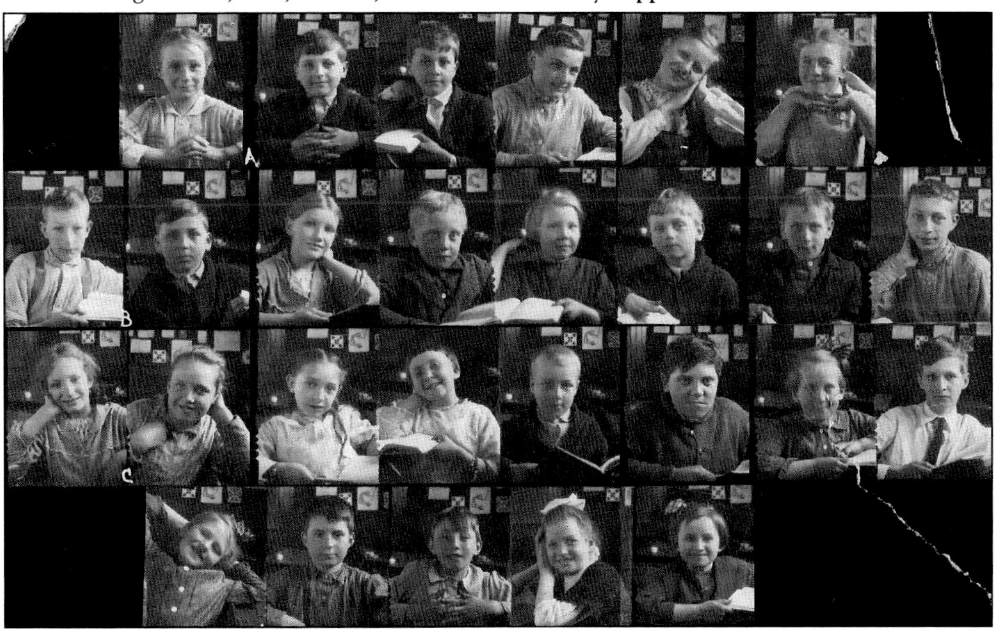

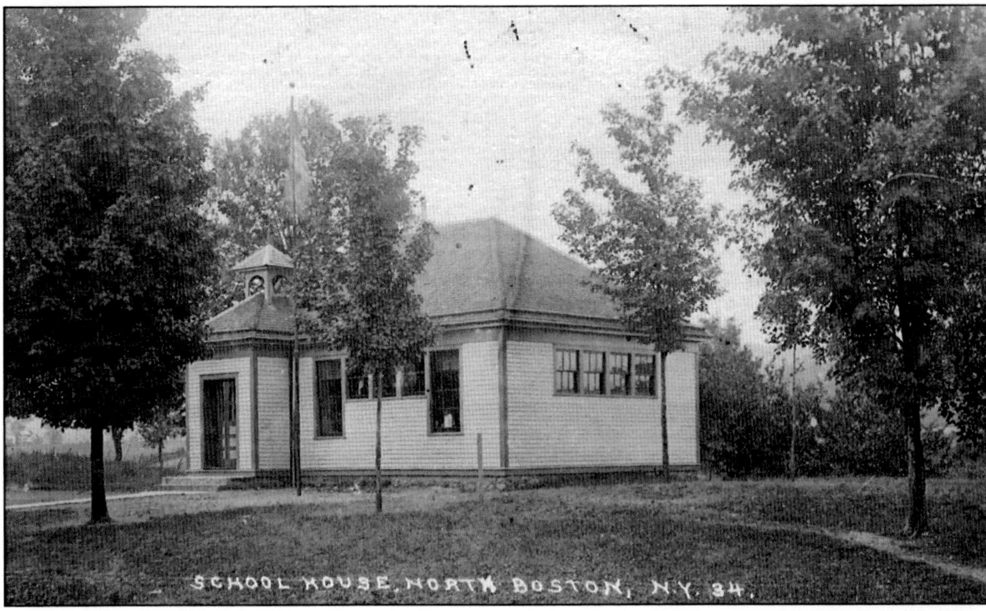

District No. 4 in North Boston was on Back Creek Road in a clearing on a little rise across the street from 18 Mile Creek. When Boston Valley Elementary School was built next door, the Hamburg School District used the old building for storage. It was eventually torn down as being unsafe in the 1990s. Some who had been students there had to wipe away a tear as the walls came down.

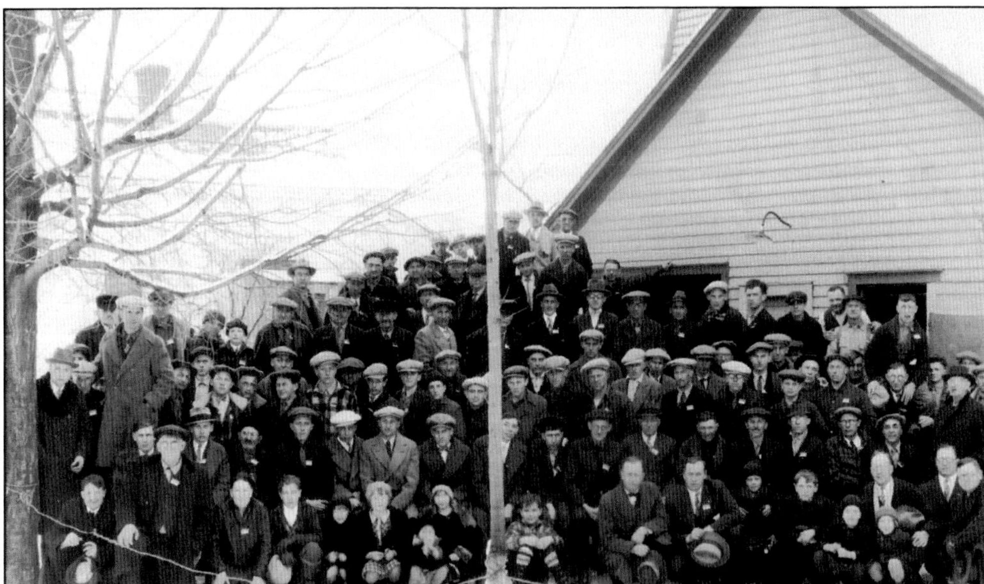

In front of the old North Boston Fire Hall, the men and boys who attended the Advance Rumley Power Farming School can be seen. Advance Rumley was a manufacturer of farm machinery in the late 19th and early 20th century. Its products were in direct competition with Farmall, Browning, and Ford. The company published books that taught proper use of its machinery and also gathered large groups together to teach them.

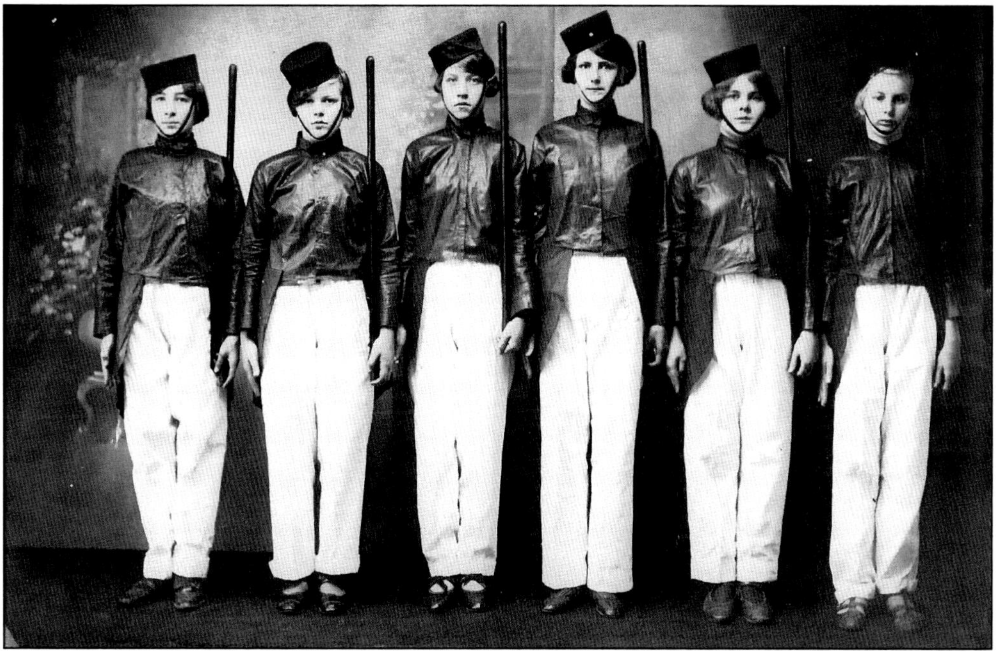

Olga Herren organized many plays in which her students would perform. In fact, she performed many times herself with the Boston Dramatic Club. From left to right are Herren's parade of the wooden soldiers, an unidentified Weber girl, Margarite Owen, Lillian Owen, Theodora Mentlewska, an unidentified Owen girl, and Lenora Northy.

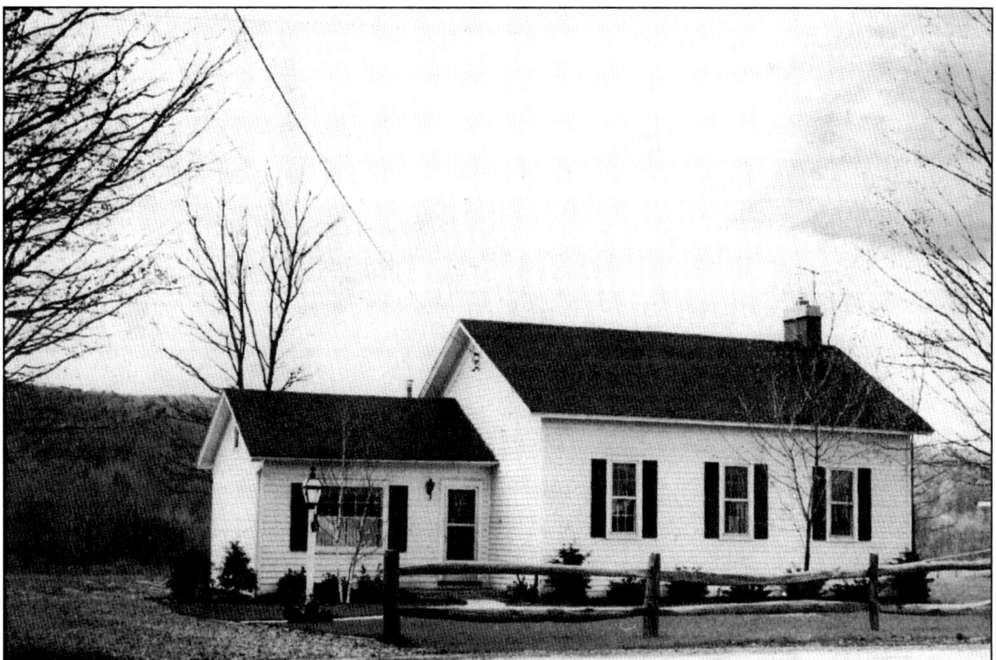

This modest residence on Boston State Road across the street from Maplewood Cemetery used to be the schoolhouse for District No. 2. Children who lived in the valley from Abbott Road to as far as Hillcroft Road would walk to school during the months of November to March.

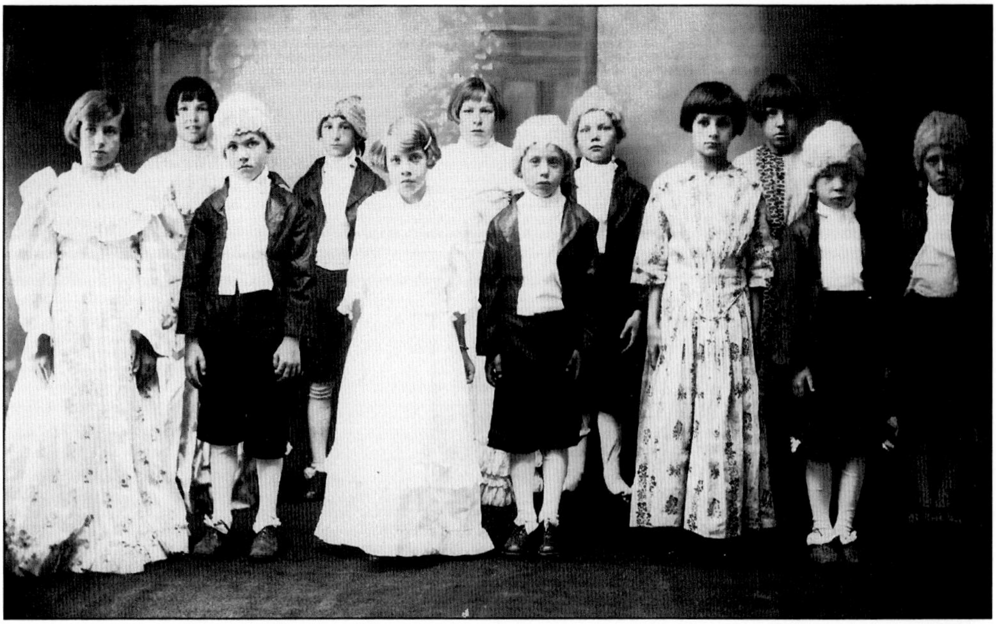

The younger children loved to "play act" and dress up in costumes too, although it is hard to tell by the looks on their faces! A tradition that began in the late 1800s, enacting the wedding of Tom Thumb was a popular fund-raiser for schools and churches. It began with America's fascination with the real Tom Thumb, a little person named Charles Stratton who in 1863 married another little person named Lavinia Warren.

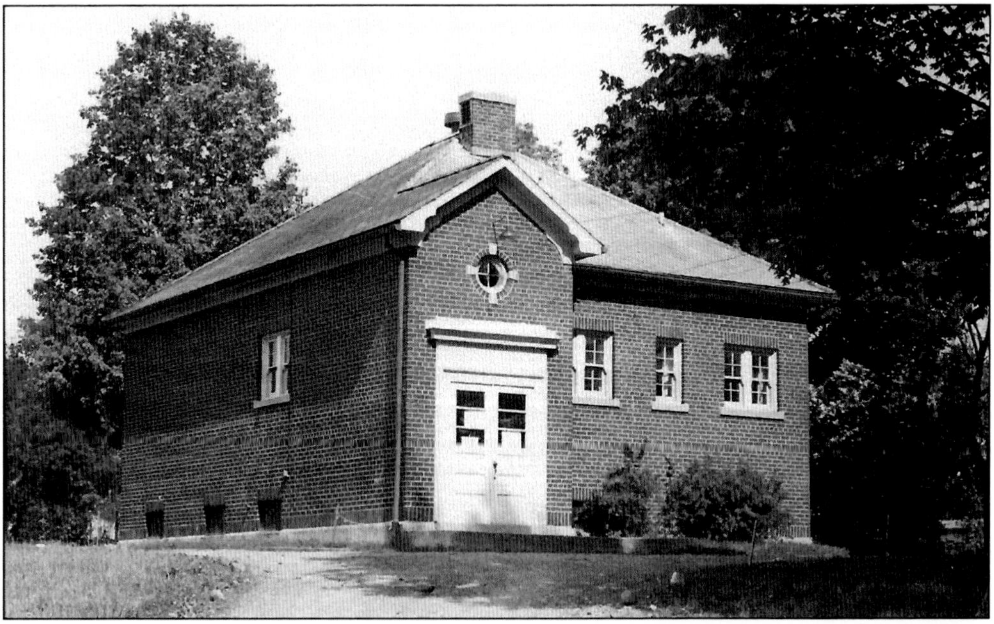

This is a modern photograph of the building that was once District No. 1. The first building burned down and was replaced with this brick edifice that is now home to the Boston Free Library. The only evidence that this was once a schoolhouse is the graffiti written on a wooden beam in the building's attic that reads, "We the boys of Boston were the first to find this hiding place. Signed: Kenneth Bower, Frank Kaczor and Harold Faulring."

Six

BUSINESSES

People today would probably not have any idea how to turn a lush wilderness into a thriving community with only simple tools and the sweat of hard work. As families in the 19th century took up all their belongings, packed them onto a wagon pulled by a team of horses, and moved west, they had no idea what was ahead or how they would even stay alive when there was so much that was unknown. But they did thrive, as they built simple log cabins, hunted deer and turkey for food, and then made decisions on how to build a community. They needed logs to build a shelter, so they started a sawmill. They needed to grow corn and wheat for food, so they built a gristmill. Their oxen and horses needed harnesses and saddles, so they built harness shops and tanneries. Then came wagon builders, hardware and supply stores, and shoemakers. One business that was very ingenious was the ashery. On the corner of Keller Road and Feddick Road there was an ashery. As the pioneers cleared the land, there was an overabundance of wood, more than they needed to build shelters. So they naturally burned all the excess and turned it to ash. The settlers carted tons of ash to the ashery and sold it for cash. Now they had money to buy food and supplies with. The job of the ashery was to soak the ash in hot water and filter it, leaving alkaline liquid called lye. The lye would be mixed with animal fat to produce soap. Some of the lye would be boiled down to produce black salts or potash. The potash could then be used to make glass and ceramics. As life got a little easier, new businesses became more discretionary. Creameries and cheese factories mass-produced the tasty commodities, hardware stores started carrying pretty lamps, fabric shipped in from New York City, and a new mode of transportation that was manufactured in Buffalo, the bicycle. Eventually there was a hat shop and millinery for dress notions. There is nothing that can be compared to simple American ingenuity.

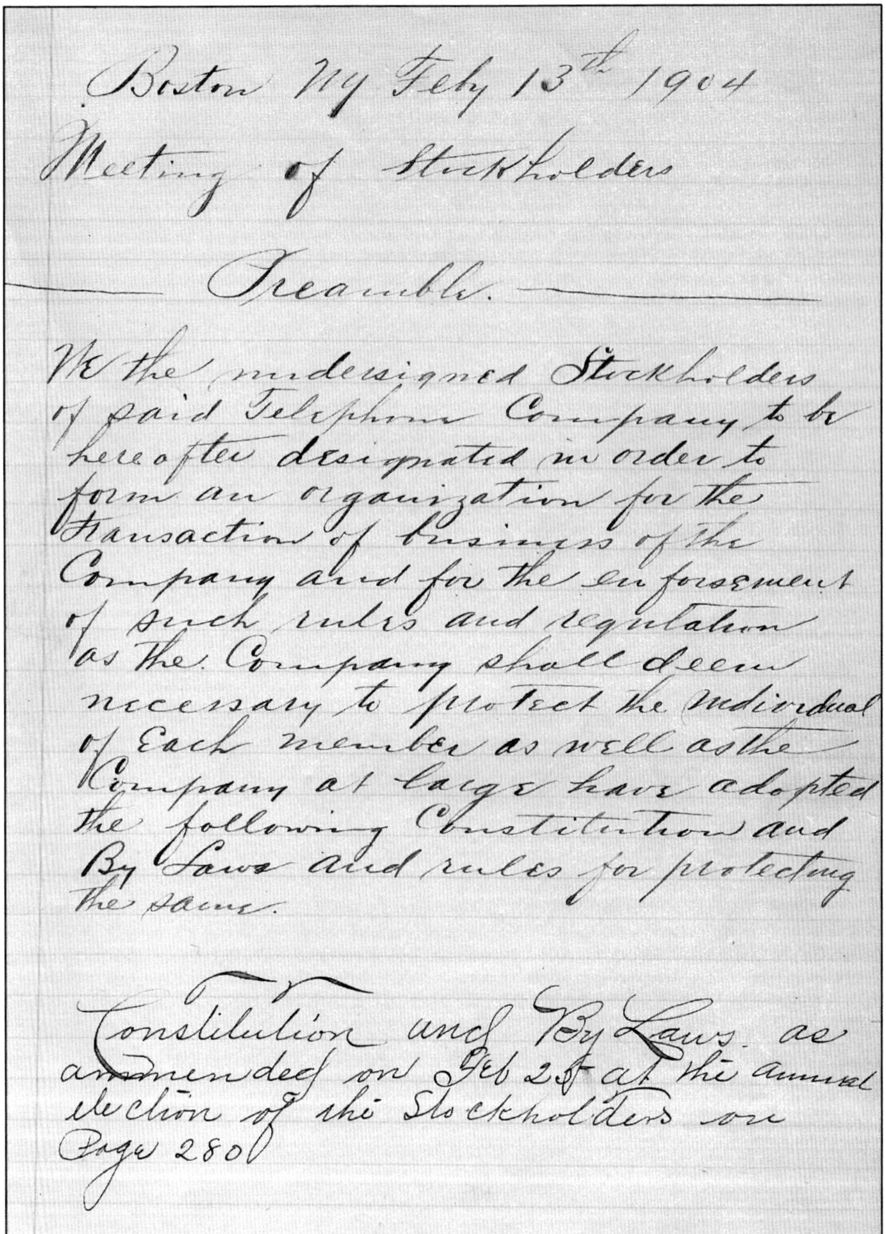

Boston NY Feby 13th 1904

Meeting of Stockholders

Preamble.

We the undersigned Stockholders of said Telephone Company to be hereafter designated in order to form an organization for the transaction of business of the Company and for the enforsement of such rules and regulation as the Company shall deem necessary to protect the individual of Each member as well as the Company at large have adopted the following Constitution and By Laws and rules for protecting the same.

Constitution and By Laws as ammended on Feb 25 at the annual election of the Stockholders on Page 280

When the B&S was winding its construction crews through the Boston hills, the contractor grew tired of going into Hamburg every time he needed to contact his boss by telephone. He tried to interest some residents in contacting the telephone companies in Hamburg and Buffalo to see if they would consider extending their lines into Boston. Those companies did not think that Boston would have enough subscribers to make the extension profitable. So the group decided to form its own telephone company and sold shares for $10 each. They eventually put enough money together to form the Boston Telephone Company, and on February 13, 1904, a meeting of the stockholders was held. They elected officers, drew up a constitution, and started setting poles and stringing wires. By 1925, there were 342 telephones in operation. On January 1, 1932, the Bell Telephone Company took over the business after paying the stockholders $32,000.

In 1905, the Boston Telephone Company had put up enough poles and wire to begin operations. A switchboard was installed in a private residence on the north side of Patchin Road. The switchboard was eventually moved to a building in Boston, across the street from St. Peter's Church. Carrie Mammoser and Mrs. Titus were the first switchboard operators.

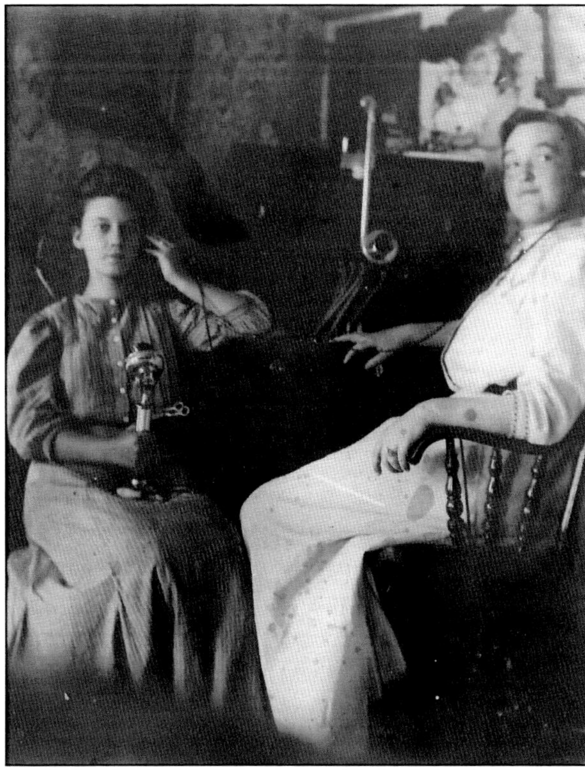

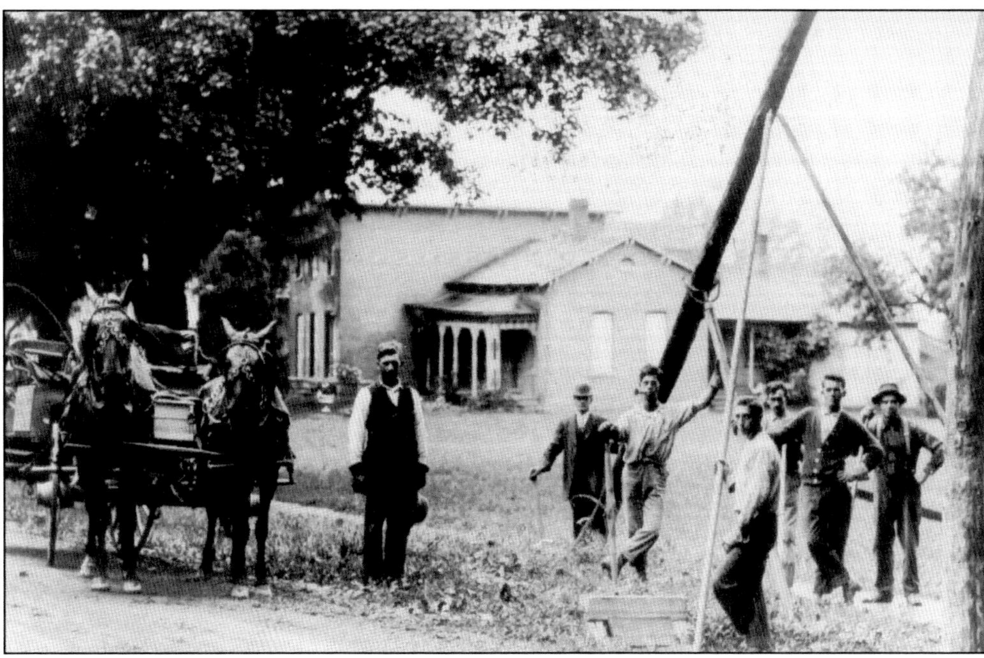

Installing telephone poles and stringing wires on them for the telephone company had not been worked out to a science yet in 1905. At least it was not in the town of Boston. It was a little like building the pyramids with just a saw and a hammer. If these fellows had just asked the railroad contractor to bring his guys down for a few days, the work would have gone a lot faster.

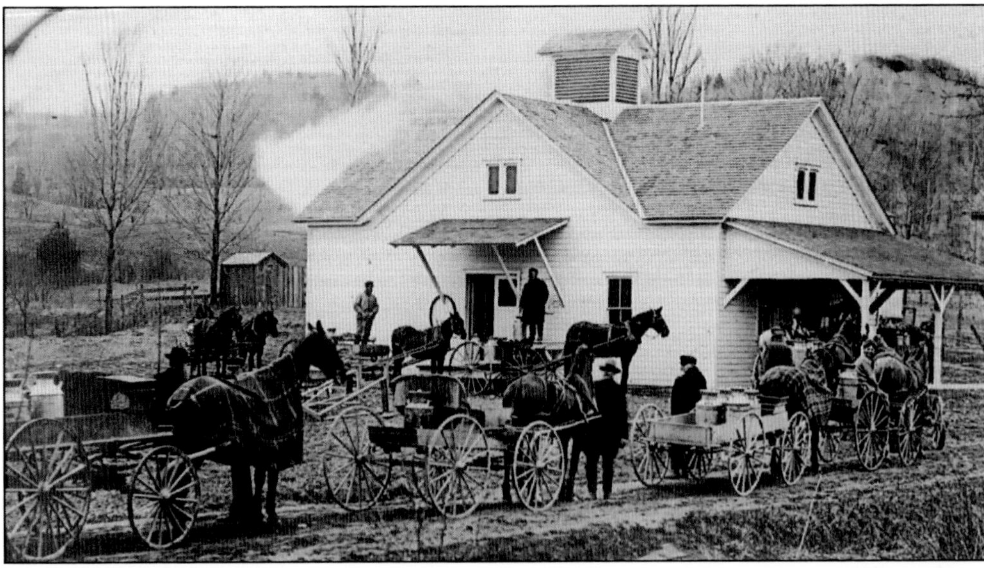

Several creameries and cheese factories were built to accommodate the volume of milk produced by all the farms in town. The Boston Creamery on Boston Colden Road was the biggest and most prosperous. The farmers brought their wagons carrying 10-gallon metal milk cans full of fresh milk and sold it or traded it for the butter, cream, and cheese they made there.

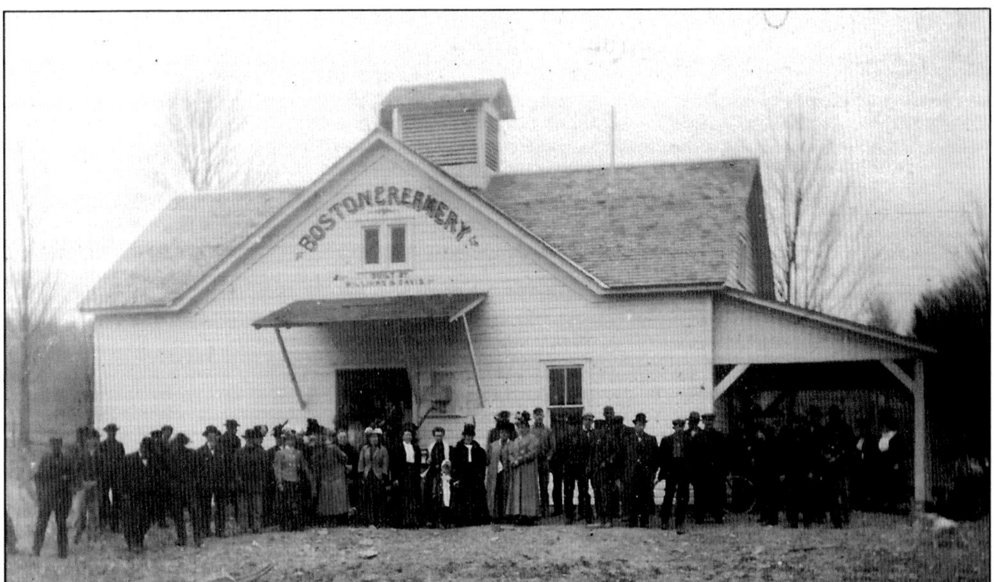

This photograph probably shows the party that ensued when the creamery decided to sell stock in its company. The name of the company was added to the building, as well as the words, "Built by Williams and Davis." The building still stands and has been remodeled as a private residence.

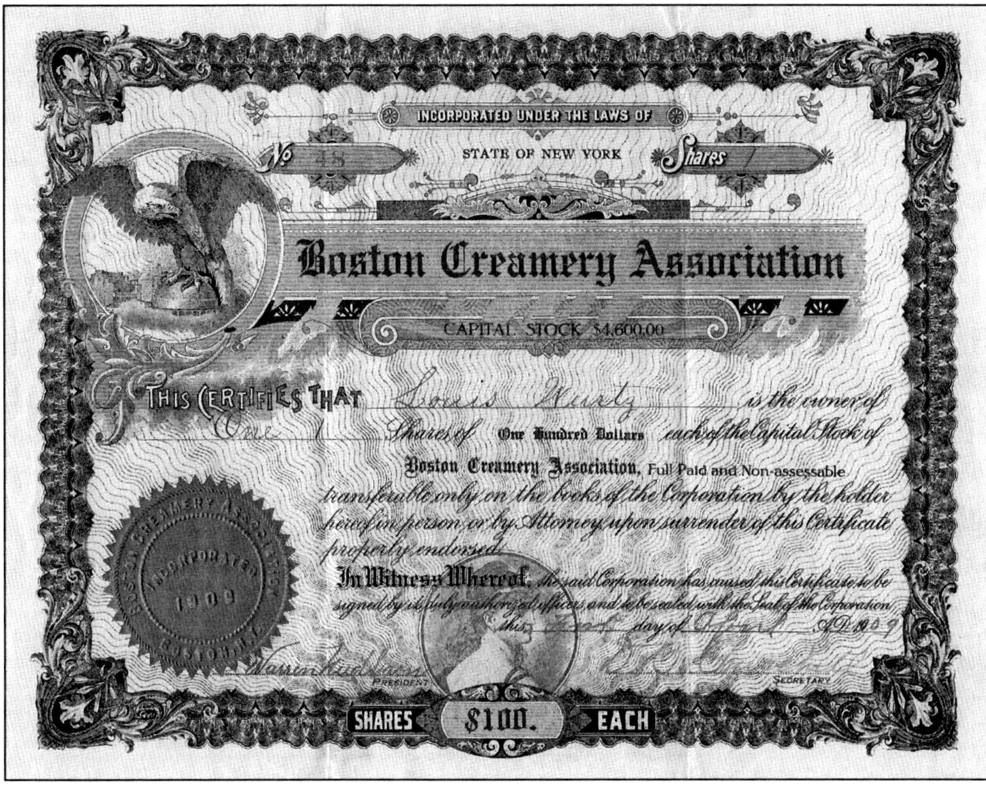

INCORPORATED UNDER THE LAWS OF STATE OF NEW YORK

No 48 Shares 1

Boston Creamery Association

CAPITAL STOCK $4,600.00

This Certifies That Louis Wurtz is the owner of One 1 Shares of One Hundred Dollars each of the Capital Stock of Boston Creamery Association, Full Paid and Non-assessable transferable only on the books of the Corporation by the holder hereof in person or by Attorney upon surrender of this Certificate properly endorsed.

In Witness Whereof, the said Corporation has caused this Certificate to be signed by its duly authorized officers, and to be sealed with the Seal of the Corporation this first day of April A.D. 1909

PRESIDENT SECRETARY

SHARES $100. EACH

In 1909, the Boston Creamery Association sold stock in the company. Business was good. It sold $4,600 in capital stock at $100 per share. That was a hefty price in 1909. Louis Wurtz, another fellow businessman, bought share 48 on April 1, 1909. It is curious how they could sell certificate 48 at $100 when the offering was only for $4,600. The certificate is signed by the president of the creamery, Warren Needham, and the secretary, D. B. Churchill. The company paid dividends to the shareholders every month. This dividend certificate shows that from February 1, 1910, to February 28, inclusive, the creamery took in 46,020 pounds of milk, made 108 pounds of butter, and produced 1,078 gallons of cream. Notice that the price of butter was 30¢ per pound.

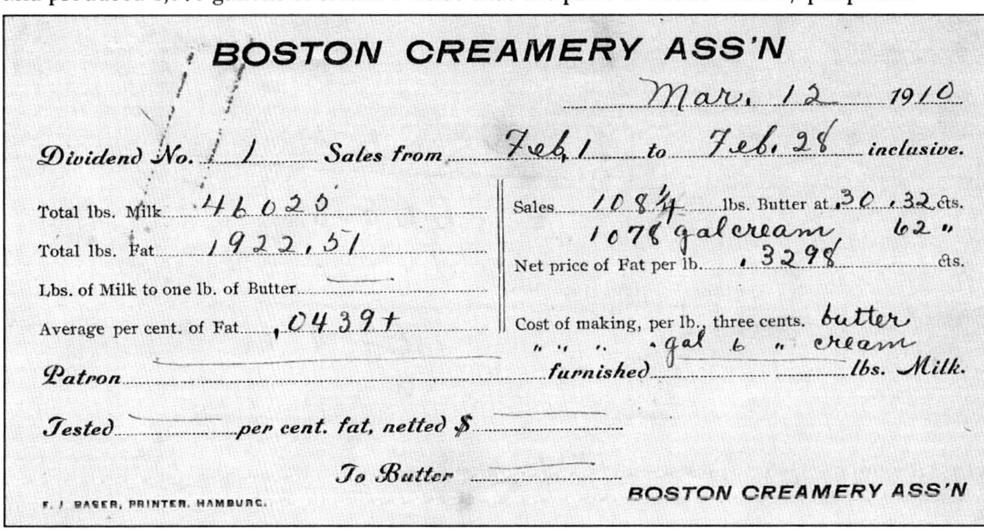

BOSTON CREAMERY ASS'N

Mar. 12 1910

Dividend No. 1 Sales from Feb. 1 to Feb. 28 inclusive.

Total lbs. Milk 46020

Total lbs. Fat 1922.51

Lbs. of Milk to one lb. of Butter —

Average per cent. of Fat .0439+

Sales 108¼ lbs. Butter at .30 .32 cts.

1078 gal cream 62 "

Net price of Fat per lb. .3298 cts.

Cost of making, per lb., three cents. butter

" " " gal 6 " cream

Patron — furnished — lbs. Milk.

Tested — per cent. fat, netted $ —

To Butter —

F. J. BASER, PRINTER, HAMBURG.

BOSTON CREAMERY ASS'N

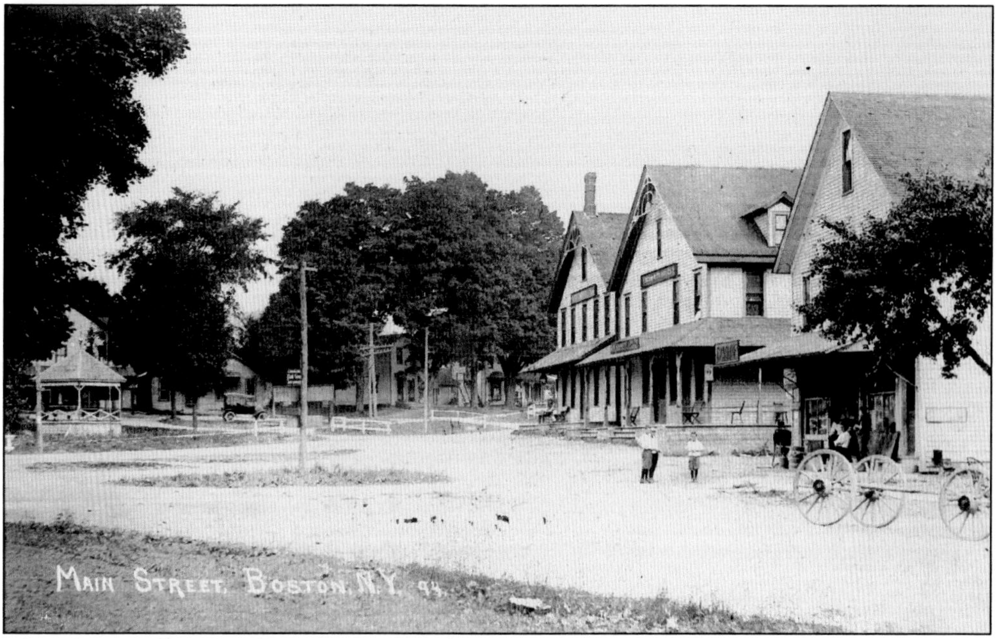

This photograph, taken between 1900 and 1920, is looking southeast from where the Liberty Tavern now stands. A partially completed wagon is in front of the wagon shop out of sight on the right. Then behind the tree branch is the general store that sold everything from Coca-Cola to gasoline. Further on is the Iroquois Hotel and the last building is the Boston Hotel. The gazebo on the left no longer exists.

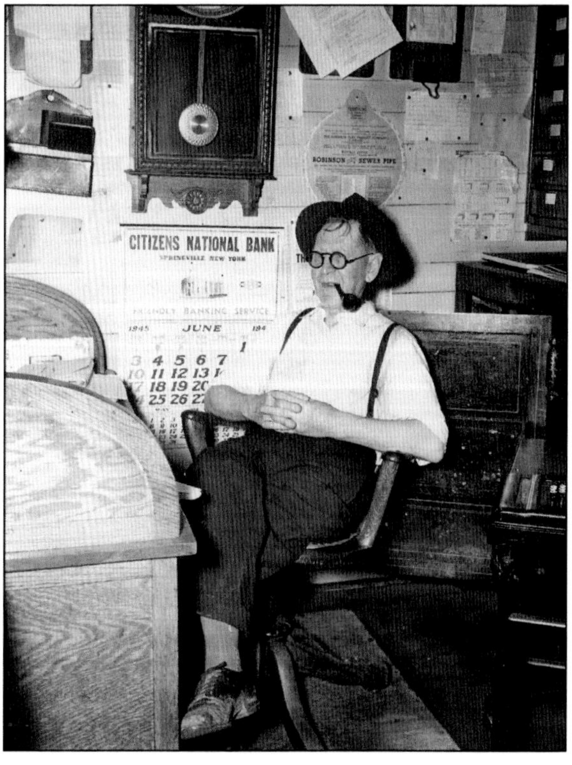

Frank Weber owned a hardware store in Boston near Boston Commons for many years. The whole Weber family owned stores in Boston for several generations. Here is Frank, relaxing with his pipe. The year is 1945, according to the Citizens National Bank calendar behind him. Unfortunately, the building that housed his store burned down a few years ago.

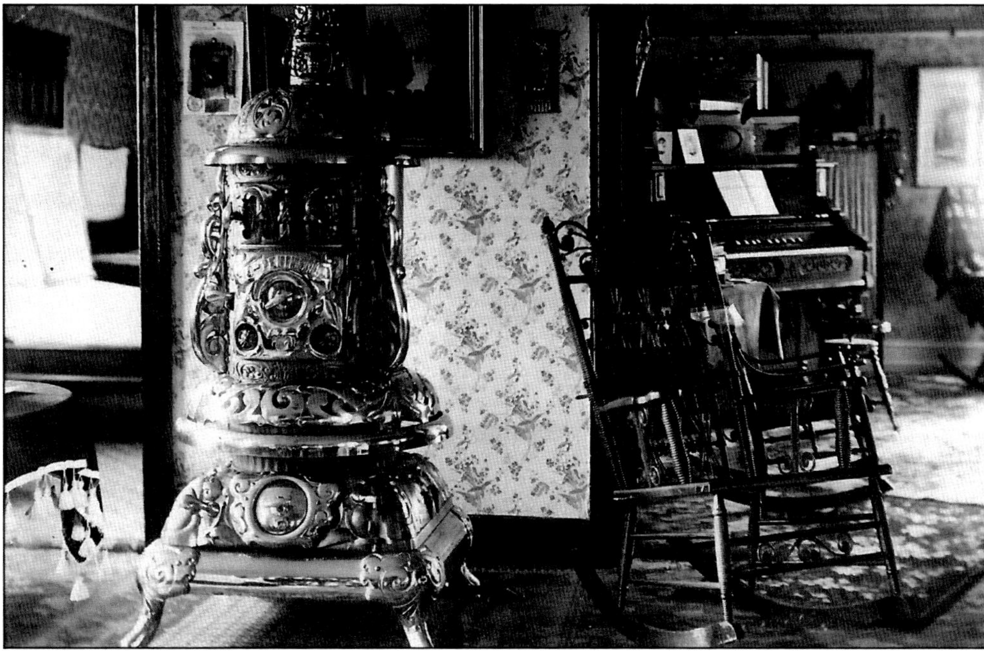

Perry Dye owned a store in Boston in the early 1900s that stood on the corner of the state road and Boston Cross Road. His store also held the Boston Post Office, an insurance business, and a Red and White store, all in the same storefront. This beautiful stove was in the front of the store, probably in the area where he sold insurance.

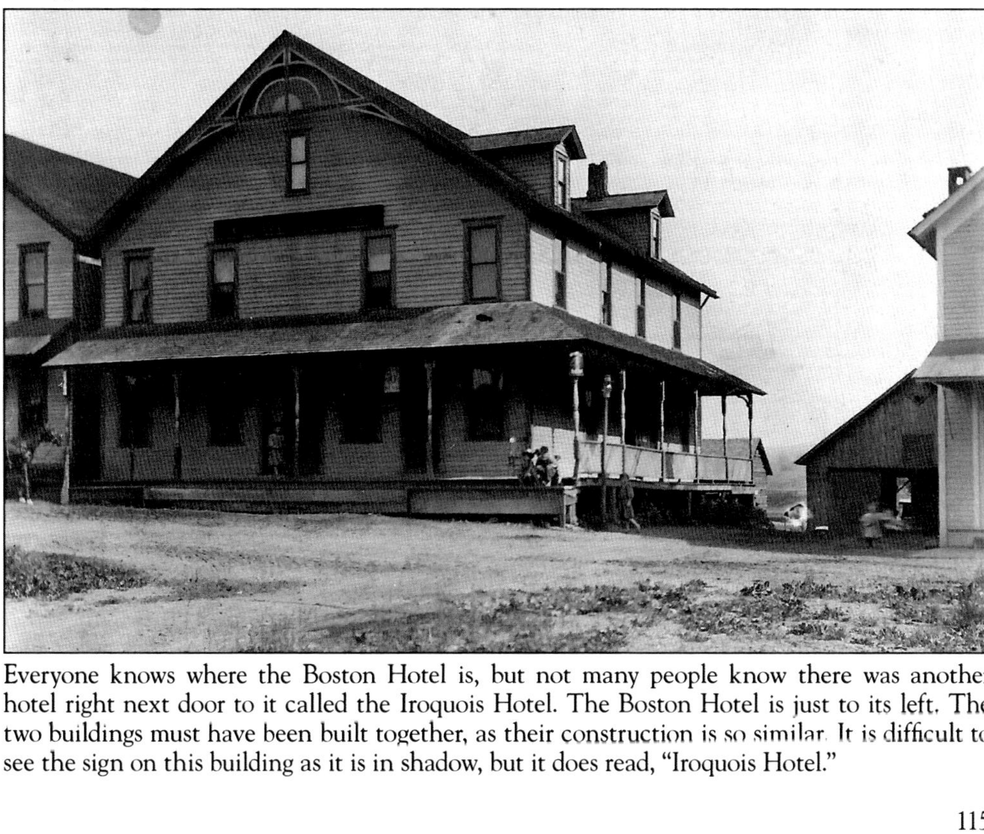

Everyone knows where the Boston Hotel is, but not many people know there was another hotel right next door to it called the Iroquois Hotel. The Boston Hotel is just to its left. The two buildings must have been built together, as their construction is so similar. It is difficult to see the sign on this building as it is in shadow, but it does read, "Iroquois Hotel."

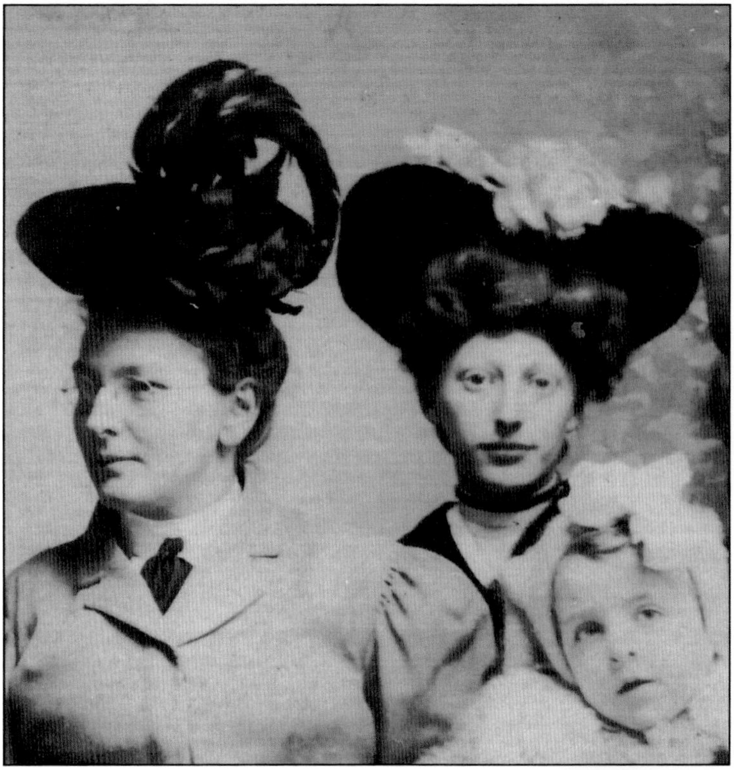

Jennie Dye was an entrepreneur when it was not even fashionable. In the early 1900s, she owned many businesses in town, one of which was a hat shop. She designed women's hats and clothing that would have been able to stand toe to toe with anything that came from the city. These ladies are modeling some of the hats that Dye designed. (Courtesy of Jane Clarke.)

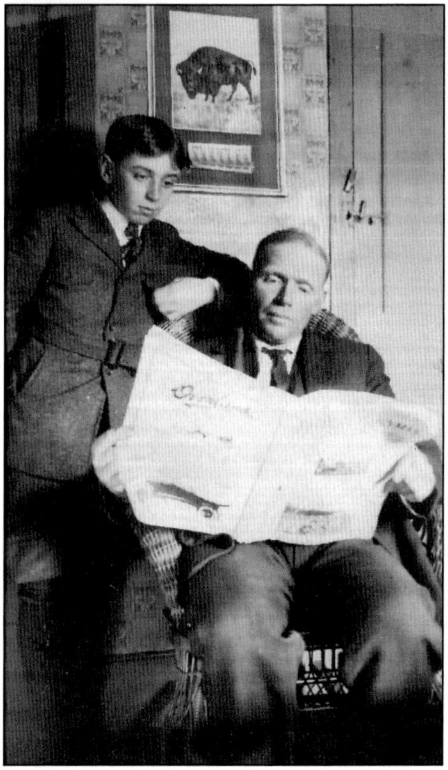

Leland and Perry Dye are deep in thought as they read the only local paper sold in town, the *Buffalo Evening News*. The calendar behind them says it is January 1920. Leland was Perry's nephew, his younger brother Earl's son. (Courtesy of Jane Clarke.)

Jennie Dye Williams's daughter Eleanore loved to come out to the store and help her mother. Here she is standing in front of the store that was at the bottom of Boston Cross Road. This lovely millinery sold notions and New Idea dress patterns. Real Victorian valentines could be found there as well. When Jennie designed a dress for someone, she would go right to their house to take their measurements. (Courtesy of Jane Clarke.)

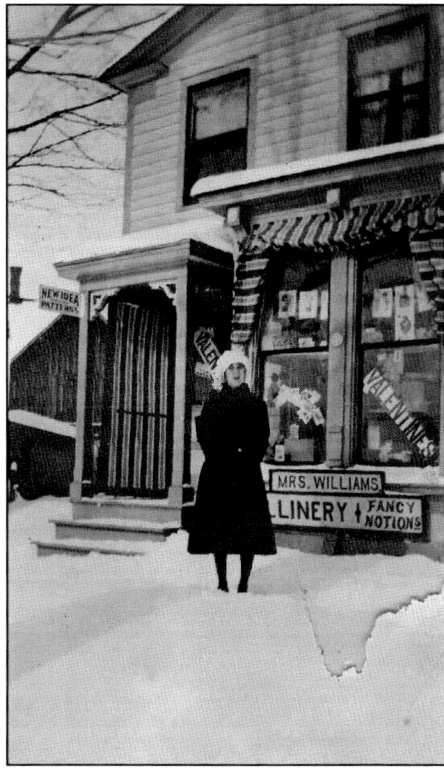

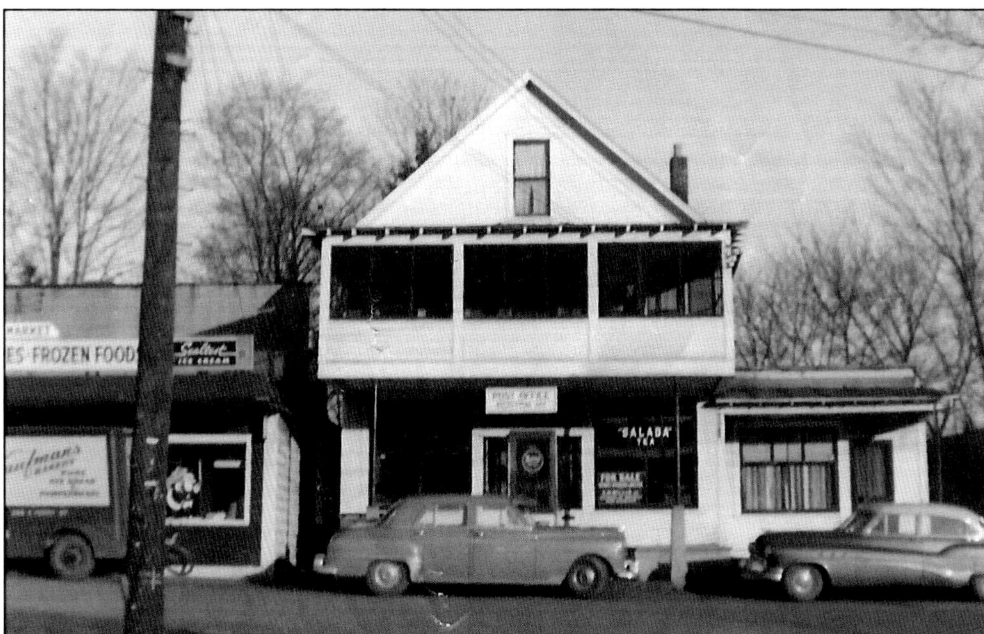

When Perry Dye passed away in 1961, his store in Boston Commons was put up for sale. There was a new store right next door that was selling brands of food that are recognizable today—fresh bread from Kaufman's, which was delivered everyday from Buffalo, and Sealtest Ice Cream. The Boston Post Office took up residence in a new building that was built down the road.

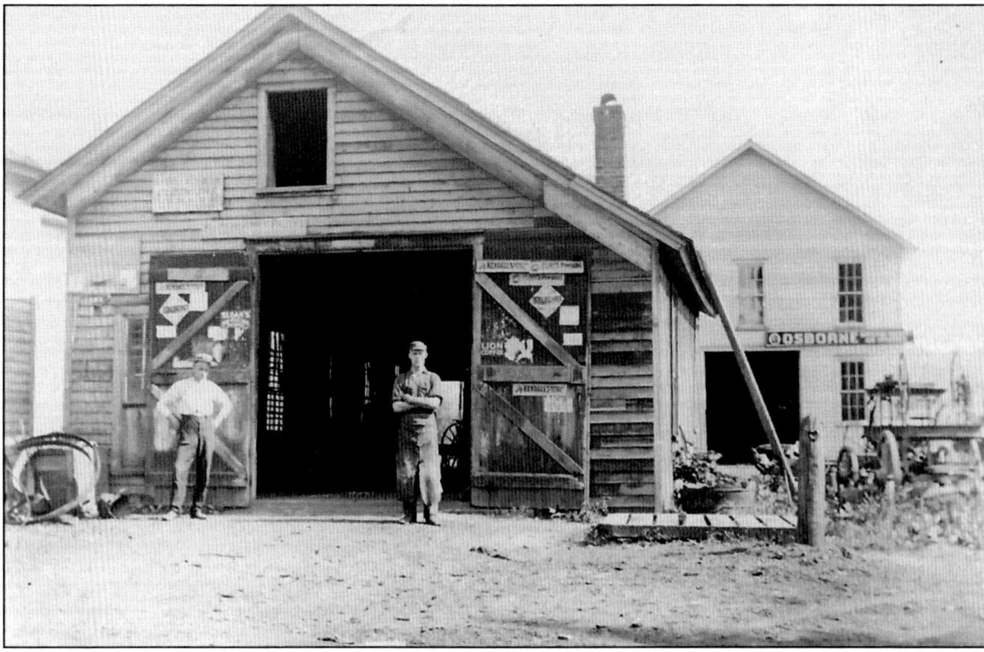

This early store carried just about anything one could ever need. The signs on the doors advertise Lion coffee, Flints powders, Kendall's Spavin Cure, Sloan's Sure Garlic Cure, Siegel and Robinson Clothiers, and Warren Paint. Just to the right of the front building, there is a large post with a ring on it for tying up customers' horses while they were inside shopping.

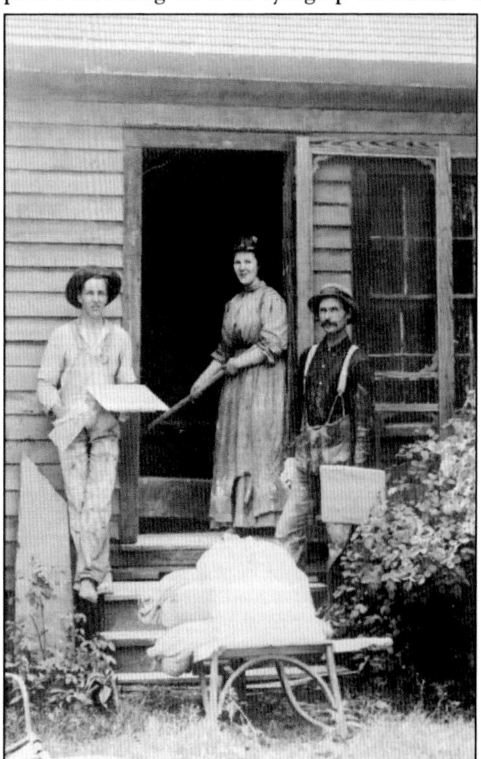

The woman in the middle of this photograph is Susan Hauth Dye. In 1916, she decided to try her hand at opening a bakery, to help other women who were too busy to bake for their own family. Susan had a successful run with her bakery and eventually married Perry Dye, another businessman. She became the postmaster for the Boston Post Office from 1921 to 1954.

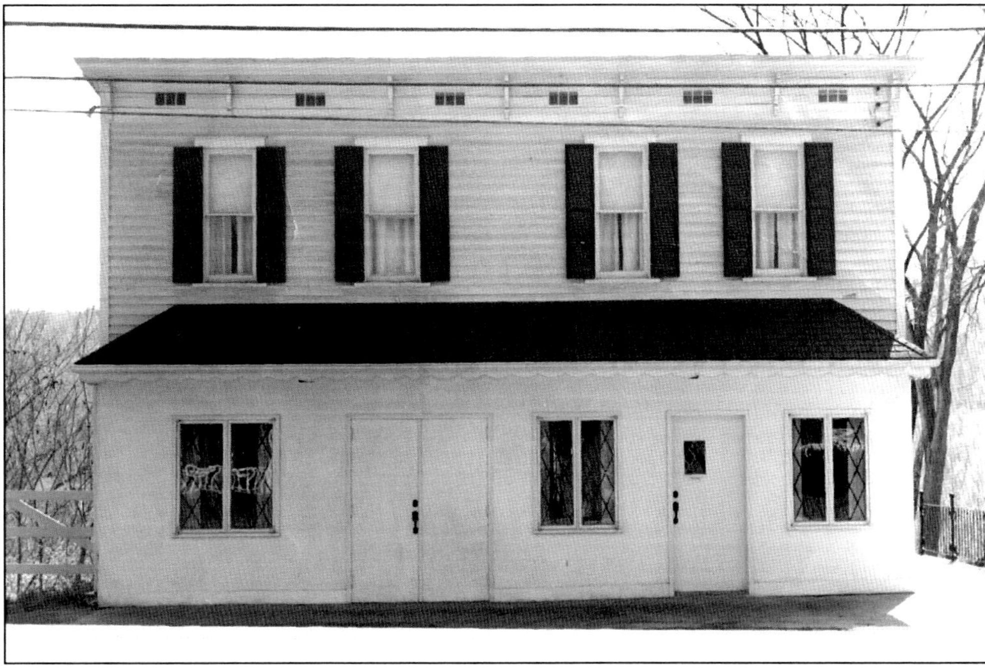

The Wurtz family has history in Boston going back over 100 years. This building on Boston State Road, just a few doors down from the Boston Hotel, was the location of several Wurtz businesses. John Wurtz in the 19th century owned a blacksmith shop, was a wagon maker, and owned a cider mill. This particular building housed the Wurtz Furniture Store and some years later, the Wurtz Funeral Home. Many furniture and cabinetmakers in those days became coffin manufacturers. In the photograph below, the Wurtz Funeral Hearse was breathtaking as it passed by. The casket of the dear departed can be seen through the etched-glass windows on either side. The clip-clop of the hooves of the white horse, wearing a jet-black shawl, was the only sound heard as someone's loved one was transported to one of the town's cemeteries.

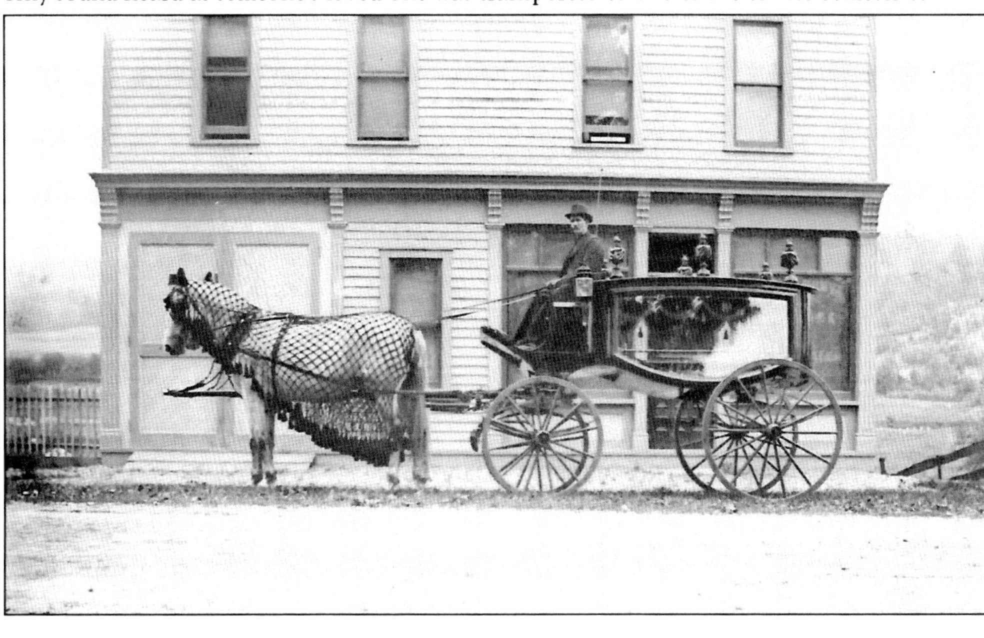

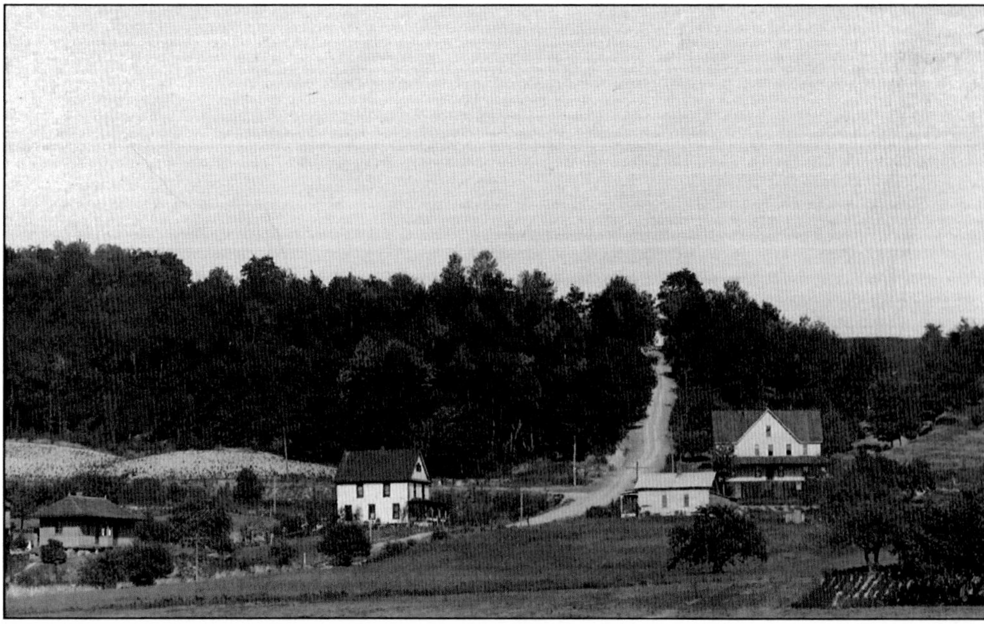

Traveling up the hill on Boston Cross Road looking east, one would cross over what is now called the power line. This used to be the path that the B&S traveled between 1906 and 1916. The building on the right is the hotel that was built at the same time as the railroad. Some of the records call it the Armus Hotel, and other records call it the Simms Hotel. It was built so travelers could stop and stay the night and maybe even visit some of the local businesses. When the railroad left, so did the hotel traffic. So much for Boston's tourist business. The photograph below shows the north side of the hotel along Boston Cross Road. The wagon is taking travelers from the hotel to the train depot for their departure from the lovely little town.

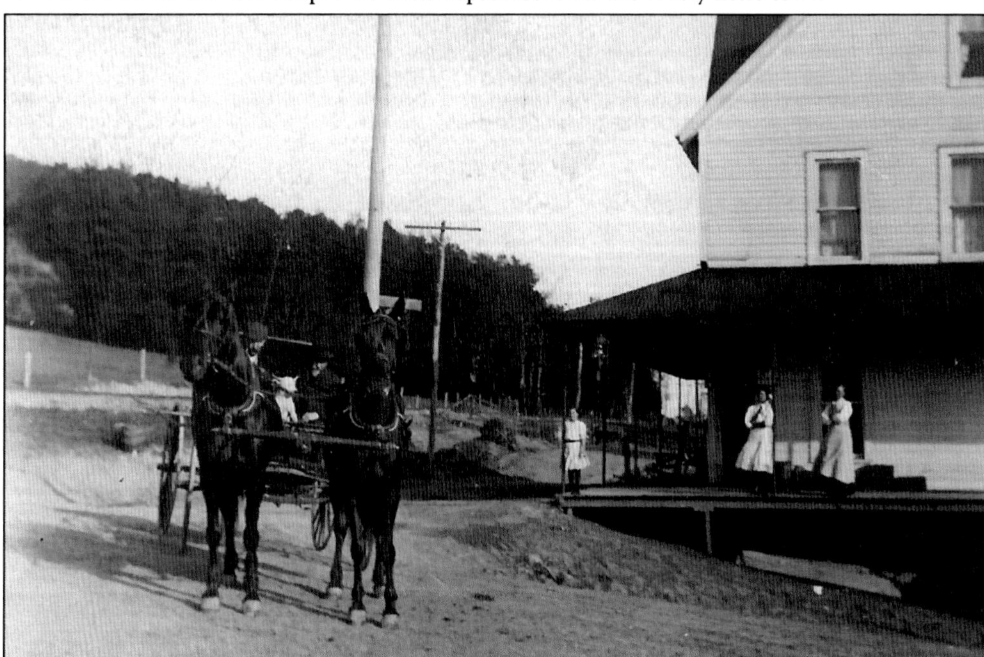

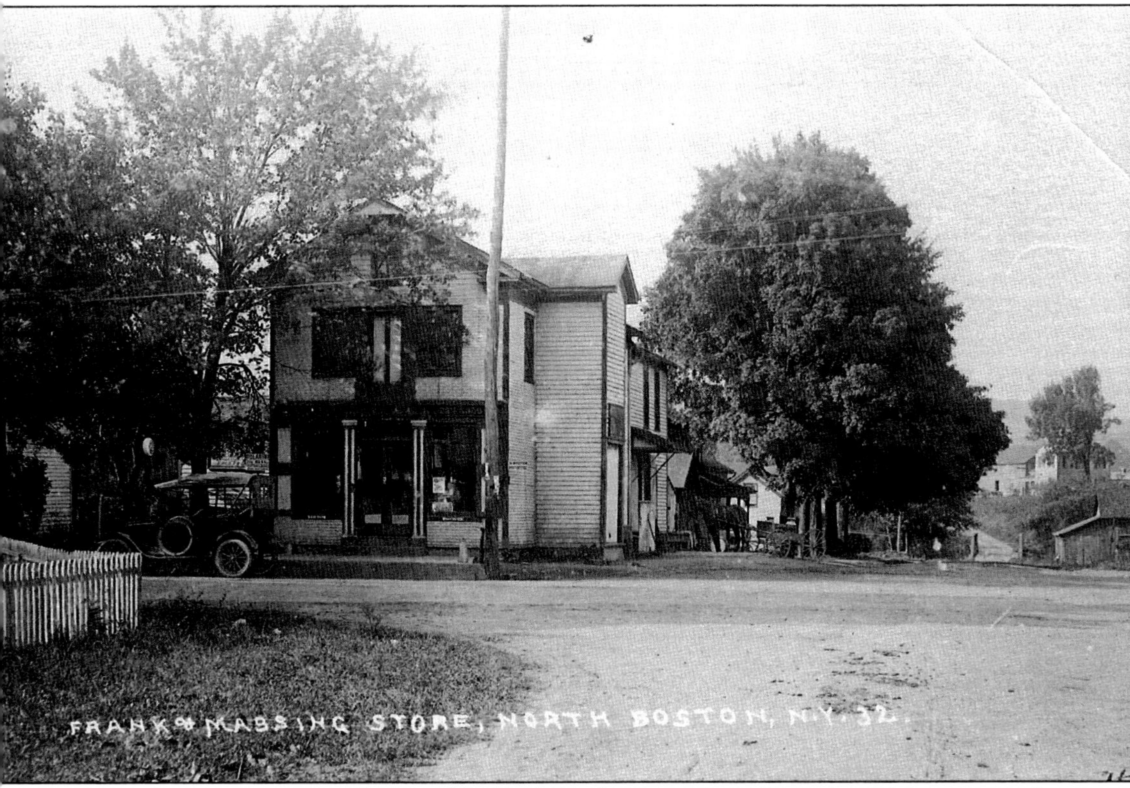

In 1932, this store was partially owned by Fred Frank. It stood on the corner of the state road and Zimmerman Road in North Boston and still stands, home to an attorney's office. The store was downstairs, and the storage area was upstairs. When Frank wanted to store some inventory on the top floor, he would load the goods on a pallet, hook up a pulley and a rope to the top ridge of the building, and pull the pallet up to the door between the two windows. Then a helper would swing the pallet into the door and unload it. It was a very tricky and time-consuming process. Eventually Frank decided to build the addition that is jutting out on the right side of the building and install an elevator. Frank believed in working smarter, not working harder. The North Boston Post Office was also housed here for a time.

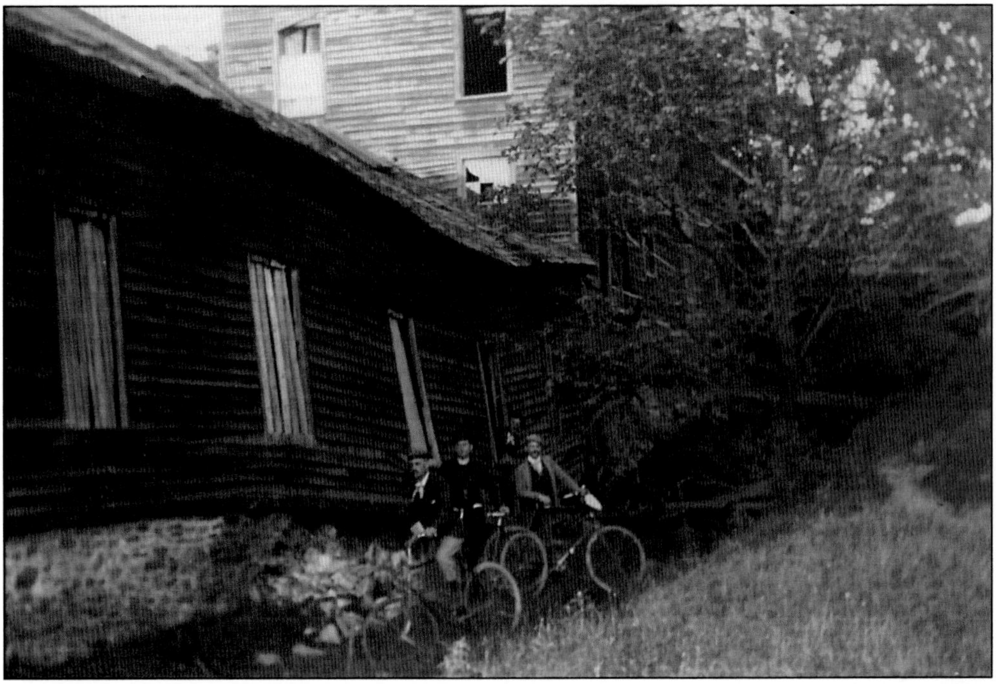

This huge crumbling building once housed a woolen mill. This photograph was taken in 1899, and the building was located along Boston State Road around the area where the Brick Oven Restaurant now stands. There are no records to show who owned the mill, but perhaps it was George Briggs's business, where he would have built his patented wool presses in the years before and after 1867.

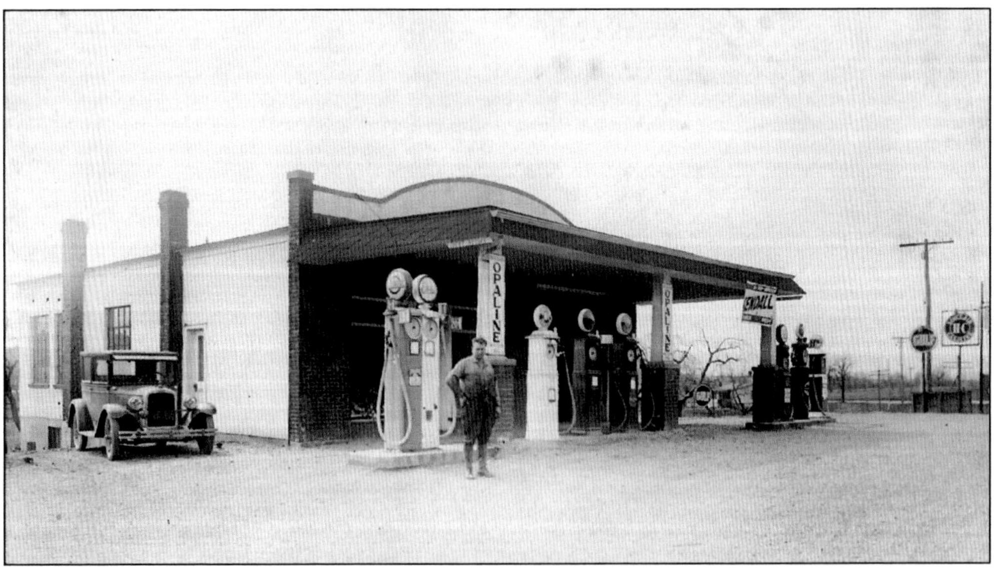

When the automobile started becoming the most popular mode of transportation, gas stations became a necessity and Leroy Pfarner was up for the task, so he opened this gas station in North Boston. According to the signs, he sold gasoline made by Esso, Kendall, and Gulf. Prices ranged from 15¢ a gallon to 20¢. He also sold Sinclair Opaline Motor Oil and offered restrooms to weary travelers.

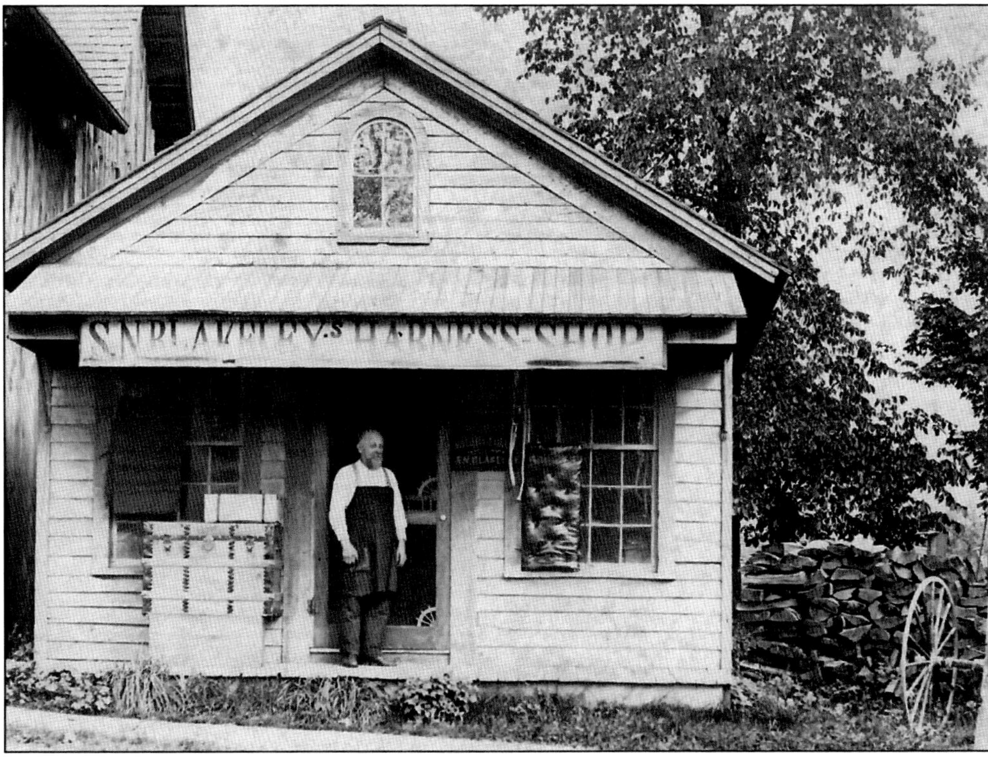

S. N. Blakeley's Harness Shop was in Boston Commons on the southeast corner of the intersection of the state road and Boston Cross Road. Down Mill Street along 18 Mile Creek was a tannery where he would buy tanned animal hides for his business. Then he would make harnesses, saddles, leather-bound steamer trunks, and cushioned seats for carriages. The sign on the door also offered his services as a notary public.

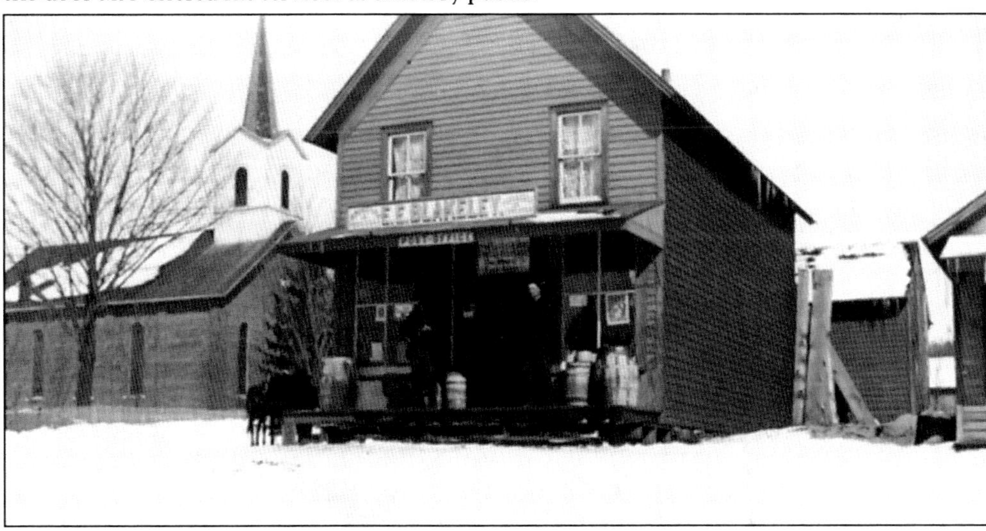

Right next door to S. N. Blakeley's Harness Shop was E. E. Blakeley's general store. To the left is the original St. John's Church as it stood in the 19th century. The store sold groceries, provisions (probably staples like flour, sugar, and lard), and medicinal cures as well as tobacco and cigars. It was also home to the Boston Post Office for a number of years.

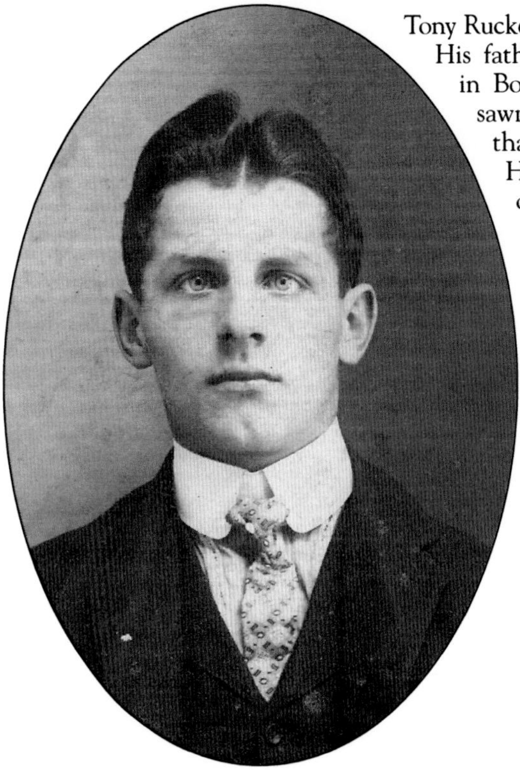

Tony Rucker came from a very business-oriented family. His father, John Rucker, owned acres of farmland in Boston and was very prosperous. Tony ran a sawmill in Boston, run by steam power rather than using waterpower from 18 Mile Creek. He was married and had three children, one of whom, Robert Lee Rucker, died a war hero during World War II. (Courtesy of Tom and Marilyn Rucker.)

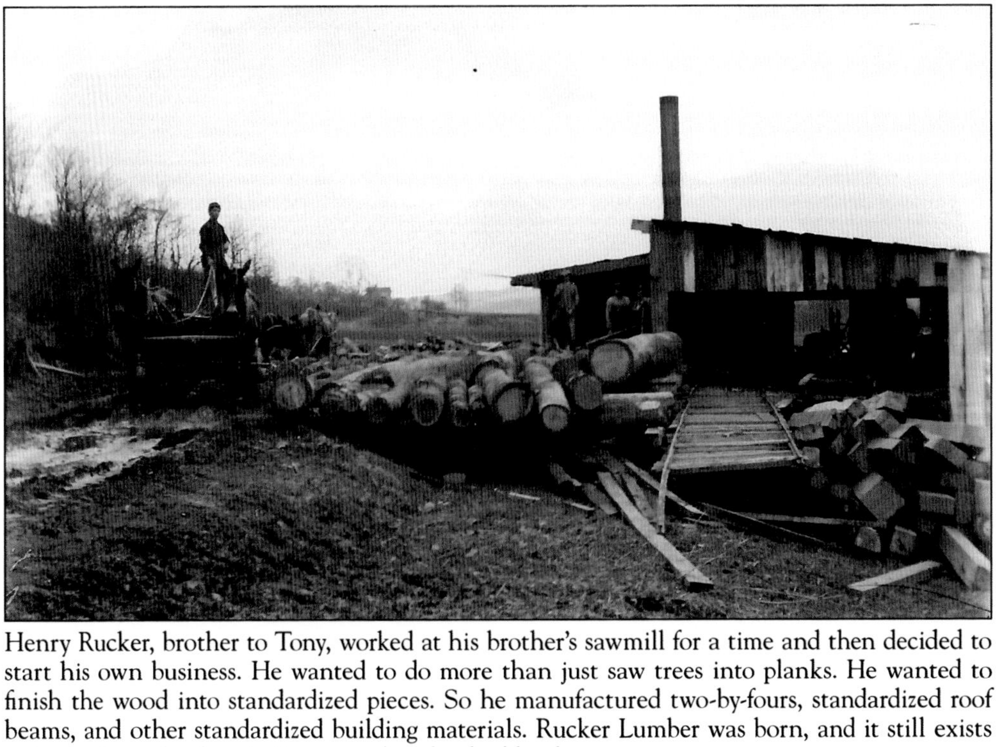

Henry Rucker, brother to Tony, worked at his brother's sawmill for a time and then decided to start his own business. He wanted to do more than just saw trees into planks. He wanted to finish the wood into standardized pieces. So he manufactured two-by-fours, standardized roof beams, and other standardized building materials. Rucker Lumber was born, and it still exists today as the only place in Boston to buy finished lumber.

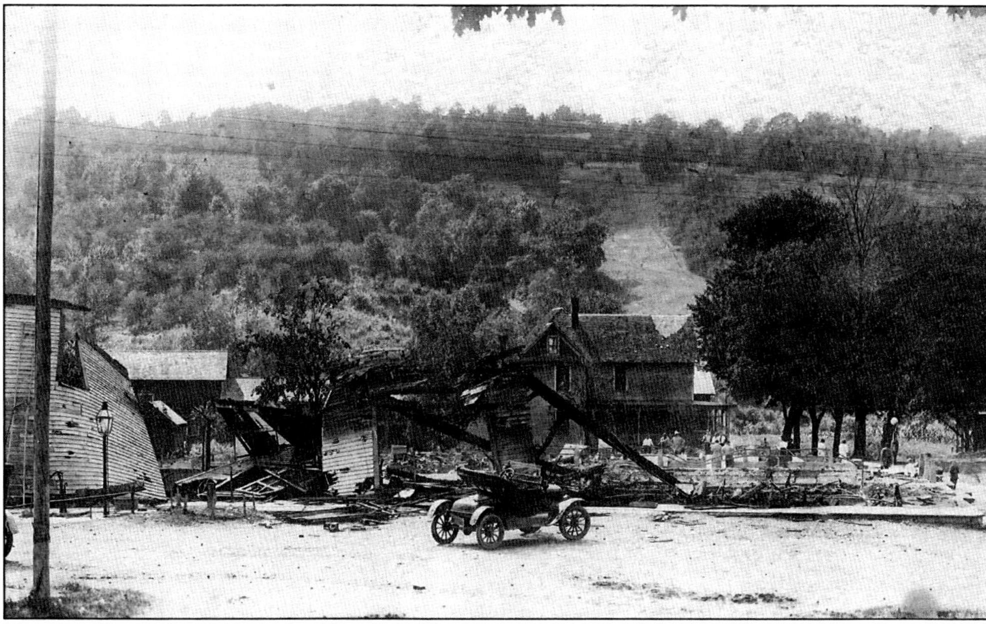

In August 1920, the unthinkable happened. A fire started in a garage down the street from the Boston Hotel and destroyed every business on that side of the street. The men valiantly fought the flames by forming a bucket brigade from the creek, but it was not enough. The Boston Hotel, the Iroquois Hotel, Hund's Hall, a barbershop, and two residences succumbed to the flames that day.

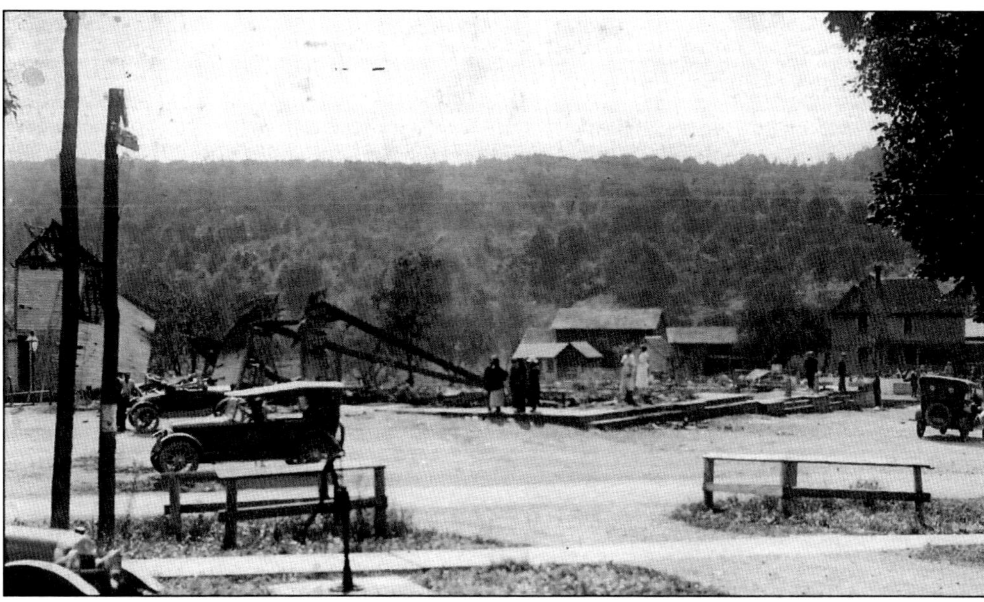

This view of the devastation is seen from across the street in front of Perry Dye's store. Looking southwest against the backdrop of the west hill, one can make out the foundation and front steps of the Boston Hotel and the Iroquois Hotel that used to stand there the day before. The hand water pump in the foreground stands in mute sadness for the loss of so much.

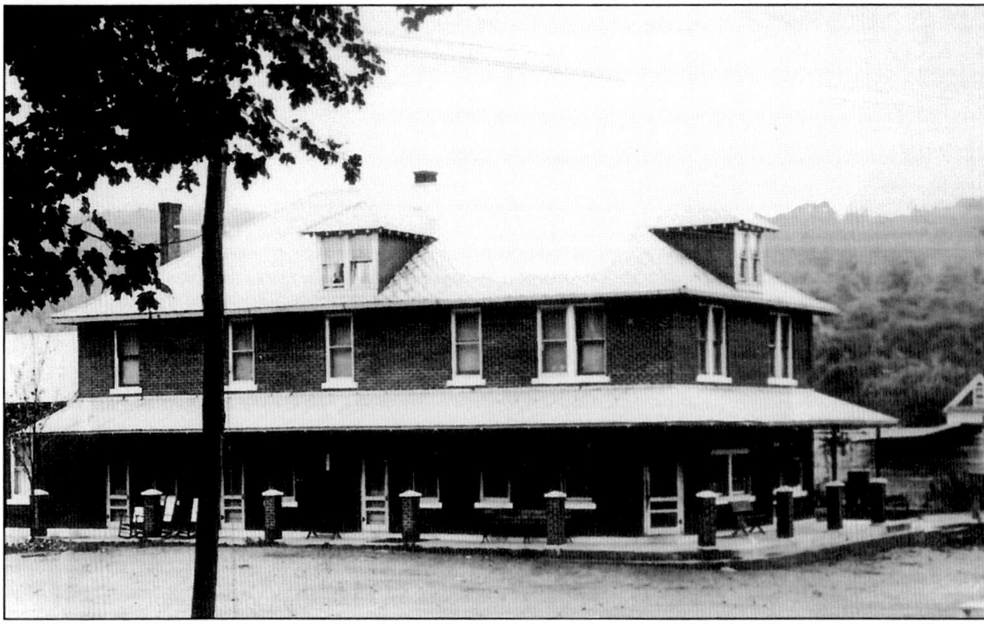

After the Boston Hotel and the rest of the corner of town went up in flames in 1920, the decision came whether or not to rebuild. They decided to rebuild only the Boston Hotel, and this time using brick. They reasoned that a brick building could not burn down. So out of the ashes rose this new Boston Hotel, which still stands today and is a popular meeting place for everyone in town.

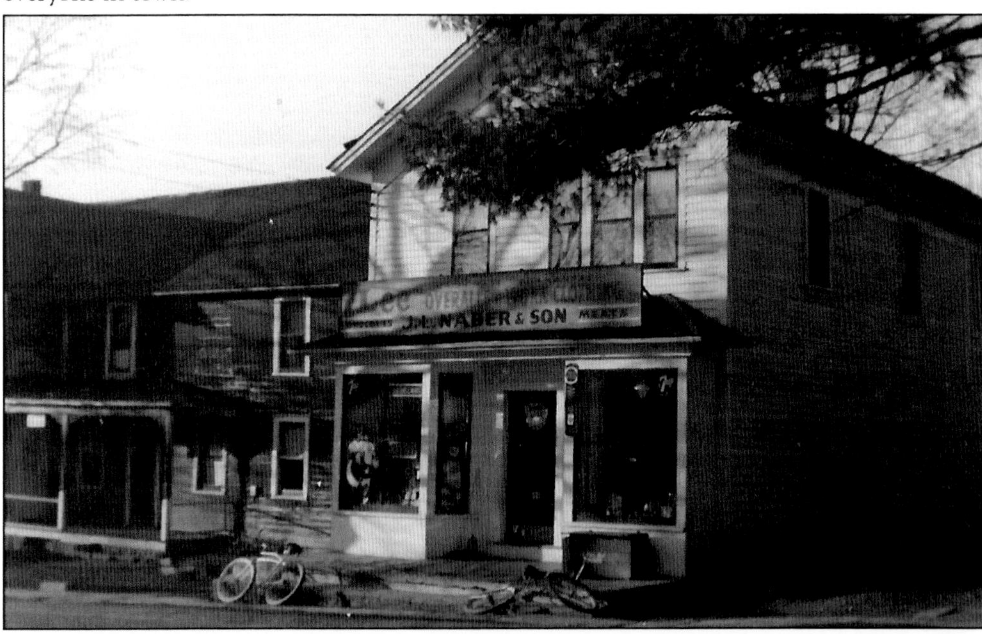

Not many people still remember Nabor's Store at the bottom of Boston Cross Road. The building was the third on the left as one turned up the street from the state road. The sign shown here above the door touts "Lee Brand Union Made and Guaranteed Overalls and Work Clothing." They also sold groceries, meats, and 7-Up. Just to the right of the door is the newspaper box, which held the *Buffalo Evening News*.

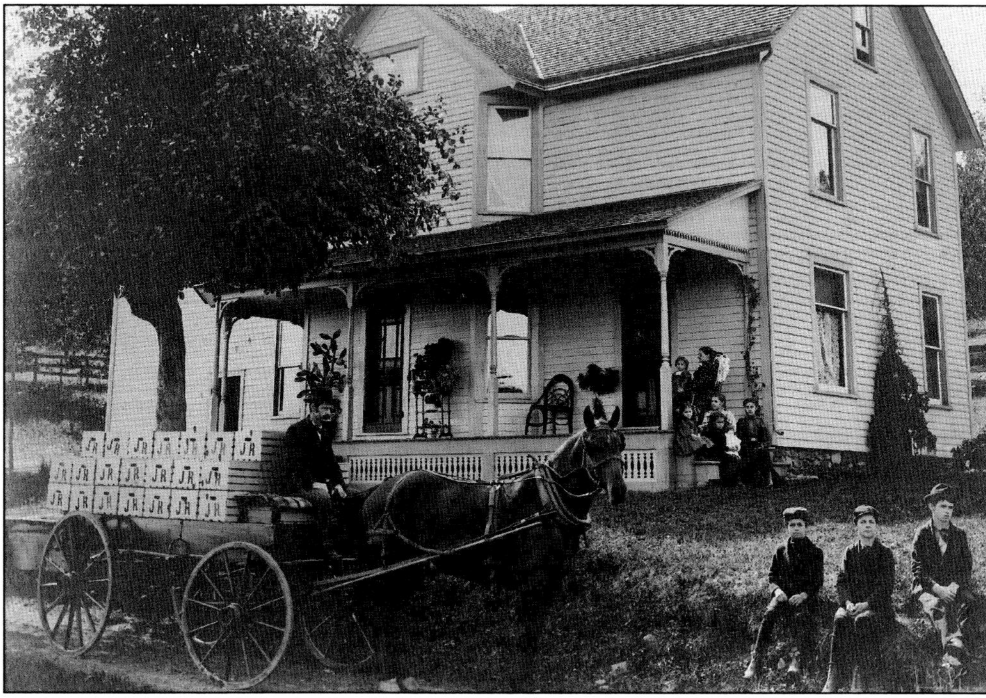

This beautiful Victorian home was the residence of the Rucker family. John Rucker was a farmer, and here he is on his wagon loaded with raspberries and strawberries ready to go to the market in Buffalo. The boxes are marked "JR" to signify John Rucker. Sitting on the ground on the right are, from left to right, Tony, Henry, and Albert Rucker. John's wife, Johanna, is on the porch with the girls, Lucy, Genevieve, Cecilia, and Salome.

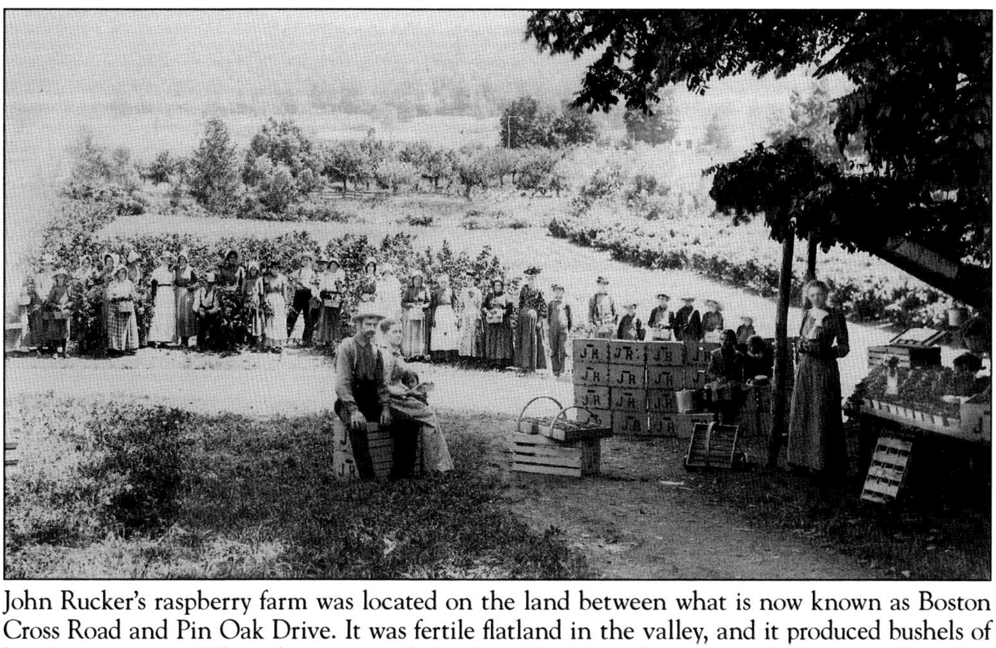

John Rucker's raspberry farm was located on the land between what is now known as Boston Cross Road and Pin Oak Drive. It was fertile flatland in the valley, and it produced bushels of berries every year. When the crop needed to be picked, it took many neighbors to pitch in, but the rewards were plenty. On the right, a roadside produce stand offers the berries for sale.

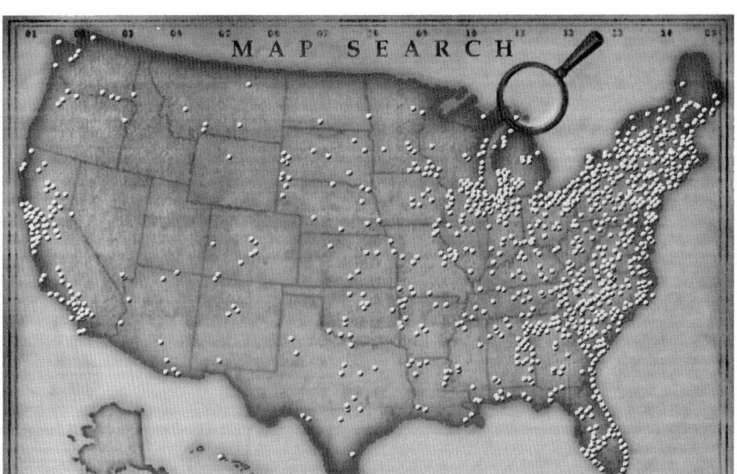
MAP SEARCH